GETTING TO GREY OWL

GETTING
TO
GREY
OWL

JOURNEYS
ON FOUR
CONTINENTS

KURT CASWELL

TRINITY UNIVERSITY PRESS
SAN ANTONIO

Published by Trinity University Press
San Antonio, Texas 78212

Cover design by Sarah Cooper
Book design by BookMatters, Berkeley
Cover images: © iStock.com/Vividus; korionov; zuperman; igoralecsander;
chriscrowley; Sorapop; Minerva Studio; Bobbushphoto; wuttichok; ritfuse;
brianbalster; Lagni

Some of these essays appeared in the following publications: a small part of "A River
in Hokkaido" in *Potomac Review*, spring/summer 2004; the second part of "Les
Femmes Belles avec Merci" in *Matter* issue 12, summer 2009; "Four Mountains" in
To Everything on Earth: New Writing on Fate, Community, and Nature, edited by Kurt
Caswell, Susan Leigh Tomlinson, and Diane Hueter Warner, Texas Tech University
Press, 2010; an early draft of "Crossing Over the Mountain" in *Waccamaw*, April 24,
2011; "Ah, Venice, Again" in *Slab*, issue 6, 2011; "A Short Walk in Anasazi Country"
in *Earthlines*, issue 1, 2012; "Death in Seville" in *American Literary Review*, fall 2012;
"Getting to Grey Owl's Cabin" in *Terrain.org*, August 1, 2013; the first part of "Les
Femmes Belles avec Merci" in *Shadowgraph Magazine*, winter 2014.

Poems by Matsuo Bashō, on pages 8–9 and 19 are from *The Narrow Road to the Deep
North: And Other Travel Sketches*. Trans. Nobuyuki Yuasa. New York: Penguin, 1966.

"Home-sickness" by Mary Mackellar on page 114 is from *The Book of Highland Verse;
An (English) Anthology, Consisting of (A) Translations from Gaelic*, translated by Dugald
Mitchell, 1912.

Trinity University Press strives to produce its books using methods and materials
in an environmentally sensitive manner. We favor working with manufacturers that
practice sustainable management of all natural resources, produce paper using
recycled stock, and manage forests with the best possible practices for people,
biodiversity, and sustainability. The press is a member of the Green Press Initiative,
a nonprofit program dedicated to supporting publishers in their efforts to reduce
their impacts on endangered forests, climate change, and forest-dependent
communities.

The paper used in this publication meets the minimum requirements of the
American National Standard for Information Sciences—Permanence of Paper for
Printed Library Materials, ANSI 39.48–1992.

ISBN 978-1-59534-261-4 paperback
ISBN 978-1-59534-262-1 ebook

CIP data on file at the Library of Congress

19 18 17 16 15 | 5 4 3 2 1

for Scott
a companion for every road

I am a nomad, not a farmer. I am an adorer of the unfaithful, the changing, the fantastic. I don't care to secure my love to one bare place on this earth. I believe that what we love is only a symbol. Whenever our love becomes too attached to one thing, one faith, one virtue, then I become suspicious.

Good luck to the farmer! Good luck to the man who owns this place, the man who works it, the faithful, the virtuous! I can love him, I can revere him, I can envy him. But I have wasted half my life trying to live his life. I wanted to be something that I was not. I even wanted to be a poet and a middle class person at the same time. I wanted to be an artist and a man of fantasy, but I also wanted to be a good man, a man at home. It all went on for a long time, till I knew that a man cannot be both and have both, that I am a nomad and not a farmer, a man who searches and not a man who keeps. A long time I castigated myself before gods and laws which were only idols for me. That was what I did wrong, my anguish, my complicity in the world's pain. I increased the world's guilt and anguish, by doing violence to myself, by not daring to walk toward my own salvation. The way to salvation leads neither to the left nor the right: it leads into your own heart, and there alone is God, and there alone is peace.

—Herman Hesse, *Wandering*

CONTENTS

A RIVER IN HOKKAIDO

Japan, 1992–95

It is fall now, and the Chitose River is high and green, the cooler rains coming in to swell it from the mountain lake at its headwaters, Shikotsuko (Dead Bones Lake). The river moves fast through the trees and dwarf bamboo, and through a shower of colored leaves when the wind comes in, a bluster of bright butterflies. These fall colors fall. They spring, tumble, and float, spreading over the river's surface like drops of paint, widening, a careless painter's palette. The colors bleed together in looping swirls—oil on water. Dragonflies spin away, setting the sky in motion, and kingfisher and grey heron where the trees are hung low to touch the water, and in those cool, quiet shaded troughs at the cut bank, salmon move upriver toward the lake, the second deepest lake in Japan.

I paddle with my friend, Noguchi, our two canoes adding two colors—blue and red. There before the Chitose salmon hatchery, Noguchi turns his boat into an eddy behind an exposed rock. The rapid below is short and straight, not much to worry over. Noguchi scans the chute for obstructions, anything that wasn't here the last time we paddled through. The route looks clear, and he positions the bow of his boat upstream at the eddy's edge, pulls three strokes hard with his paddle, driving the bow of his boat into the oncoming current. The fast water takes the bow out, pushes it, spins it, the boat turning and turning, as Noguchi peels out leaning, his bow now facing downstream. He takes the rapid head-on. I see his boat drop into the wave-hole. He vanishes a moment, a moment more, except for his black helmet visible above the river's horizon clouded with spray. His boat takes on speed, hits the bottom of that hole where the water dropping down begins to press up as the boat buoys, and, with Noguchi's hard final stroke, punches through the peaking wave. Downstream, he finds another eddy behind an even larger rock, turns in out of the current, faces upstream again, and looks for me to come down.

I peel out of the eddy, following Noguchi's line, and run the rapid clean and fine, catch the same eddy behind the big rock, and there we sit like bobbing ducks, my hand resting on his shoulder, the river moving fast around us.

"Ka-to," Noguchi says, his pronunciation of my name, "I want a more bigger waves."

I nod in agreement. "But it's a pretty morning," I say.

"Yes, of course. Pretty morning. You see the salmons?" he says pointing to the shallows along the left bank.

And I do see them. They are there and there and there, crowded against the rocky shore. I see dorsal fins exposed to the open air, their backs curved ellipses outlined by the water, like the hull of a canoe. The salmon are funneled into a tight chute, all of them trying to move upstream at once. They thrash and turn and push. They are running out of time. Or, time is running out of them. Noguchi and I both need to get home soon—our workday is about to begin. In turn, we pull up into the faster current along the outside edge of the eddy, push out and away, our boats back into the fast water moving down.

I came to Hokkaido, Japan, in March 1992 to teach English at a small private school. It was my first trip out of North America. I didn't know much of anything. In the grocery store, I wondered: is this a bottle of bleach or a bottle of milk? The head of the school paraded me around the city to shake hands with officials. They spoke rapidly in Japanese, sizing me up with their eyes like a racehorse, or a used car. When I walked to school in the morning, people stopped to stare at me, or they pointed and shouted, "Hello! Hello! Hello!" or they ran away, frightened.

During those first months in Hokkaido, the Chitose River was good to me. It felt like home. It relieved me from the sensory overload that comes in moving abroad. It offered me a structure I knew, a system I understood. The river was my panic hole, what the writer Jim Harrison defines as a "place where you go physically or mentally or both when the life is being squeezed out of you or you think it is, which is the same thing."

Canoeing is not an outdoor sport; it's an art. At least I would have it so. It is balance, timing, intuitive knowledge of your body and the river, and harmony between those parts. To be a good canoeist, you must give up the idea that the boat is powered by your body. The boat is an extension of your body—the canoeist is an aquatic satyr: half human, half canoe.

New paddlers and nonpaddlers commonly mistake the boat Noguchi and I paddle for a kayak. The C-1 looks like a kayak—it has a closed hull, and the paddler wears a spray skirt to keep the water out of the cockpit—but it is clearly a canoe. The primary difference between the two (beyond the shape and size of the hull) is that in a kayak you sit on your butt and use a double-bladed paddle, and in the C-1 (as with all canoes) you kneel and use a single-bladed paddle. The kayak is hard on the lower back. The canoe is hard on the knees. The C-1 is more difficult to keep upright, because your center of gravity is higher, and it's more difficult to move forward in a straight line, but it is easier to roll. A canoeist will tell you that the C-1 is "half the paddle and twice the man." Or the other way around, that the kayak is "twice the paddle, and half the man." To be fair, they are distinctly different boats attracting different paddlers.

During the cold months, Kazuko and I frequented our favorite Korean restaurant, Aridan. Kazuko took a taxi, and I walked across town and through the new snow. When I arrived, I would find her there drinking beer with Mama-san, the owner, at our regular corner table beneath the Kirin beer poster. One night I stared languidly past Kazuko at this poster of a young Japanese woman in a swimsuit with a mug of beer. She said, "You like skinny girl?" and then could not stop laughing.

At the first bend in the river, I come clean through the eddy line, plant my paddle and pull up into the slack water, then push forward with my knees and body pulling the boat up on the paddle, gliding, and peel out into the current. Noguchi and I take turns in the fast water paddling circles in and out of the eddy. On my final run I gain speed across the eddy line, lift up on my downstream knee, sink the stern and, as the bow comes up, pivot back 180 degrees. A pivot turn. Balanced on that delicate edge, the bow coming straight up out of the water, I hold it, hold it, hold it, paddling in a circle, a pirouette, and then lose it, and crash, and go upside down. In the water upside down, I have about twenty seconds or so to roll back up. If I can't, I will have to pull the spray skirt away from the cockpit and come away from the boat. Or drown. Beneath the water, I roll forward, my chest pressed against the deck of the boat. Now I'm looking up through the water at the sky, as if lying on my back in a field of bluebell blossoms. I reach out and up with my paddle on the left side, find the surface, feel the surface with the blade, then, like a beaver slapping its tail, press down on the surface of the river and pull my body and boat upright. My head comes out of the water last. The water is cold as it comes off my back.

Hokkaido is home to the Ainu people, who were here long before the Yamato Japanese came up from the south, from Honshu, in the late nineteenth century. The story of the meeting of these two cultures is not unlike the story of the meeting of Europeans and the native peoples of North America: a long, bloody negotiation.

Kazuko loves to laugh and drink beer and forget her worries. She is in her late forties now, but young at heart. If she stalls at all in her energy and gaiety, it is her increasing concern about her fiftieth birthday. "Pretty soon," she says, "I'm just old lady." She is not tall but is fit and gracious and very beautiful and rich. She has full red lips painted in heavy red lipstick, and through the evening, the lipstick pushes forward into a crest of broken pieces from the friction of her beer glass. Her light black hair is shoulder-length and pinned back in a soft curve over her forehead. Sometimes in winter she wears a padded Chinese jacket, which accents her form, her face, her gleaming dark eyes. She doesn't have any children, and it isn't clear to me whether she ever wanted any, though a Brazilian friend married to a Japanese man told me not having children was the great tragedy of her life. Maybe so, as Kazuko negotiates the world through the prism of a tragic melodrama, a sad joy from a secret pain. I'm reminded of Vermeer's painting *Girl with a Pearl Earring*, the open question in her eyes, her mouth willing and ready, but unable to ask it. One night in a taxi as she dropped me at my apartment, she took hold of my arm and said, "When you are back to America, don't forget my name. Don't forget. Write about me."

At the place the river runs wide, the place we know as Big Eddy, I ferry across the current, making pivot turns and running back along the speed. When I am tired, I paddle to the dock and haul out like a seal. I have brought sweet bread from a local bakery, and Noguchi, strong coffee in a thermos. We cast off our helmets and rest in the sun. The clouds are building at the edges, and it might rain soon. A grey heron tows its broad-backed shadow over the water, and I look up craning my neck to watch it go. I stretch out, use my helmet for a pillow, and close my eyes against the sun. We both have to go to work in a few hours—me to the English school to teach, Noguchi to run the family business, a third-generation tailor and retail men's suit shop, mostly fine Italian suits for businessmen—but for the moment it is possible to rest this way with the boats idle on the flat water, and stare up through the raining leaves against the blue.

The Chitose River is a mountain river with its source at Shikotsuko, the deepest lake in Hokkaido (1,191 feet deep), and second only to Lake Tazawa (1,388 feet deep) in all of Japan. Shikotsuko is a volcanic caldera, like Oregon's Crater Lake, and the mountains around it are still active volcanoes: Tarumae, Eniwa, Fuppushi. This means the lake is surrounded by hot springs. In the language of the indigenous Ainu, the name of the lake means "hollow" or "depression." To the Japanese, the name means "dead bones." No wonder, as it is said that the bottom is covered in a forest of ancient, skeletal trees and that the lake is popular among people. When a body sinks to the bottom, it is entrapped by the fingery branches, and the cold freezes it, makes it heavy, at that great depth. People who go down do not come back up. This is great news for suicides who want to disappear. A friend claims to have once brought a corpse to the surface while fishing for lake trout. He thought he had a big one, and he did.

With all these broken spirits flinging themselves into the depths, Shikotsuko is crowded with ghosts. Ghosts appear commonly in photographs, and are spotted along the highway to the lake. Several people I know claim to have seen an old woman with long white hair running alongside their speeding car at night.

After a day of canoeing on Osarugawa, a river running down from the Hidaka Mountains into the Pacific a couple hours east of Chitose, Noguchi and I sit naked in Biratori *onsen*, a hot-spring bath. The Saru River valley is home to many Ainu people, and the village of Nibutani has a beautiful Ainu museum and cultural center. The hot-spring pool is shallow. I stand holding a thin, white vanity towel to guard my nether region against strained courtesy, as the water circles my knees. The air is chilling, despite the sun. When I sit, it warms me through, closing in around my heart and lungs. Noguchi hands me a can of Kirin beer. He raises his own. "Kanpaii," I hear him say, "Cheers to our good day." The beer is bitter and cold. Noguchi moves over there against the stone wall dividing the men from the women. His eyes fall closed in relaxation. He sinks under, the water closing in over the top of his head. We are outside, naked on the earth and under the sky, the cold creek rushing by the hot pool, welcome and warm here seated on the bottom. My birth is a time too distant to remember, but so near as to be almost yesterday. This is Mother Earth's water, a primal seeding. I feel the crust of the planet beneath me as Noguchi pushes up out of the water, his head emerging like a fish, then his shoulders, his eyes pinched closed, his mouth opening to take a breath, as if for the first time. He looks at me like a puppy, happy and wild and free. He drinks his beer. His thinning hair now points straight up from sinking under. I sink lower into the steamy water. A pool of sunlight. Early spring. I feel the deep fresh refreshing, and all my muscles warm, go soft.

> Bathed in such comfort
> In the balmy spring of Yamanaka,
> I can do without plucking
> Life-preserving chrysanthemums.
> — Matsuo Bashō

In Chitose, I looked out my apartment window one morning in April to find a fresh spring rain melting the winter snows. The rain came in against the window, then turned away, falling in long lines on the quiet river, rolling by, rolling by. Across the river in the cedar trees lining the bank at the Shinto shrine, the jungle crows gathered against the wet cold. One flew out of the trees and dove down, then spread its wings at the surface of the water, pulled up, and landed in the trees again. Another followed, swooped, pulled up, landed. I saw something in the water go under—a little duckling separated from its mother. The duckling swirled in an eddy as the ravens dove from the trees. With each pass, the little duckling was forced to dive under. After a dozen or so passes, the duckling went under and did not come back up.

Kazuko and Mama-san welcomed me at Aridan. I removed my boots and stepped up onto the tatami to sit down. Mama-san called out for three mugs of beer. She drank with us, a few swallows, then made polite excuses and returned to her work. No, no, we complained. Drink with us. Drink with us. Then she bowed and apologized and told us her liver was bad, and the doctor said she should not drink. So she lit the gas grill at our table in preparation for the food she was to bring.

Mama-san brought kim-chee, collecting all the tender ends of the cabbage leaves in one bowl for Kazuko. Then she brought a plate of vegetables, and two plates of raw meat, one of various cuts of beef, the other of beef tongue, because tongue was my favorite, thinly sliced, and lightly grilled, with a piece of kim-chee and bathed in the strong *yaki nikku* sauce.

The meat tasted very good against that cold night. Kazuko and I ate and drank until we were too tired to eat anymore. Then Kazuko ordered a spicy Korean soup. Even with such a bellyful of meat, I could not refuse the delicious soup.

Like most hot springs in Japan, this one has a small shop with a restaurant, and you pay about five dollars for a bath. You can rent towels and purchase toothbrushes and toothpaste, razors, shampoo, conditioner. There is a room for undressing, a room for washing, and a room for bathing in the several indoor pools, one of which will likely contain some curative tea, ginseng for example. And then an outdoor bath, the natural spring water collected in a simple stone enclosure.

As Noguchi and I entered through the sliding doors, I noticed chrysanthemums growing along the steps. The smell of sulfur surrounded us like a warm blanket. The contrast was distinct, an invisible line between flower and sulfur. I knew then that I would hold on to the difference in that moment for many years to come.

This time of year, the Chitose River swells with meltwater from the deep snow in the mountains surrounding Shikotsuko. It comes down from the mountains fast and cold and clean, raising the lake level and the river. As mountain snows melt—the snows from up high, where the Hokkaido brown bear lives—the river rises, and the little rapids we paddle become pushy, testy. If the water level continues to rise, the eddies where we slide out of the current to rest in our boats vanish. The whole river from one side to the other becomes a moving highway. The banks rise into the trees, and the river, like a wolf, rips trees from their roots and topples them along the banks. They create dangerous strainers, which can pull in a canoe and trap it in the branches. It's easy to drown in a river like that.

I am at ease here in this hot-spring pool, my two hundred bones and nine orifices. The men's side is empty except for Noguchi and me. I sit on a stone, the water completing the circle around my shoulders. I wet my vanity towel and fold it into a long rectangle, place it on top of my head. The soft murmur of women's voices comes through the gap in the wall. A bird passes, flying fast upriver. Pied kingfisher. A birch leaf breaks loose and settles on the surface of the pool, a water ring moving out around it. If no one disturbs this leaf, it will sink to the bottom and become part of that thin layer of organic matter settled there. I move my hand across the bottom of the pool, stirring up a cloud of detritus. It mixes and rises to the surface, then settles again, falling like soft rain over my bare legs.

The Ainu believe that every river in Hokkaido is home to nature spirits called *kamui*, and the chief nature spirit resides in the upper reaches of the river near its headwaters, usually somewhere in the mountains. These mountains are also home to the chief bear spirit, who makes a journey each spring into a nearby village to give himself to the people, his flesh and hide and skull. Likewise, the dog salmon is not just a fish, but food sent by the *kamui* of the sea. The Ainu call this fish *kamui chep*, which means "divine fish," or they call it *shiipe kamui chep*, which means "grand food divine fish." It is through the sacred window of the Ainu house that the fire god, who cooks the food for the people, communicates with the *kamui*. If the people treat bear and salmon with respect, they will be happy, and the *kamui* will send them into the villages again the next year.

Sometimes Kazuko's husband, Shigeru Watanabe, would join us at Aridan: a big man with a round happy belly, thick black hair combed just so, and dark, heavy eyebrows. He owned many businesses, and it was said that he was the wealthiest man in Hokkaido. Kazuko and Watanabe did not live together. He lived on the family estate, and Kazuko lived alone in an apartment, not far downriver from me. They were not legally married, and their relationship was something of a secret, the kind of secret everyone knows about and talks about, but only in whispers. The problem was, as I understood it, one of inheritance: who would get the family fortune when Watanabe died? To complicate matters, Kazuko was born in China during the Japanese occupation. Her father was an officer in the army, and her mother may have been her father's Chinese mistress. Watanabe had many mistresses too, so the story went, and was publicly known as Chitose's rich bachelor. So Kazuko was born of a mistress, and became a mistress herself. When Kazuko and Watanabe were together, they were happy, and they had been together now for more than twenty years.

Sometimes at Aridan, Watanabe would sing for us in German, or in English, or even in Japanese. Kazuko would sing with him. He kept a worn slip of paper in his breast pocket with the lyrics of his favorite songs. His favorite of the favorites was "Green, Green Grass of Home." He had sung these songs many times, and he didn't need the paper to remember anymore, but he would take it out just the same, and cradle it in his thick hands like the petal of a flower.

At the onsen, a young woman came out from behind the counter to greet us. Her mouth was softened by her wet lips. Her hair, shoulder length, was perfectly straight. She wore black, thigh-high socks over her thin, shapeless legs, and a denim apron, the strings tied tight at the small of her back. She smiled unexpectedly when Noguchi said: "Two for a bath, please." She held out her small, white hand. I put a thousand-yen note in her open palm, while Noguchi pulled two cans of cold Kirin beer from the vending machine. I stood there dumbly in her presence, my heels hanging painfully over the back of the little onsen slippers, a noticeable imbalance in my sway. Caught in her gaze, a moment passed, and her mouth opened softly to speak. "This way, please," she said, motioning toward the blue curtain with her hand.

That morning Noguchi and I paddled together, the speeding water humming against the bambooed banks, as we worked our canoes at Big Eddy, practicing rolls and pivot turns. We played that way in the water for an hour before our knees went sore and our arms grew heavy. We stopped to rest on the fishing dock. When we collected ourselves, we poured hot tea into our cups.

Here was a moment of certainty. Drinking hot oolong tea at the Chitose River. I sat cross-legged on the dock, the tea steam rising up around my nose. I could feel some anticipation in Noguchi's manner, as if he wanted to say something. The giant *fuki* already covered the easy hills along the roads, up through the shrinking snow, short, early bulbous flowers that glowed nuclear yellow. If you put your nose into the *fuki* blossom, you could smell spring coming on. It's a fine flower in miso soup. For a taste of spring, crush just a little over the surface of your bowl, and take in the flower and the soup in a breath.

One evening as we were laughing and drinking at Aridan, Watanabe noticed a waitress who worked for one of his restaurants dining with her boyfriend. He greeted them at their table. He ordered another bottle of Kirin beer and poured their glasses full. I saw in his face then a kindness and humility that comes only with a surety of knowing yourself, as in the face of the Roman-nosed sumo, Musashimaru. Watanabe talked with the young couple briefly, and then he bowed low, his nose all the way down to the tatami. When the young couple got up to leave, they found that Watanabe had paid their bill.

A long time ago, so this story goes, an Ainu man went to sea to fish. A great wind came up, and he was lost for many days. He nearly died. The island he found was full of people, who took him in and cared for him until his strength returned. One day, the chief of the people told him they were traveling to his land for trade and that he could at last go home. He was also told not to look at the people during the voyage. If he did look at them, the people would be very angry. The man was surprised by the hundreds and hundreds of ships traveling to his land. When they arrived, the chief revealed his true identity: "I am not a man, but the chief of all salmon. In return for saving your life and returning you to your home, you must worship me and honor me with offerings. Don't forget." This is why the salmon is such a revered fish among the native people of Hokkaido.

At the onsen, Noguchi and I left our slippers on the wood floor and stepped up onto the tatami in our socks. The clothes lockers were wide, flat wicker baskets arranged on an open wood rack. We undressed, side by side, leaving our coats and clothes and everything, our wallets, his car keys, my favorite Italian walking boots, right there in the open. Walking naked into a hot springs with your clothes and boots and wallet unattended in a public place releases feelings of a special vulnerability. What if someone came along and took our stuff? What if someone found my favorite boots appealing? He might simply put them on and walk away. Noguchi must have noticed something in my face, because he said, "Don't worry, Kato. No Japanese want it. Boots too big."

When I was sick in bed, Kazuko took a taxi to Aridan and asked Mama-san to prepare a soup for me. She came to my apartment and knocked on my door. I answered. It was snowing out, and the snow fell white on her beautiful black hair. She looked like an angel, or maybe a witch. She thrust the pan through the opening and said, "Spicy Korean soup. You know this type? Good for health. Drink all." Then she hurried away into the waiting taxi.

Clouds sifted over the hot-spring pool, closing off the sun. The air temperature dropped. The sun returned and played over the water again. Noguchi sat near the outside wall, the creek moving fast behind him. He looked half asleep, perfectly at home.

"How's your wife?" I asked.

"OK."

"Really?"

"No. No good," he said.

"I'm sorry."

"I have to decide."

He looked defeated then, like there wasn't anything after deciding. "Well," I said, unsure how to comfort him, "there are many fish in the sea."

"What's that? Fish in the sea?" he said. "Like a tuna-something?"

"No," I said. "It just means there are other women in the world. You will be OK."

"Oh. I see, Kato." Then he said, "I don't like divorce."

"No. Of course not."

"And I don't like alone."

"Well," I said. "You can catch a new fish."

"Ah, Kato," Noguchi said happily. "I see. Many fish in the sea. So I must fishing!"

"Yes, right. But you shouldn't say that to anyone," I said. "It's not very good to say. People will be angry if you call a woman a fish."

"Oh, really," he said. "Not good in English. OK. Thank you, Kato." He paused. "But I have my son. And she is crazy. She is Jehovah's something. Really bad. And her parents too. They hate me."

"That's bad."

"Yeah, really bad. And I have a son, too. She will take him."

I was quiet while he drank from his beer again and then set the can in the rocks behind his head. He looked out into the creek, and everything reminded him of divorce. He couldn't think of anything else. And trying not to think of it, he thought of it, and it came back to him again and again until he decided to think of something else.

"Let's go fishing," he said. "Let's enjoy our life."

"OK," I said, and that's how I knew he had decided.

"OK," Noguchi said. "Only one problem, Kato. Japanese parent. Really strange. If I am single, maybe they think I am gay."

Long ago in an Ainu village, the people ran out of food. They were starving. Everyone died except a brother and sister. The sister sent her brother out with their father's inheritance to buy food. In the wilds, he met a man and a woman. They were both very beautiful, divine even. They fed him all the whale meat he could eat. When the boy tried to pay for the food, the divine man said: "The food is yours. But I want your father's inheritance. I will go and get my own treasures to trade with you." When he was gone, the divine woman said: "I am the bear goddess. My husband is a dragon, and a bad man. When he returns, tell him you want me, not his treasures. He will be angry and go away. Then we can be together." When the dragon husband returned, the boy did as the bear wife had said. Just as the words left his mouth, lightning flashed, and a thunderclap boomed in the distance. The dragon husband vanished. The boy married the bear goddess, and that is why bears are half human.

People say the ghost of an old woman haunts this onsen. You can feel her presence when you are relaxed. She starts low on your back, just above the pelvis, a cold freeze in your muscles, and moves up like a draft to the shoulders and back of the neck.

The story goes that long ago, an old woman died in one of the pools. All day people entered the pool where she was dead. It is amazing she did not float up or turn over face down in the pool. Some children finally became suspicious. Hadn't they better wake her? It isn't healthy to fall asleep in the hot springs. A young girl shook her gently, saying, "Obasan. Obasan." That's when the young girl felt the chill of death. She froze, unable to take her hand away. She screamed. Her mother rushed to her side. The girl was weeping, her fingers still wrapped around the dead arm. Then, to their amazement, the old woman opened her eyes and looked right at them. In the heat of the onsen pool, her eyes had swelled up like huge boiled eggs.

On New Year's Eve, Kazuko and I took adjacent rooms in the Noboribetsu Grand Hotel. A porter met us in the lobby, and carried our bags upstairs. Kazuko planned to have a bath before she did anything else, so we collected our toiletries and changed into our *yukatas* and walked together down the hallway on our way to the bath. Kazuko put her hand in my arm. People looked at us, as they passed. Kazuko giggled and said, "Tee-hee. They are wondering about us."

Noboribetsu is the most famous hot springs in Hokkaido. It is a small village built on a hill where the tourist shops, restaurants, and hotels have grown up around it. The water rises from the earth at Jigokudani, which means "Valley of Hell." Steam and sulfur cloud the air. For some years, Jigokudani has been a popular site for suicides. Whole families have taken their lives here, plunging together into the bubbling pools. But mostly people come to Noboribetsu to bathe in its curative waters. From Chitose, it's three hours by car. Naturally, Kazuko hired a taxi.

We reached the entrance to the bath. Kazuko passed through the red curtain, and I passed through the blue curtain. Mixed bathing used to be common in Japan, as the bath has long been a family affair. Men and women used to bathe together unmolested, even wash each other, daughter washing father washing mother who sits in front of the mirror washing her face. No problem. These days, except in a few traditional onsens, men bathe with men, and women bathe with women. This new modesty might be blamed on the influence of the Puritan West. I don't think it's an improvement.

Dai-ichi Takimoto Hotel, not far from our hotel, has the largest bath in Hokkaido. Inside are dozens of hot-spring pools, each with different curative properties. The men's bath is downstairs, and the women are upstairs. From the women's bath, a balcony looks over onto the men's bath, like the mezzanine in a theater. If they wanted, the women could stand at the balcony and watch a hundred naked men who have no place to hide. But they don't. When the hotel first opened, the men's bath was upstairs, and the women's bath was downstairs. If they wanted, the men could stand at the balcony and watch a hundred naked women who had no place to hide. And they did.

After the bath, Kazuko was warm and red, tired from her long stay in the hot water. I went to her room for supper. We ordered in. We asked for a traditional New Year's meal, *osechi-ryori*, various dishes presented in lacquer boxes. Each dish represents a good wish for the next year: happiness, long life, good health. Like that. We drank cold sake and then cold beer, and ate the dishes to our good futures. And we laughed a lot. We were very tired then, and very happy.

Early spring mornings in Hokkaido are cold. I am out of milk and bread again, so I walk to the Seven-Eleven, through the dirt alleyway and across the highway, which draws west into the higher, still snowed-in country around Shikotsuko.

When I step out of my door, the feral cats scatter like leaves. They huddle against the sun-hardened snow on the roof of the tin shed outside my apartment. I have been feeding two of them all winter, and on warmer days, the female tiger stripe comes through the open window into my tatami room while I work at my desk. She explores the apartment, as long as I remain seated. If I move, or try to coax her to my hand, she turns and hurries out. Later, in the spring, she brings her five kittens inside. They are dark and wear the marks of the Manx that howls from under the cars in the late afternoons. The kittens wrestle and roll in the sun on the tatami, while mother waits, a silhouette in the windowsill. They are not so shy, and I can sit on the floor with them and they will bat at my wiggling toes.

On my way for milk, I walk around the corner and down the alleyway, my wet hair stiffening in the cold against the back of my neck. I pass the empty lot where, two days ago, a backhoe leveled the house to the ground. Today not even the great pile of twisted pipe and splintered lumber remains. It is a smooth, graded lot.

I walk by the small city hospital. Most mornings a car is parking or unparking, and the people inside stare at me with amazement and fear. They stare, and sometimes I stare back, until they realize they are staring, and look away.

At breakfast on New Year's Day, Kazuko and I drank sake from square bamboo cups, and made a walk through the maze of tourist gift shops to Jigokudani, the Valley of Hell, where the hot-spring water boils, and steam and sulfur vents from the center of the earth. Looking onto those pits, Kazuko said, "Beautiful. Ugly. I think I stay here until I die."

On our way back to the hotel, we stopped at the shrine. It was not a building, but a little Shinto kiosk, with cars speeding by behind us on the road.

"Now we make-a-wish," Kazuko said.

We each pitched a hundred-yen coin into the offering box.

Walking along the Chitose River one summer night in the rain, I stopped near the bridge leading into Aoba Park. The river makes a dogleg here and swirls into a wide pool. The rain came softly, and I watched the fish-marks on the river. On the opposite bank, a red fox in the rain. It stopped to look at me. I felt something pass between us, and then the fox wasn't there anymore.

I felt happy then and also sad, walking back to my apartment in the rain.

The old woman at Seven-Eleven greets me with "good morning" when I enter. Her face is deeply creased. Her hair is tied in a neat bun. And her two gold teeth flash when she smiles. I know where the bread and milk are, but I pass through all the aisles like a child in a toy store. In the cooler, I find melon milk next to the orange juice. I find a nondairy creamer called Creap. Here are scores of instant noodles, dried squid, and a fried spaghetti sandwich near the bento, a ready lunch. When I have my milk and loaf of bread, I inspect the oden steaming at the counter: various boiled sea creatures, eggs, vegetables, and odd-shaped soy products in light soup.

Back home, the cats are on the tin roof again. I say hello to them as I pass. Inside, my apartment is warm and dry. Spring light plays against the tatami. I slide the window open just enough and set down a bowl of milk. I hear the water boil, and the room fills with that familiar smell when the toaster chimes. I work at my desk, listening for the sound of cat-feet on the floor.

> Early dawn,
> Young white fish
> Shining in ephemeral white
> Hardly an inch long.
> — Matsuo Bashō

You already know this. Salmon are anadromous fish, traveling up freshwater rivers and streams from the sea to lay their eggs in the fall. The female will carve out a depression with her tail in the riverbed. She lays her eggs while a male circles, waiting. When she is finished, the male releases his sperm over the deposit, fertilizing the eggs. And here the eggs remain all winter, the tiny salmon growing inside. In the spring, before the snow has receded into the sun, the salmon hatch and grow and swarm. Many become food for heron and kingfisher and for larger fish. The survivors travel downstream through spring into the summer sea. Their body chemistry transitions from fresh- to saltwater. Salmon live for about three years at sea, and then, drawn by some urgency inside them that they can do nothing about, they begin the journey back to their birthplace, back home, to spawn.

You also know that they will die. Salmon come from the sea to the river to lay their eggs and die. The flesh and bone melts into the streambed that made them. They live their whole life in preparation for this one moment, this one returning, this one good death.

We peel out of the eddy, my red C-1 river right, Noguchi's blue C-1 river left, our boats carving an arc around the rock in the middle. We float side by side, attending the shallows for salmon.

I feel the fall air tightening my face, but I am warm and comfortable inside my dry jacket. The stiff nylon jacket crackles when I take another stroke, guiding my canoe downstream. I spot salmon, here and here and here. I see their bright backs beneath the water, their rolling motions in the current. I see healthy vibrant fish that run up the river when my boat passes by, and I see dying, decaying fish. The banks, shallows, and eddies are littered with broken corpses.

A dragonfly lands on my foredeck. It sits a moment, flexes its four wings, and turns its head like a mechanical cuckoo before rising again on cool air as I reach my paddle forward. It doesn't flee like a bird but lingers like a fly, flying around and around and landing on the shaft of my paddle. I stare deep into its bulbous eyes. Do you know you will die soon, dragonfly? Do you know your life is about to slip away?

We paddle down, in no hurry, drifting as slow or fast as the river. I make strokes with my paddle, moving the white blade like smooth ivory through the soft water. The sound is so light, it is even quieter than no sound at all.

Noguchi has pulled up into an eddy behind an old log. He points into the pool, and I slip in behind him to have a look.

"Salmon," he says. "Big one."

A long, fat, male drifting in the pool, his flesh coming apart. It rolls onto its side, then rights itself. Its tail is torn and ragged. All the fins—dorsal, pelvic, anal—are torn and ragged. The fish turns over again, and the eddy takes it in a circle. We paddle on.

Just downstream, we slip into the dead water of a wide eddy, our boats brushing the sandy bottom. On the bank, overhung with branches and long tendrils of leaves, Noguchi points up. "Wild grapes," he says. "Here. Taste them."

To get to this hot spring, Noguchi and I walk up a shallow riverbed, following other walkers as we go. The river drains over wide flat shelves of rock, pooling here and there. The farther you go toward the source, the hotter the water gets. At a bend in the river, we arrive. Twenty or thirty people crowd into a few little pools. Everyone wears a swimsuit.

"Why is everyone wearing a swimsuit?" I ask. "I thought people always undress for the hot springs."

"No, not here," Noguchi says.

"Why not here?"

"Here, no people do it," Noguchi says. "But naked maybe no problem. Please try, if you have a confidence."

Morning ice bends dwarf bamboo down, the leaf tips riding the surface of the Chitose River. Shush, shush, shush. Shush, shush, shush, as a kingfisher speeds downstream and the jungle crows crowd the tall trees, laughing, because salmon are traveling into the mountains from the Japan Sea, and the birds expect the universe will provide a free lunch. I plant my paddle into the slack water at the top of the eddy, pull my C-1 forward and up and in beside Noguchi, who washes sideways with my motion to make room for me. We bob side by side in our boats, arms clasped like brothers.

Not all rivers are created equal, but all rivers are equally created, and it was here on the water I felt most at home in Japan. My friendship with Noguchi grew because we both love to paddle.

"Try pee-vot!" Noguchi calls to me.

"OK," I say, and peel out, the bow of my boat riding up on the fast water, riding up on the edge of upright and downright upside down, until I go just too far and crash and roll and roll back up, laughing. "Oohh!" I hear Noguchi say. "Head, maybe like a ice cream!"

It is a beautiful time of year on the river, with grey heron standing in the shallows around every corner; the water, gray too with the fall snow and the overcast Hokkaido sky. And the salmon, moving upriver in great bands of bright red and streaks of gray, the lot of them sweeping across the river in one motion like a dragon's tail to avoid our boats coming on.

In later weeks, when the early snows have melted in resurging summer sun, and the trees have lost all their leaves, the salmon are spent of eggs, milt, and life and lie broken in the shallows like hulls of rice, scoured, to be swilled away.

We find a deep pool downstream, and I pull my spray skirt back to fish out my diving mask, a window on a salmon's world. I pull it over my nose and eyes, give Noguchi my thumbs-up, and turn my boat over into the deep pool. I hang from it, as if suspended from a fishing bobber with my one big breath to keep me down. I can see the roots of trees at the under-river edge, a few small trout, and the bottom designed with stones. And there in this green watery world is a broad-backed male salmon, its lower jaw hooked like a boxer. It looks tired and spent, its skin graying like an old man's hair. I watch it for as long as I can, sculling in its fins to keep its place, a kind of active sleep. The fish doesn't seem to notice me. My chest tightens, and I pull up on my paddle as quietly as I can, the cold water pouring off my shoulders and helmet.

I draw a few deep breaths and enter that world again. I hear water underwater, and there is Noguchi hanging under his boat like me. We smile because our faces are masked and gravity drawn, and he says something that sounds like bubbles. We roll back up, laughing. How silly we look upside down in our boats. And how terrifyingly good we are at getting into places we really don't belong.

I draw breath again and go under. The salmon is there. I take one hand off the safety of my paddle and search the deep for the fish. I lay my hand across the crest of the head. It doesn't move, this fish in my hand, and I draw down its back with my fingers as smooth as the current of water that freshens the space between us. I near the end of my breath as the motion of my touch threatens to press the fish away. I stretch out my reach until I feel myself coming loose from my seat upside down.

Without warning, a red wave consumes me, salmon by the hundreds bucking and pulling from side to side, coursing, speeding, forcing the water out ahead. My pulse quickens as the big fish stream by, bigger than life, bigger than me, around my chest and under my arms and across the glass of my eyes. I have to breathe, but I force myself to stretch it out longer. I let go of my paddle to free up my arms and raise them now upside down to the bottom into the world under the river where the coursing salmon sing like God's choir, and then I'm falling free, out of my plastic boat, out of the confines of my technology, and floating, flying, gasping for breath at the surface, and I dive deep down again spreading my arms and legs wide like wings, like fins in the current-air as the fish and my heart with the planet pulse home.

AFTER FAN CHENGDA:
A RIVER DIARY

China, 1995

(1) In Guilin, that southern Chinese city on the great Li River, which flows a broad, smooth braid through those famed limestone towers covered over in greenery, I was in love; I was in love with being in love, in love with my youth, and in love with the road, so I followed my friends onto a flat-bottomed tourist boat that spring for a pleasant day standing at the rails and gazing onto the verdant countryside of rice fields and spires of stone. From the rooftop deck we could see both up and down the river, where we had been and where we were going, while off the back of the boat the kitchen boys prepared our lunch, heaving great buckets of slop over the rail to the fishes. And up and down the stairs between the decks came the staff women, dressed in their black pumps, sleek black skirts, and tan-yellow blouses buttoned up the front, the sleeves squared off at the elbows, cut low in the neck to offer those two lovely bones of the clavicle. For any young American man (such as myself) the roselike lips and coarse black hair of a Chinese woman offers a foregone exoticism. It was a pleasure to be young and alive because all the years before, I could not know that not being young and alive was an eventuality or that sometimes sorrow grows so unerringly in the heart as to break it or about betrayal. And in the tension of this dif-

ference now, I felt alive and mortal and powerfully fragile, so that any failure was a delight and any success was a boon, and nothing I did or did not do mattered at all in the long round of the expanding universe.

My companions, Kraig Donald and Kazuko Osogami, were happy too, leaning into the Chinese past and future, so easy with the idleness of the day, as if they had just finished their work and deserved a rest. Kraig and I were both English teachers in different schools in Chitose, a little city on Hokkaido, the most northerly island in Japan. Kraig grew up in Braintree, about half the distance between London and the North Sea. He was a large blonde man, a soft man, with an easy intelligence, a Prince Valiant haircut, and a buffoonish laugh, which I rather liked. He smoked, socially,. and possessed an urbane sensibility that I associated with London. He taught me, among other things, to look at my own country from the outside. Apparently, not everyone thinks America is the greatest country in the world. "God," he'd say, "an American. Bloody disgusting." Or "Americans are so fucking belligerent," at which he'd turn to me to check himself: "But you're different, of course." He had pierced his nose since coming to Japan; and one night, in a confusion of alcohol and darkness, he walked through the glass wall next to the glass door of a Tokyo hotel—walked through so that the glass separated into a million little sparkles on the pavement. Upon impact, that little stud in his nose pierced his septum, and, after having it forcibly removed, Kraig argued against but finally paid for the damages. It was the hotel's fault, he initially said. Without proper lighting, that door was nearly invisible.

It was Kazuko who had dreamed up this journey into China, a Japanese package tour of Shanghai, Guilin, and Beijing, with a group of mostly retirees and honeymooners. She had long wanted to travel in China, for it held the distant nostalgia of home. Born near Beijing during the Japanese occupation, Kazuko held on to a few faint memories, a remote agitation somewhere in the blood that this landscape, this language was home. Kazuko's husband, Shigeru Watanabe, a businessman with a diverse portfolio of investments and ventures, was locally known as the richest man in Hokkaido. He was also locally known as Hokkaido's rich bachelor, for he was not legally married. Kazuko regarded herself as a kept woman. She loved Watanabe fiercely, and he loved her. When I spent time in their company, they would laugh and smile and hold each other's gaze, and then Kazuko would clap me about the shoulders in a joke, and sometimes Watanabe would sing. This trip to China was his gift to Kraig and me, for Watanabe lived on the family estate, and he kept a modest apartment for Kazuko in town. He traveled a great deal on business, breezing in and out of her life, which, by my count, encouraged the passion of their love. One evening outside that wonderful Chitose restaurant that specialized in Korean yaki nikku, a quiet snow falling on the metal roof, Watanabe issued this charge: "Please," he said carefully to me, "take care of my wife."

(2) The river journey would take us from Guilin to Yangshuo, a day-long passage with lunch. We would pass through the famed karst mountains, which the twelfth-century Chinese official Fan Chengda (1126–93) called "worthy to be rated first in the world." Perhaps you've seen this dramatic landscape in the movies: It's featured in *The Painted Veil* with Edward Norton and Naomi Watts (worth your time). It appears in a few scenes in *The Joy Luck Club* (not bad, a little schmaltzy). And in *Star Wars Episode III: Revenge of the Sith*, it is the planet Kashyyyk, or the Wookiee Planet C (not sure you should bother).

A karst landscape is a highly complex system of spires, shafts, sinkholes, caves, and disappearing streams made up of limestone, dolomite, or marble and sculpted by water. Limestone, which makes up the karst mountains of Guilin, is a nonclastic sedimentary rock, which means it is mostly composed of marine fossils laid down by an ancient sea. Once that sea receded, water—carrying enough carbon dioxide to form a weak carbonic acid—dissolved this limestone bedrock and, over a few million years of rain and rivers, left behind dramatic, if not weird, formations which people find highly romantic and will travel thousands of miles to have a look at. Auden, that English poet of considerable powers, thought it curious that we do so, for the karst landscape, like love, "dissolves in water." His poem "In Praise of Limestone" offers this bleakness:

> "I am the solitude that asks and promises nothing;
> That is how I shall set you free. There is no love;
> There are only the various envies, all of them sad."

So off we went, the boat pulling away from the dock, Kazuko and Kraig at my side, and the great Li River drawing us downstream. We stood at the rail watching the cormorant fishermen work the gray waters from simple bamboo punts with a basket fixed in the center. The cormorant dove for the fish, while the fisherman did fairly nothing at all. When the bird surfaced, he took the catch from its mouth. The cormorant was fishing for itself, not the fisherman, only it couldn't seem to remember that the fisherman had tied a cord around its neck, just tight enough that it couldn't swallow.

As the tour boat made mid-channel, the wind came up, and Kazuko expressed her agitation. Dressed mostly in white, with a white cap over a white cloth neckshade that flowed down along her dark oriental hair and up around her square chin, her lips full and red (she looked like the Queen of the Nile), she took up my arm and said: "Kart. Take me inside."

Most Japanese people pronounced my name "Ka-to," but Kazuko spoke English well enough to know she had to try for a hard consonant at the end, but then there was that issue with *L* and *R*, so famous among the Japanese. You know: Fa Ra Ra Ra Raaaaa, Ra Ra, Ra, Raaa.

"It's perfectly wonderful out here. Let's stay outside," I said.

"No more, da-me," she said, mixing the two languages. "Take me inside. We take-a beer soon."

"How about after we reach Elephant Trunk Hill," I said, checking our route. "It's not far. And we can't miss it."

"No," she said. "Kart. OK. You stay here. You like outside, *dakara*. I know your mind." She turned to Kraig. "Kray-g," she said. "We go inside. OK? Take-a beer now?"

"OK," Kraig told her, and they went below to take a table at the window.

(3) Fan Chengda, one of China's greatest poets and travel writers, made his living as a government official during the Southern Song dynasty (1127–1279). He served as military governor of Guangxi province from April 1173 to February 1175, so he lived and worked in Guilin. Fan Chengda's *Treatises of the Supervisor and Guardian of the Cinnamon Sea* is the seminal work on life in Guangxi during the Southern Song. In those days, Guilin (literally "cinnamon grove") was considered a remote backwater, the post many government officials desired least. It was thinly populated, and most of the people were not Chinese but members of various indigenous groups. Though the Chinese had begun to arrive during the Qin dynasty (221–206 BCE), the region had not yet entered the "cultural orbit of Chinese civilization," writes Fan Chengda's translator, James M. Hargett. In fact, according to another historian, Guangxi did not come into "firm Chinese control" until 1949. The region was thought to be "infested by miasmas and malaria," writes Hargett, "populated by spear-wielding, tattooed, and aggressive 'barbarian' peoples, and home to dense forests infested with savage beasts, venomous snakes, and leeches detachable from the body only by fire." Naturally, Fan Chengda fell in love with the place right away.

According to Fan Chengda, a miasma is "caused by mountain mists and watery poisons, together with foul exhalations from wild grasses and steamy swelter from lush vegetation. People who have come down with miasma look like they have malaria." He goes on to report that miasma "relates to the blazing quarter [the south], where the pulse of the land is dispersed and the air is drained. People are baked by its constant heat." The treatment? Monkshood, as well as "pinellia, atractylodes, and agastache formula."

Fan Chengda was not particularly productive as a writer during his stay. That came later: he wrote the whole of *Treatises* during the journey to his new post in Sichuan. In the book, he says he found a life-giving "peace of mind" in Guilin and, upon departure, remained "deeply attached." Among the many reasons for his enduring attachment is "the wondrous nature of the [limestone] hills," which he describes as "jade bamboo shoots and jasper hairpins, forests of them extend[ing] without limit."

(4) As we approached Elephant Trunk, I had myself become intoxicated by the wondrous hills and stood at the railing in quiet awe. I could feel the lush greenery and wet stone that would soon tower over me as we entered Ox Gorge. This place felt old, and full of an alien history that I might come to know only at its surface. It also felt new. Despite Fan Chengda's claim that the pulse of the southern lands is dispersed and the air is drained, I felt a vital energy here, a frenzy and voraciousness for the shiny and new. But not just here on this tourist boat—everywhere in Guilin, and everywhere in China: in the streets, shops, and markets; in the flow of tourists buying up food, alcohol, and trinkets; at the museums, the tombs, and the Great Wall, where a crowd gathered as Kraig and I batted about a hacky sack; at the monuments to the three thousand years of glorious Chinese civilization. The whole country was perched on the edge of a terrifying capitalism, and here I was sailing gaily through the center of it.

Elephant Trunk Hill is so named because this mound of limestone features an arch at the river's edge that looks like an elephant's trunk drinking from the water. Atop the hill is a pagoda built during the Ming dynasty (1368–1644), and though old, it was not here during Fan Chengda's day. The space through the arch is known as River and Moon Grotto. Fan Chengda writes that the summit is "upright and orderly, just like the great disk of the moon." It is the symbol of Guilin, and as we passed by, I put my head back momentarily to gaze up at the sky. This was the life I had dreamed of, a traveling life, in which my constant movement offered a changing vision of the luminous world. I wanted to look back on my life from a ripe old age and think not on the years that I had passed but on the distances I had traveled and on the places I had seen.

Fan Chengda was no different, for along with his *Treatises*, it is his travel writing that distinguishes him. Capitalizing on a new form of

travel narrative emerging in China at the time—the river diary—
Fan Chengda wrote accounts of his boat journeys both into and out
of Guilin. The story of his journey in, *Diary of Mounting a Simurgh*
(*Canluan lu*), takes place over 115 days, in which snow, rains, and
swollen rivers forced him to abandon his boat and travel overland.
The story of his journey out, *Diary of a Boat Trip to Wu* (*Wuchuan
lu*), translated by James M. Hargett, features, among other things, a
ten-day ascent of Mount Emei, during which he bathes in a strange
light known as Buddha's Glory. He also includes an account of the
annual slaughter of fifty thousand sheep in honor of a third-century
Chinese engineer; a confession of his fondness for lychee fruit; and
a small dragon spotted on the river's shore. But it was from the
summit of Mount Emei that Fan Chengda found the pinnacle of
his experience: "The mountains stretch and sweep into India and
other alien lands. . . . This magnificent, surpassing view tops everything I have seen in my life."

Such travel narratives were little more than catalogs of the sights
and sounds of a journey coupled with history and tall tales. They
were most often arranged chronologically, with one entry compris-
ing one day. Entries could be brief—just one line—or could go on
for hundreds of Chinese characters. Critics remark that not only
are his travel narratives among Fan Chengda's greatest achieve-
ments, but his prose is itself a journey, a dynamic and moving
force that reflects the motion of the boat in which he travels: "The
scenes described," writes Hargett, "are almost always shifting, and
the angle from which objects and places are observed is constantly
changing. . . . Scene after scene, in rapid-fire succession, flash right
before the reader's eyes."

(5) Downriver we went, past the Forest of Odd-Shaped Peaks and
then Daxu Town, which dates back to the Northern Song dynasty
(960–1127). Near the head of Ox Gorge, I went below to join my
friends. When I arrived at the table, Kazuko looked up at me with
her dark, shining eyes. She raised her hand for a waiter. "Biru," she
said, and then, "xiexie," and winked at me.

"That language sounds good on you," I said.

"Oh, yeah? You really think so?" She giggled.

"Yeah, it really does, Kazuko," Kraig said.

"Xiexie," Kazuko said. "And how you like massage last night?" she asked me.

"You didn't show up," I said.

"No. Of course I know that. Did you en-joy?"

"Yes," I said. "Very nice."

(6) It had not been, in fact, very nice. In the Park Hotel in Guilin—where Fubo Hill stands sentinel, and inside its cave the Han General, Ma Yuan (14 BCE to 49 CE), tested his sword, and where a dragon once lived illuminated by a pearl—Kraig, Kazuko, and I returned from the streets laden with gifts for people back home. At the head of the stairs leading down from the lobby, Kazuko noticed a sign that read: Massage.

"Very good for health," she said. "Six o'clock. Don't be late."

At six o'clock, I went downstairs. At the entrance to the shop, a long, lovely woman stood at a podium in front of the open doors. Her eyes were a little glassy, and she held her shoulders square, her long pearly white arms bent at the elbows where her black hair dropped over them, her chin pointed up bathed in red light. Everything around her was red. The door was red, the walls and the hanging things with long tassels from the ceiling were red, the very air was red. She looked like a crane ascending into the clouds at sunset.

I waited for Kazuko. And I waited. I began to wonder if she was already inside. The reader board gave a price of 250 yuan for a sauna and massage, and I had 400 in my pocket. Since I had the cost covered, I thought I might as well. The woman in red showed me the way in.

The red hallway opened into a darkened red room where a dozen men, younger and older, wore white towels and reclined in lounge chairs, smoking. A young Chinese man appeared at my side. He was my age, maybe younger, and he wore a fine black suit.

"Hello, sir. Nice you come here to this place. We have a nice sauna here," he told me. "Very nice for relaxing. Inside you change clothes."

Two young boys approached me in the dressing room. One reached for my waist as I was removing my pants. I pulled back, startled. He giggled like a girl. He thrust out his hand. I shook my head. I could undress myself. Then another boy snatched up my favorite Italian hiking boots.

"Shine!" he said. "Shine! Shine!"

"OK," I said.

I wrapped a heavy cotton towel about my waist like a skirt. The man appeared beside me again. "You like shiny shoes!" he said, smiling. "Come this way, please. Right this way, sir."

I followed him to the sauna.

"Go inside," he said. "Very nice. Very hot and nice inside. Good for health."

I opened the door and entered the steam-filled room. I sat down on the wood bench and drew the steam into my lungs, exhaled. Inhaled. Exhaled. Beads of sweat came down from under my hair, fell over the arch of my nose and dripped onto the wood slats.

The door opened. It was him again. He stood before me in the steamy room, wearing his nice suit.

"By the way," he said. "Sorry to disturb you, sir. I must ask a question. You want the regular massage? Or the really, really good massage?" He wriggled his white fingers in the air.

I didn't have a lot of money. Honestly, I wasn't expecting to pay. Kazuko always paid for everything, and it was nearly impossible to stop her. Over the two and a half years in her company, I completely surrendered to this luxury.

"I'll take the regular massage."

"No," he said. "You don't understand me. You want regular massage, or the really, really good massage?" He said it more slowly this time.

"I'll have the regular massage," I said. Sometimes, like a terrier, your mind grabs onto an idea and won't let go.

"No!" he said firmly. "Listen, please. Listen to me. You want reg-u-lar ma-ssage, or reeeally reeeally gooood ma-ssage?" He wriggled his fingers in front of me again.

Honestly, I didn't get it at first. I was a fairly innocent guy from rural Oregon, and this was my first visit to a place where I might be offered what was being offered. There's a first time for everything.

Surprised, and worried over money, I told him I'd take the regular massage.

"OK," he said. "But the regular massage isn't good."

He left me, and I sat quietly, sweating in the sauna. But I was agitated now, a little worried, not relaxed at all. The sauna was too hot, and I felt vulnerable and exposed in my towel. My clothes and my favorite Italian boots were inside that little dressing room, guarded by two hermaphroditic boys who wanted money for service. Shine shoes? Shine shoes? Right. The regular shine, or the really, really good shine?

I opened the door and went out into the dressing room.

"Please," said my host, materializing out of thin air, "put this on." He handed me a blue cotton shirt and a pair of blue cotton shorts. "Come with me."

He led me through the front lounge and into a small room in the back. A group of women assembled in a line. "You must choose," he said.

This was a moment beyond my star, and I was wholly unprepared. It seemed that everything in China was for sale, including these women. I was embarrassed for them and embarrassed for myself. I would not walk up and down the line, look at their teeth as if they were horses, test the sturdiness of their legs. I would not. Yet I had little to trouble me, as I had but asked for the regular massage. Why should I feel guilty? I pointed to the first woman in line. She giggled and they all giggled together, then she took my hand forcibly and led me away.

The room we entered was empty but for the two of us and a couple dozen massage tables covered in crisp white sheets. She had me lie down on a table in the middle. She stood over me, and I felt her black hair fall over my chest. She wore a black dress with lace curving in low around her neck, opening her chest to my view. Her eyes were black too. The red and the black. Her mouth was lovely and red, and her hands looked strong. I was surprised at myself for feeling excited. I had chosen well. She said something in Mandarin, and I responded in Japanese, then in English. She shrugged her shoulders and went to work. The regular massage, remember. It was fine. It was regular. I overcame my little surge of excitement and went back to feeling like a regular guy doing a regular thing. I relaxed a little and let the tension go.

She spoke to me in Mandarin, and I said a few things in Japanese, I don't know what, and then she said a few things more, I don't know what. We started to laugh. We laughed a little together because we were having a conversation and not understanding, although the circumstances made it seem possible to know what the other had said. Everything was OK and regular, and I felt like a regular guy, and I think she felt like a regular girl.

I began to think about what she did for a living, what she did for men who came into her room. It was an odd thought about such a regular girl. But also, I really didn't mind it. I wondered where she lived and how she had grown up. Was she Chinese from the north, or from one of the several local Man tribes? Then she hopped up on the table and put her knees into my back. She sat on my back and worked her hands through my shoulders. My neck went lax and my arms tingled by my sides. Did regular girls do this? I thought they might. I hoped they would.

When it was over, she stood beside the table. She seemed to be asking me to consider her again. I sat up. Our eyes met smilingly. I shook my head. She looked down and then offered me her hand and led me out of the room.

Then it was him again, interrupting our pleasant walk.

"My friend," he said. "That wasn't very good, I know. How about you and she once more time with the really, really good massage." He picked up her hand and put it in mine, offering her like a pastry. "You see," he said, "she likes you."

I shook my head.

"How about it!" he said.

"I don't have enough money."

"It won't be much more."

"How much?"

"About two hundred."

"Yes," I said, "that's not much." I paused, realizing I was considering it. Then I said, "I didn't bring enough."

"So?" he said. "OK. It's settled then. You go back again with her." I shook my head.

"All right," he said. "All right. But I am sure that wasn't very good. How about a tip for the girl, then."

"How much should I tip her?"

"One hundred."

I gave it to her, and she smiled and departed. I didn't want her to go, because I was beginning to reconsider.

"Now, how about tip for me?"

"For you?"

"Yes, of course."

"For what?"

"For service," he said. "It should be about double as the girl."

I only had 300 left, and the front desk would ask for 250.

"Double?" I said.

"It is for my service," he said. "It's a very good service."

I handed him fifty.

He threw his hands up in the air and groaned. This happy guy wasn't happy anymore, and suddenly he couldn't speak English. He spoke hurriedly in Mandarin, perhaps cursing, and ushered me to the dressing room. The boys hovered like flies as I changed my clothes, and one handed me my polished Italian boots. They looked very fine. I gave them each ten yuan.

I stopped at the front counter to pay. The crane woman would not look up at me. I put everything I had left on the counter, and she swept it off into a basket with her hand.

Back in the room, I told Kraig about my adventure.

"So, you said no," Kraig said.

"Right," I said. "I said no."

"Why did you do that?"

"I don't know," I said, really wondering. "Maybe I should go back for another try?"

Later, in Beijing, in the hotel Jing Da Du, Kraig would be invited to accompany the Japanese men in our tour group for a circle jerk. A few were newly married, and the others were married and bored. They ushered Kraig into a back room in the hotel bar and formed a circle with a Chinese woman to the left of each man. Each Chinese woman would reach across her body with her right hand and work the man on her left. Well, that's my vision of it anyway. She could also work the man on her right with her right hand. Of course, if she was left-handed, then it all gets fouled up. Anyway, we will never know for sure, because even though the married Japanese men would have paid the bill for Kraig (they were keen to see how things shaped up for an Englishman), he turned them down.

"So, you said no," I said to him that night.

"Yeah," he said. "I said no and came right back to the room."

"How do I know you really said no?" I asked.

"How do I know *you* really said no?"

"Good point," I said.

"Well, we'll probably be remembered as the two guys who said no."

"Probably," I said.

(7) Back on the Li River, lunch rolled out on carts across the dining room, and the people on deck came inside. There wasn't much to do but eat and drink and watch the country slide by from the windows. Seated at the table, though, I couldn't see the sky or the tops of the karst mountains bending away and leaning over the river. The limestone towers of Ox Gorge are reported to look like oxen, especially the formation known as Nine Oxen Ridge or Nine Oxen Playing with Water, where the river bends along a series of long sandy beaches. Others claim the formations look like horses, or

lions, or tigers, or even dragons. To me, however, they are mounds of mashed potatoes, and they remind me of "Hakone," one of my favorite woodblock prints by Hiroshige from his Tokaido Road series. Dragons or potatoes, all I could think about was getting back outside. We were missing the best part of the river.

Most of the fare from that lunch is lost to me, as so many things are, and I wonder now what dishes were served, what new and exotic tastes I encountered. Did I sample Fan Chengda's favored lychee fruit? I think I did. According to his *Treatises*, he didn't care much for the lychees of the region, claiming those from Min are far superior. And he mentions the dragon lychees. When steamed, they taste like longan (as if anyone knows what that is). But do not eat them raw, Fan Chengda advises, "for this will trigger the onset of epilepsy or apparitions of monsters." Maybe someone had such an apparition when looking out on the karst hills? And did I taste the soft plums he writes about or perhaps the human-faced fruit? Or the more auspiciously named goat-droppings fruit, the taste which Fan Chengda claims is "not outstanding"? Or, my favorite, the rubbing-and-scratching nuts, which are "sweet but slightly astringent"? I could have eaten the barbel fish: "very fatty," and "full and wonderful." Or the shrimp fish: "tastes like shrimp but lighter and more wonderful." Or the goby fish: "In shape they resemble black carp" and, along with the shrimp fish, are "regarded as precious," both of which come from the Li River. Were the fishermen along the river banks catching the fish we ate? What did we drink, aside from the beer? Perhaps the local wine Fan Chengda calls "auspicious dew," made with "clear and cool water" from a local well. So many questions, and all of it lost. What a pity.

And what about the cinnamon, the source of Guilin's name? If some of these dishes were seasoned with cinnamon, who would know, as meat dish after meat dish arrived at our table, smothered in a dark, gooey sauce. Were we eating chicken or beef or horse or dog? Likely one of each. Truly, Guilin is famous for its cinnamon trees *Cinnamomum cassia*, which Fan Chengda calls "a wondrous tree." Its use as a spice and a medicine dates back at least four thousand years. In the Southern Song, however, most of the cinnamon trees of Guilin had been cut down (lord knows why), and the spice came from afar. They have all grown back since then, though, and in late summer and fall, the *cassia* blooms and the city is overwhelmed by the sweet scent of cinnamon.

(8) Outside again, gliding through Ox Gorge and its towers of stone, I waited at the rails hoping to see something new, something changing, something fantastic. The upper reaches of the river out of Guilin are densely populated, with towns and cultivated fields crowding the banks. Ox Gorge, however, is far too mountainous to support many people, the great humps of limestone cutting off easy overland access to form a wild green wilderness. The river itself is the pathway in and out, as it was in Fan Chengda's day. River travel was more dependable and often faster and cheaper than overland travel. In the Southern Song, the Li River was part of a great network of navigable riverways, where boats moved goods (silks, pottery, salt, teas, rice) and people, especially government officials. The road system was also well developed but could pose a formidable challenge if the weather went bad. Though river travel had its dangers too (winds, dangerous rapids, low or high water), it was the way the country moved. The government rules regarding the travel of an official of Fan Chengda's power and influence allowed for an entourage of up to four passenger boats and one luggage boat. Fan Chengda often traveled with his wife and two sons, and sometimes other family members, all supported by staff and attendants: six from traveler's service, two from the letter and memorial service, and fifteen from food service. A large group of well-wishers would travel with him for the first several days of the journey, along with a soldier escort of 330 men, for pirates worked the waterways.

Another bend in the river, and we came by Immortal Stone and its companion Wangfu Rock, also known as Yearning for Husband's Return Rock. These two formations come with a story. Somewhere in the Chinese past, a young couple and their baby were transporting goods on a small punt to Guilin. They had very little food, but when a destitute man appeared, they gladly gave it away to help him, expecting someone farther upriver would do the same for them. They traveled on and grew hungrier and weaker, and at last the husband climbed to the top of a hill to look for help. He scanned the river for other boats, and in his extreme worry, he turned to stone. His wife waited and waited for him to return. Finally she climbed up the hill. At the place she discovered his lithified body, she too turned to stone.

(9) The river drew us down, and with Kraig and Kazuko at my side, I took in the smoky, humid air on this early spring day. We could see other tourist boats like ours on the river, in front of us and behind, more evidence that China's markets and monuments were open for business. Meanwhile, along the banks of the Li, peasant farmers worked their fields and paddies with nary a stitch on, barefoot and oblivious to the passengers at the rails who gazed at them as if at zoo animals. What did these farmers care about the rising smoke of China's industry? They had always worked these fields, and while the government and the corporations grew rich, they would still be working these fields. They worked these fields as a symbol of its past, bucolic icons of a quaint agrarian Confucianism, or a tourist attraction.

I wondered if these farmers were Chinese, or descendants of one of the several tribal cultures indigenous to this region. Fan Chengda devotes a great deal of attention in his *Treatises* to these cultures, which collectively he calls the Man Peoples. They include the Yao, Lao, Li, and Dan peoples, as well as the Man. He writes about them to work out how best to govern, how best to bring them into the fold so that they may be of service to the Southern Song. Perhaps we must not judge Fan Chengda too harshly, as he grew very fond of Guilin and its peoples and found them fascinating, yet of the Man he has this to say: "Their manner is fierce and ferocious; their customs and habits are preposterous and strange. It is not possible to completely rein in and rule them by means of the teachings and laws of the Middle Kingdom, so for now all we can do is to bridle and halter them." I hear in Fan Chengda's tone a bold reverence for the Man, just as I hear his frustration as a governor. Indeed, these cultures do sound fierce and wondrously strange. Consider the following string of customs and behaviors:

- Fan Chengda reports that after a Lao woman has given birth, her husband will lie down next to the newborn and pretend to give birth himself. If he does not do this, his wife will be met with sudden illness.

- The country of the Black Warrior Lao is "filled with miasmic poisons. Those who come down with such illness cannot drink any medicine. So they knock out their own teeth."

- The Man hate foul smells, so they defecate into a hole and then cover it up, like a cat. They also use feces to "deal with people whom they despise. They fling chamber pots at these people, who invariably leap onto their horses and flee in alarm."

- When a relative dies among the Li peoples, "no one cries or eats rice porridge. They eat only raw beef, which they regard as the ultimate way of expressing profound grief." They then put the dead into a coffin, pick it up, and begin walking. They cast raw eggs before it. "The place where the chicken egg does not break is selected to serve as the grave site."

- Apparently, both the Li and the Yao are fond of killing. When Li men drink together, they keep their knives by their sides. "If either says anything inappropriate, they then get up and try to kill each other."

- Yao men are "suspicious and ruthless and treat death lightly. They can also endure hunger [for a long time] when they are away in battle. They ascend and descend the precipitous mountain trails as if they were flying."

(10) I wondered whether the cranes were still hanging around the Li River. Had they gone north? Probably. The red-crowned crane, the largest and heaviest of the world's fifteen crane species, spends winters here (among other places), and Fan Chengda mentions it in his *Treatises*. He calls it the gray crane and says its entire body

"is a gloomy gray color." Gray cranes "are also able to sing and dance." He is referring to their courtship dance, which may also be performed spontaneously at any time for no apparent reason. Fan Chengda reports that the laws of the day prohibited the capture or trapping of rare birds, and thus many fascinating birds, rare and otherwise, lived during the Southern Song. Fan Chengda writes of parrots, peacocks, and cockatoos, as well as the hill mynah ("capable of human speech" and "compared with a parrot, much cleverer"), the halcyon kingfisher (people "dry their flesh and sell it"), and the magic falcon, which nests in holes in trees. People like to block off these holes with wood, which forces the bird to dematerialize and pass through the tree's trunk to enter its nest. It does so only after performing a ritual dance. Upon finding its hole blocked, the magic falcon drops to the ground at the foot of the tree and performs the *yu* step, dragging one leg as if in a limp. After this dance, it can enter its nest. People then sprinkle ash on the ground to retrace the bird's steps, hoping to learn its magic. Would you not want to learn to dematerialize too? But the clever little bird, which is probably a kind of woodpecker, or possibly the Eurasian kestrel, erases its tracks with its talon, so no one may stumble on its secret.

(11) On the top deck, the Li River spreading before us, Kraig and I watched the honeymooners in our tour group as we came by Crown Cave and Half-side Ferry. It was a bright, clear day, and the day went on being bright and clear as the couples held each other's hands and peered over the railings at the water passing under the boat. One couple in particular—a most handsome couple, she in her lacy white dress, which bent around her knees and made visible the form of her body in the river wind, her white, impossible shoes, and her slightly broad and flattened nose on her angelic face; and he with his smart black slacks and white business shirt, his glowing gold watch, his Tom Cruise haircut—seemed truly in love. He made goo-goo eyes. She giggled and kissed his forehead. She put her hand on the small of his back. He dropped his hand onto the convex mound at the back of her dress. It was a little show for us, the other pas-

sengers, to suggest that their lives would be better than ours. They would be true to each other, and their money and good fortune proved they had been chosen by a benevolent providence. I watched a few birds pass overhead, three flying together in the bright air.

Choosing a bride was a very different affair in Guilin in the Southern Song. "People in villages are violent and brutal," writes Fan Chengda. "Men kidnap the wives and daughters of others and run off with them." This he calls Abducting a Partner. The couple flees to some remote backwater, where they may live happily ever after, at least until another man appears who then abducts the woman again. Poor creature. She might be abducted several times in her lifetime and never see her family or relatives again.

(12) Not much was happening on the deck of that tourist boat as we navigated the river. It felt a bit ominous, like the soft pool before a rapid. I wondered what would happen next.

Among the peoples of Guilin, there is a way to discover what would happen next, or at least whether that next thing was good or not so good: divination with chickens. According to Fan Chengda, "They take a young rooster, hold it up by its two legs, burn incense and divine through prayers, and beat the chicken to death." The two thigh bones are removed, cleaned, and bound with a cord. Then, by inserting a piece of bamboo into the bundle, somehow the diviner can determine if a person is auspicious or inauspicious. Some people also divine with chicken eggs.

(13) At the Painted Hill of Nine Horses, it seemed nothing at all was going to happen. This wonderful wall came up before us and towered over the boat. Its story is that Sun Wukong, the Monkey King, left his heavenly horses unattended. They escaped into the wild green hills and grazed on succulent grasses and bright flowers. One morning while they were standing in the Li River, a god discovered them, and took them home to heaven. They fled and smashed into this great wall of rock, and both turned to stone.

A beautiful story, sure, but honestly, folks, it all becomes rather like looking at clouds and seeing a dragon or a hat or the face of the ugliest woman you ever loved. A child's game, and little more. Farther on, we passed Yellow Cloth Shoal, a wide chunk of stone beneath the river's surface that looks like cloth drawn downstream. And then rising from the river's surface are formations that look like a monkey with a watermelon, a bear lying on its back, and a woman holding a baby, reportedly the Crown Prince. Instead of these visions, one might also see, respectively, Magic Johnson with a basketball, a dead horse, and Saturn devouring his children. The mind can go completely wild. Or the mind can be dulled by too many romantic stories of lovers turned to stone, fairy princesses, and fathers making noble sacrifices to save babies. It's easy to feel youthful and in love with the world when the day is new, but to sustain that love into the afternoon and on toward evening, to wake every morning and find your true love beside you and be in love with her, to go to your job and joyously follow the routines of your boring day, to sit down to a meal and say thank you and really mean it, to love your life enough to want to keep living it: that is the impossible work of the world.

(14) The day was wearing on, and Kraig and I needed a coffee. So over the final miles of the Li River tour, we sat at a table below decks with Kazuko and drank one cup, and then a second. After passing Carp Hill (yep, rocks that look like carp), then Camel Crossing the River (rocks that look like a camel crossing the river), and Snail Hill (a snail, of course), we neared Yangshuo, the end of our journey. Here, the famed Green Lotus Hill holds another such story, something about a carp and a fairy who fall in love, and because love is impermanent, the fairy panics and tries to find a way to guarantee that she can stay with her carp lover forever. As you have likely guessed, for some mysterious reason, the fairy turns to stone. In that way, if you look on the bright side, she got her wish.

The hill is famous for its many pavilions and for the statues and Chinese characters carved in the limestone walls. The most famous is the carving of the character "dai," which stands at nearly twenty feet high and ten feet wide. "Dai" means both "area" and "young generation." As part of a longer phrase, "dai" translates to mean that the youth of the area should work hard to maintain its beauty and to contribute to the country. What a pleasant thought, as our cruise on the Li River came to an end.

(15) Back in Guilin, Kraig and I walked the city at night. The tour group had kept us busy all day, and now we wanted to explore a little on our own. From the Park Hotel, we came down across a bridge over the foulest body of water I had ever seen, perhaps part of the old moat around Guilin, or one of the canals dug for water transport a thousand years ago. In the dark, at the water's edge, we heard singing frogs and watched a man set frog traps in the thick night stench. Did he catch the same frogs we ate for supper in the hotel? We had eaten other treasures too—in particular, blackened swallow, a plate rimmed with little charred birds, which must be eaten head first, beak, eyes, and all. The taste was bitter, sour, like vinegar. Kraig couldn't quite stomach it, so he ran his chopstick through its eyeholes, like performing some voodoo rite.

Out on the streets, we passed dentists drilling teeth at night, people hovering over card games under dim electric lights, and bicycles coursing in and out of the traffic, the taxis, buses, cars, trucks, and the uncountable people, many walking barefoot. A young man stopped us to ask if we could light his cigarette. He wore little round glasses, like James Joyce, the left lens with a crack down the center.

"A light?" Kraig said. "But you have a lighter in your hand."

"Sir, yes I do. But this lighter is for trade. Would you like to trade?"

"Why not," Kraig said. "This is not an English lighter, though. I bought it in Japan."

"This is not a Chinese lighter," the man said. "I traded with a German."

His name was Li Yuan, and with this introduction he launched in on a series of questions. He asked about freedoms in America and Europe, and about the movie *Forrest Gump*. He believed that in America, what happened to Forrest Gump happened to everybody.

He asked if in the West people could go to a library and read any book they wanted for free.

"Yes," I said. "That is true."

"And you can truly read any book?"

"Right, you can read any book in the library."

"In England too?" he asked.

"In England too," Kraig said.

"I have lost my most prized book," he said sadly.

"What's that?" Kraig asked.

"*Siddhartha* by Herman Hesse."

"Oh, yes. Wonderful book," I said.

"Sir, would you please send me another?" He handed Kraig a small slip of paper prepared with his name and address.

"You want a copy of *Siddhartha*?" Kraig asked.

"Yes, sir."

"Why? Can't you find one here?" I asked.

"Sir, this is not possible. This is not a free country."

A small crowd gathered to watch us. A couple of Chinese soldiers walked by. Then they walked by again. Li Yuan appeared nervous. China was opening up, sure, but it wasn't open yet, and maybe it never would be. Li Yuan's chance was slipping away, so he came to the point.

"A man I know said he can take me to America if I pay him one thousand dollars. I do not have this money," he said. "But I am working to save it."

"I don't know," I said. "I'm not sure I'd trust this man with your money."

"I know," Li Yuan said. "Maybe I would waste my money. But I have to try something. I feel like a prisoner. Maybe you can help me."

"I don't think we can help you," Kraig said.

"Please sir. You must help."

The soldiers walked by again.

"No," I said. "We cannot help you."

"At least, please, send me this book," he pleaded.

"I'll send you the book," Kraig said.

"Yes sir, thank you," Li Yuan said. "Thank you. And if I write to you with some questions, is this OK?"

"I'll send you the book," Kraig said. "That's it."

"OK, sir. Thank you."

"All right," Kraig said, and he put out his hand to say goodbye.

Li Yuan shook both our hands excitedly, and we parted.

It was late, and as we were to catch an early flight to Beijing, Kraig and I turned back toward the hotel.

"Are you really going to send him the book?" I asked.

"No," Kraig said. "Probably not."

We went on, crossing over the stinking waters again, and up the hill toward the many lights of the hotel.

AH, VENICE, AGAIN

Italy, 2009

There's nothing new to say, nothing more pleasing
said Henry James, than to hear it said.

— Robert McNamara, "Of Venice"

Everything has a beginning, a time when it wasn't what it is. The universe was born out of the Big Bang, and before that there was no space, and there was no time. Our galaxy and solar system have a beginning. The earth has a beginning. And you have a beginning, an origin point before which you were not anything at all. But one can hardly say this about Venice. Perhaps it is the one true exception, or rather, it is exceptional, the exception's exception, the city that was a nation, the swampy mudflat that became a marble island, the dwarf that grew into a giant. And it has always been so. You can never come to the end of Venice, the way you can never come to the end of Shakespeare or Mozart. So why bother with this great theme, why tap out yet another story of this place out of time? The point isn't that someone will say something new about Venice (certainly not me), but that its vastness allows everyone to say something.

Before arriving in Venice, however, I was in Spain, teaching travel writing in my university's study abroad program in Seville. It was all going swimmingly—our group kept hours in the university center for classes, then roamed the country on weekends, tossing in a rogue journey to Lisbon. Then, during Semana Santa, all my students and colleagues fled for northern climes (Paris, London, Rome), and I (what was I thinking?) hung around Seville like a starving dog. I spent a few days with two Hungarian brothers who were two years into a six-year walk around the world (another story, really) and spied on the endless robed processions processing through town. And yet a bad case of cabin fever blew in over me.

I couldn't sleep. I had already watched a half-dozen DVDs on my laptop, read a wonderful book by Laurie Lee, and written page after dull page in my notebook. It was midnight one night, maybe it was Thursday, when I found myself pacing back and forth from the window to the door in my little flat. What was I to do? I put on my shoes and grabbed a handful of cash. I thought I might walk about town to gas off, but I'm not a night person so much, not a city boy, not a barfly. I made a few turns around the cathedral, passed through the old Jewish quarter and across the tip of the Jardines de Murillo. I hungered for something natural, a bright star overhead, a tree to sit under, an empty land out in front of me. I did the only sensible thing: I bought a bag of potato chips and ate them all in one go. I couldn't make a habit of this, what with the dangers of chemical preservatives and high cholesterol. So the next day, when my friends Carmen and John, along with their young daughter, Maria, invited me to join them on a trip to Venice, I accepted.

It was raining as I entered Venice from the north. I say the north because if you take the shuttle bus in from Marco Polo International, you step out into the Piazzale Roma on the north end of town, north-west end really, and if it is raining, then the first thing you do is buy an umbrella. You're going to walk to your hotel, of course—wander is more like it—across the ancient city through ancient streets and along ancient canals; and if it is raining, then you buy an umbrella. My friends would be in late that evening, as we had booked different flights. I had the entire day to myself. Oh, glorious! What would I do with this expanse of time? What could I do? I bought an umbrella at the first kiosk I found, a spring-loaded shade of a goodly size with a nice tartan pattern, red and black, a pattern I'd never consider if I were traveling in Scotland, but this wasn't Scotland, and this pattern was hip in the way that things are hip when out of place. I sauntered off, protected from the rain.

The umbrella is an ancient tool, older than Venice herself. It likely grew out of Egypt some three thousand years ago, as many things did, for royalty, as usual, a symbol of those beings living on a higher plane and overshadowing the lower worlds—a vault of heaven over the pharaohs. In ancient Greece, the umbrella was associated with Bacchus and the sexual reveries of his followers. It soon lost that symbolism and was used as a pedestrian shelter from sun or rain (call it parasol or umbrella, respectively). Later, something very exciting happened. In 1177, so the story goes, Pope Alexander III blessed the Doge of Venice, Sebastiano Ziani, with the honor of bearing his umbrella on arranging a meeting with Emperor Frederick of Germany. So I carried my umbrella boldly through the city, neither pope nor doge nor pharaoh, just an ordinary guy from Oregon, lifting it high over a sea of umbrellas, tourists probably, a gangway of bright colors fustering down the narrow streets.

There are no cars in Venice, no bicycles either. The pace of Venetian life is at walking speed, slow and of the body, the feet and knees and quads, the hips moving in their gentle gait, the shoulders squared and the head up, an outward view, a bright and peaceful forward progress at about three miles per hour. We don't know, or we don't realize, how the speed of modern things—our cars and trains and planes, our iPods and iPhones and e-mails, our enslavement by the clock—takes us away from ourselves, hurries us along to death. In Venice, I felt alive and easy, happy and hungry, maybe even younger than I was, part of something larger than myself, like Big Bang all over again. I guess in summer the canals stink of mortality, a thousand years of human refuse slowly decaying in the bottom's black mud. Yet on this day, the rain freshened the city and my sheltering sky. I was perfectly in my element—nothing to do but saunter along, explore museums and buildings and waterways, have a coffee, gaze at people and their shoes, watch the clouds roll in or roll out, and see the ancient waters of the black lagoon cover over the smooth Piazza San Marco.

My map foretold my way. I decided the Museo d'Arte Orientale was just my style, and I might as well have a look at its companion, the Galleria d'Arte Moderna. The latter I breezed through as I thought I might, an expressionist this and that, a modernist such-and-such, a Dadaist doodad—I didn't really get it. In the Oriental collection I found weapons—any boy's dream—spears and swords and daggers. I wandered the corridors with a dozen other dreamers slavering over those gleaming blades. I wondered, as anyone would, which one of these points, inert behind a glass casing, had pierced a man's heart. But there was too much of it, and it wore on me, slowly, slowly, so I turned to other treasures: scrolls and bowls, armoires and porcelain delicates, lacquerware, and a row of instruments, including the koto and shamisen. I guess some madman, Prince Henry II of Bourbon-Parma, Count of Bardi, collected all this stuff, some thirty thousand items, on his travels in Asia between 1887 and 1889. Imagine setting out on a journey with empty pockets, and then carrying a museum home. Do I need to say it?—Travel light . . . or don't travel at all. Then again, this collection is one of the most important from Edo period Japan. I suppose we should say three hallelujahs in praise of the wealthy and obsessed.

On I went along the Grand Canal, headed for the Pescheria and the Rialto Bridge, only I did not know it then. I didn't have a guidebook and had read virtually nothing about Venice. That came later. I had only my little map and knew only that I had to reach the Piazza San Marco to find my hotel. Carmen, who was somewhere in the sky with John and Maria, was reading *Venice Is a Fish* by Tiziano Scarpa, and later I did too. As it turned out, I was doing it right: "The first and only itinerary I suggest to you has a name," Scarpa writes. "It's called: *at random*. Subtitle: *aimlessly*. . . . *Getting lost* is the only place worth going to." Amen.

I wasn't so much as lost, but I certainly didn't know where I was, and where I was turned out to be the fish market. It's a produce market too, only who can deny the smell of the fish, and the great

wet eyes ogling you from their briny ice beds? I cruised through the
bustling aisles to survey the goods, the fishmongers taking names
and cutting off heads. The floor was slick with slime, and my shoes
became like sliders on a curling sheet. I moved effortlessly, lilting
along in a lope. Nothing much happened here except the surg-
ing energy and excitement of buying a dead fish, coupled with my
awareness that people have been doing so in this very market for
about a thousand years. When I reached the produce, I became
entranced by the shiny fruits, the rounded hard mounds arranged
like sins for the taking. I bought three apples, I don't know which
kinds, all different, and took one of them into my mouth without
washing it. I was fascinated by the pieces of fresh coconut at various
stands, broken at random and set up on little tiers with water running over them. Why I didn't buy one, I will never know.

At the Rialto Bridge I thought I'd reached a major monument,
and of course I had. Perhaps you are worldlier than I, so forgive me,
but I knew nothing about this place, this point, this high bank of
Venetian culture, apparently one of the oldest parts of the city. But
I know about it now. The marble bridge runs up over the Grand
Canal, a major point of crossing, where people pause at the pin-
nacle to have a look at the forever city down its main waterway.
Lord Byron loved this city too and lived here in his self-exile from
England, from 1816 to 1819. He called it a "fairy city of the heart."
He was famous for his prowess in swimming (among other things)
and passed under this bridge more than once, stroking his way
up the canal. In his third famous swim he was in contest with an
Englishman, Alexander Scott, and a blowhard, Angelo Mengaldo. I
suppose Byron was a blowhard too, but on this day at least his lusty
strokes spoke for him: he outraced his two opponents over a distance of four and a half miles from the Lido up the Grand Canal.
Mengaldo dropped out before they reached the Rialto, and after
that Byron swam alone. In a letter to a friend he wrote, "I was in
the sea from half past 4—till a quarter past 8—without touching or
resting." I suppose we might say three hallelujahs in praise of nobles
who are physically fit.

Gazing out from the bridge in the light rain, I found that the day was wearing on. I descended the other side, walking the smooth marble steps where, from the time of the bridge's completion in 1592, some millions of shoes have worn away every imperfection in the stone. It wasn't too far or too long after that when the light came tumbling in, the clouds parting their seams, and though it sounds like I made it up, I stepped out into the Piazza San Marco in the splendor of the midday sun.

Can you imagine it? At heart, I'm just a mountain man trapped in a paved-over world, as I heard it, or, at least, "isn't it pretty to think so," but I do give thanks for the beauty of the world's great cities. San Marco is, as you'll hear or read over and over if you visit, the only piazza in Venice, with its cornerstone the Basilica di San Marco and its five stately domes, consecrated in 1094. It was the private cathedral of the doges until 1807, when it finally opened to the public. Most buildings in Venice face the canals on which they were built, but the Basilica faces the center of the piazza. If you've seen other cathedrals in Europe, as I have—especially Saint Peter's in Vatican City, Saint Paul's in London, and the Cathedral of Seville— you may be tempted to pass this by, reasoning that if you've seen those three, you've seen them all. But have a look at the façade, the dazzling mosaics, and know that inside even greater splendor awaits you. All other places of worship pale in comparison, except perhaps the sun setting on the Grand Tetons.

I sat down on a movable gangway, used in the square to make a path when the water rises. The water was rising after the rains, and in places across the piazza floor it bubbled up from the underground and pooled. These gangways were for walking on, of course, but everywhere they had become benches for weary amblers like me. I sat down, the Basilica at my fore; over my left shoulder, the Torre dell'Orologio, with its two bronze Moors who strike a bell with great hammers on the hour; over my right shoulder, the 99-meter-high campanile, and, beyond that, statues of the city's patron saints—Saint Mark and Saint Theodore—who show the way out to the waterfront and the sea.

This is where my story stalls, where I met this splendor at early afternoon and sat idle in the center of it for more than one hour. I really had no idea what to do next except sit there and take it all in. And so I did, but it was far too much, and it wore on me, slowly, slowly. Scarpa is right again: "Too much splendor seriously damages your health."

To repair that, I went for a walk, out between the two saints and up the Riva degli Schiavoni toward a park near land's end. I still had some five hours, maybe more, before my friends arrived, and I was in no hurry. So I wandered, as is my habit, up along the waters and out along the ways. I saw various lovely sights: statues forgotten in the trees, green grass and black waters, strollers with happy faces, the outline of San Giorgio Maggiore beyond the quay, a puppy straining against its lead. I returned to the piazza the way I had come and crossed back over the footbridge, whereon stood a collection of teenagers smoking and laughing before the Bridge of Sighs. Then I did all that was left to do. I went uptown a few streets to pay too much for food I could cook better at home, checked into my hotel, and settled in for a short rest. Ah, Venice!

At nearly 11 p.m. there came a knock at my door. My friends, obviously. I went out with them, for they hadn't dined. This time, *they* paid too much for food that was modestly fair. Ah, Venice, again.

Morning in Venice is the finest hour. I woke before my friends and popped out to a little café on a corner and ordered coffee with milk. This wasn't the sort of place you'd find a seat, in fact there were no seats at all, only little shelves scattered about the walls where you might set your cup for the three seconds you need a place to set it between the three seconds you need to drink it. I stood near a pillar outside the café. The place was jam-packed, lots of men and women in suits, nary a tourist anywhere. I felt not like an insider but not quite like an outsider, so happy and welcoming were the baristas. I drank down my coffee, ordered one for the road, and returned to the lobby of the hotel.

Let me introduce you to my friends. John is a tenured professor of Spanish language and literature, specializing in the Golden Age. He's an American, from the Midwest no less, whose boyish good looks compete with his professional pragmatism. Carmen is a Spaniard, a Galician to say true, and also a professor of Spanish language and literature. She is slight, like a willow bow, but she is mighty, like Toshiro Mifune. She knows something about everything or everything about something, take your pick. So usually when I travel with these two, we will make our way through a museum of this or a gallery of that, and all look to Carmen for answers. She has the kind of mind that holds on to everything she reads, so after she had taken on Scarpa's book, we were on the lookout for everything she read. The number one dish, for example: bigoli with salsa. The anti-pee devices on the street corners around the city. The fact that the city itself is built on millions of piers, which are upside-down trees, "larches, elms, alders, pines and oaks," driven deep into the slime at the bottom of the lagoon. "How do you lay solid foundations on slime?" Scarpa asks. That's how. Even the basilica is supported by such piers, which, after all this time, have mineralized and turned to stone. So Carmen knows all this from her reading, and John now knows it from Carmen. Not wanting to leave me out, bless his heart, John lectures me on these points as we make our way about the city as if he invented Venice himself. But why, I ask, referencing Scarpa's title, is Venice a fish? Neither Carmen nor John seems to know.

We head south and west with the day, Maria complaining all the while of the great toll the walk is taking on her soul and body. She can be the hardiest of trekkers—I once climbed a mountain with her in New Mexico—but today we drag her about the city from museum to café to museum, and she's just about had enough. She does this little thing, because she's eight years old and bored to death, where she steps in front of me, walks a few steps, and trips me up. So I stumble to keep from knocking her down, regain my composition, start again, and walk now out on the edge of the four of us in the mainstream of the crowd. She's just not paying attention is all, and it's not her fault. So, on we walk, and there she is again, trip-

ping me up, me tripping up, and finding a new space now to walk
without knocking her down. Then it happens a third time, a fourth,
and I realize the little rascal is doing it on purpose. She loves this
game. She mostly considers herself a Spaniard like her mother, so
the game is, as I take it, Trip the American.

"Look, Maria," I say, trying to distract her. "You're in one of the
greatest cities in the world. Imagine all your friends back home in
Texas who will never see such gorgeous palaces, such solemn tem-
ples, such great works of art! And here you are seeing them all, and
you're only eight."

She turns and gives me the how-did-you-get-so-dense look, gazes
back on the amazing city, and says: "But they wouldn't want to."

We wend our way through the crowds, headed for the Gallerie
dell'Academia, Carmen and I stopping here and there to consider
various glass trinkets from Murano to take home to friends. For
John, spending money is like bleeding. When Carmen stops near
the front doors of a shop and says something benign like "Shall we
take a look?" you can see in his ashen face that he is a dying man,
the bloodletting so severe his head swoons and he has to turn in
circles to keep from passing out. You would think John a saint, however, when even at such peril to himself, he opens the shop door
to show Carmen in. We finally reach the bridge over the Grand
Canal, both Maria and John near death's door. I expect to see the
ferryman waiting for them, but it's just us and some other tourists,
passing over without incident.

This gallery is a must for anyone who likes art, so say the guide-
books, and so I'm optimistic as we go up the stairs into the first
exhibit. It's the usual splendor and beauty of famous galleries in
Europe, and we walk about looking at one priceless thing after
another.

"Look," John says, his excitement audible, "this is the lion of
Saint Mark!"

As God is my savior.

"Look," John says, "you can see how the angels are flying up to
heaven here. Remarkable!"

And so let's remark it.

"Look," John says, "there's a dog in this one. See it right here? A dog."

And by god it is. John has a particular affinity for dogs in paintings, as he's written an entire book on the subject, focused especially on that one painting in the Prado you probably didn't miss but now don't remember: *Las Meninas* by Velázquez.

"You see," John starts in, "I like dogs in paintings. And now that I'm on to my next book, this stuff here is really important to me. I'm writing about the 'beast within.' Do you follow me? You look at all these paintings, look at all this art, and there is this representation of 'the beast within.'"

"I see," I said.

"It's really hard what I'm doing, because I'm inventing a new language to talk about it," John says, trying to provoke me. "We don't have a language to talk about it."

Had I any measure of dangerous spontaneity, I'd have doled out that wonderful line from the Brad Pitt movie *Snatch*: "In the immortal words of the Virgin Mary: 'Come again?'"

And then John does, without a prompter: "I'm inventing a new language," he says, "a language that doesn't now exist to talk about 'the beast within.'"

"John," I said. "I don't understand. How can you be inventing a new language? Do you mean the topic is unknown, or new, or obscure? What does it mean to invent a new language?"

"I mean I'm inventing a new language. We don't know yet how to talk about 'the beast within.'"

"Sure we do," I say. "The idea has been around for ages. We've been talking about it for near forever. Vampires. Werewolves. Tarzan. Isn't it the oldest story in books? What about Enkidu? Besides, this beast within is really just a deep part of the mind. It's the unconscious, where the dragons live. All those stories of heroes—Beowulf, King Arthur, *The Lord of the Rings*, for pity's sake—are just retelling the same damn story."

"Well, yeah, I suppose you can say that. But what I'm doing is new."

"John," I say. "It's not new."

"Yes it is."

"No it isn't."

"Yes it is."

To be fair, John knows exactly what he's talking about, and I have a nasty habit of (1) arguing for the sake of arguing; and (2) never admitting that I'm wrong. So perhaps it was the saint in John again that moved him to accept the ignorance of his friend: "Let me explain . . . ," he said.

Sometime later, Carmen cruises by with Maria at her arm and interrupts John's focus by rolling her eyes as if to say: Really, boys, can't you just shut up? You're ruining my day. Then she turns back and says over her shoulder: "Really, boys, can't you just shut up? You're ruining my day."

"But Carmen," John protests. "We're having an intellectual conversation."

"Puh-lease. Just have a look at the art," Carmen says. "This is gorgeous in here, and you two are talking about nothing."

"It's the place," John asserts. "We're inspired by the art!"

"Somebody help me," Carmen says.

Our conversation goes on for a bit longer, carries on into the next gallery, John claiming he's inventing a new language, me claiming he isn't, until Carmen, utterly disgusted, disappears with Maria through the maze of rooms.

Half the day goes by, and we've moved halfway across the city, on into the galleries surrounding the piazza, the Museo Correr, looking at an exhibit of gargantuan paintings that are maps of Venice. They're beautiful, and I like maps. Maria is utterly bored, and so exhausted she can hardly stand up. She crawls around on the floor picking at imperfections in the ancient tiles, lolling about in her lethargy. I've been carrying my umbrella all this time, and a security guard chastises me for it: the hard steel point must not touch the priceless floor. Then she's after Carmen for the same thing, and so we decide to head for the Café Fiorian, one of Byron's favorite haunts, to bolster our energy.

Maria is now poised in front of a great map of Venice, where we assemble behind her. The map shows the city from above, its outline and the outlying waters. No wonder, you realize, that the splendor of Venice and its great power arose from the sea. The city itself is stationary, planted in the black mud of the lagoons, while its navy and merchant vessels go anywhere and everywhere at all speed. Some of the world's great explorers, don't forget, are Venetians: Giovanni Caboto, Nicolo de Conti, and of course, Marco Polo. And don't forget the Festa della Sensa, or the marriage of Venice to the sea. Every spring, the mayor of Venice (the doge in the old days) rides a barge to the Port of San Nicolo, where he flings a gold ring into the bouncing waves.

We all stand together gazing upon the map, and we all see a map, except Maria, who sees a shape, a shape made by the city of Venice, which is so stupidly obvious now but was impossible for me to see until then, until Maria calls out, "Mama. Look! Venice is a fish!"

At Café Fiorian, Carmen and I each pay thirteen dollars for a coffee with milk, and John and Maria choose a tea service with little sand-wiches light as air, which runs about forty bucks. But since Byron did, we do too. Apparently Byron took his breakfast here, and I go about the café's interior in search of his portrait. Established in 1720, Café Fiorian was already one hundred years old in Byron's day. I wonder if some of the furniture doesn't date from that time. Did Byron sit in this chair, or that chair? Did he sit in my chair? Or, rather, I in his? But then my modest family history rears up, and I ask: is one place better than another because someone who thought they were better than others ate there? I don't find the portrait I'm looking for, so I return to the table for my coffee. It's good, but not that good; I can make equally tasty coffee at home.

What about Byron in Venice, anyway? I've read some of his story, and it's sad and desperate and rounded by folly. He fled England on charges of incest and sodomy, never to return again. He loved Venice, it seems, and boasted carnal pleasures with over two hun-dred women. He swam the canals home at night after carousing until the second cock. He was unusually productive, and life here seems to have transformed his artistry. He wrote much of his great poem *Don Juan* in Venice, and *Childe Harold's Pilgrimage*, *Beppo*, and *Ode to Venice* are all works set in and inspired by it. Despite his grand adventures and endless exploits, in his private time, it seems, he loved his dog best, a Newfoundland he called Boatswain. In his poem "Inscription on the Monument of a Newfoundland Dog" (Boatswain died in 1808), Byron writes:

> But the poor dog, in life the firmest friend,
> The first to welcome, foremost to defend,
> Whose honest heart is still his master's own,
> Who labours, fights, lives, breathes for him alone.
> Unhonour'd falls, unnoticed all his worth,
> Denied in heaven the soul he held on earth.

These are wonderful qualities in a dog, indeed, and perhaps Byron aspired to them himself. But he was his own best enemy, as any student of literature knows. We have in Byron's work and the work of many others after, the Byronic Hero, a great talent ringed with admirable passions but flawed in the grandest ways. The usual description goes thus: a distaste for society and social structures, including an absence of respect for rank and privilege (both of which Byron possessed); thwarted by love, death, rebellion, exile, a dark secret past, arrogance, and overconfidence; and a lack of fore-sight, all rolled into a poetic self-destruction. Ah, Byron!

One of the most fascinating parts of his life was his death. In 1823, he traveled to Greece to support the independence movement from the Ottoman Empire. After investing a great sum of his own money to refit the Greek fleet, he planned to help the politician Alexandros Mavrokordatos attack the Turks at Lapanto. But he fell ill to fever, recovered, and fell ill again. The usual remedy of the day was a good bloodletting to excise the poisons from the body. Covered in leeches and pierced by the doctor's needle, he died on April 19, 1824. There was a great storm blowing afoul over his final days. Byron moaned and shivered, and went in and out of delirium.

He muttered to himself in Italian and in English as the rain fell ceaselessly and the wind banged at the windows. As he realized his great life was flying off, he came to desire the end. He wanted to die. A friend reports that he considered asking God for mercy but then came to his senses and spoke aloud: "Come, come, no weakness! Let's be a man to the last."

I wanted desperately to resist the tourist's silly love affair with the gondola, which was in its day the primary means of transportation in and out and around Venice. The city once supported some ten thousand gondoliers, but there are a mere five hundred or so now, and most of them cater to tourists. You can take a traghetti, a gondola serving as a ferry, across the Grand Canal for minimal cost, but you can walk over a bridge too. I happened to be on this bridge or that as a gondola passed under, and looking down on the sleek black boats, I saw fine couples enwrapped in each other's company, a family of four, a single man or woman, an empty boat too. They came smoothly under me, the long lovely line of them cutting a brave path through the glassy water, the gondolier calling out to the other boats beyond his blind spot, pushing the gunwales away from the canal walls with his foot. It did look, if I may say so, romantic and quintessentially Venetian. I guess Byron had a private gondola and gondolier, as the wealthy and famous keep a stretch Hummer with driver these days. Would I ever have another opportunity? Unlikely.

And so it came to pass that on passing a handsome young wheeler-dealer near the Rialto, Carmen was drawn aside by his angelic face and, using hers, struck us a deal. I don't recall the price. It was expensive, but not offensive, so we took it. John, though his veins were nearly dry, offered up his euros smilingly.

Our gondolier wore all black—black shoes and trousers, a black vest—but for his black-and-white-striped shirt, the shirt you've seen in movies and thus hope to see on your gondolier. His face carried a stern look, his cheeks drawn down by creases along each side of his nose. His arms were beautifully shaped, long and muscled beneath his snug sleeves, and his hands were hardened by the soft wood shaft of his oar. He had hair, you could see that, the peak coming in tight to the brow, but he wore it shaved, right down against the dark bone of his head.

"You speak Italian?" our gondolier asked.

"A little Italian," John said. "Carmen speaks it best. No, we don't speak Italian. We speak Spanish."

"Oh, Spanish," he said, in English.

"But he doesn't," Carmen said in Spanish, pointing to me.

"German?" the gondolier asked of me.

"English," John said.

"Then I will speak to you in English," he said, though he was already.

"Ah, this is Venice," he said pushing off from the moorings. "For one thousand years, this city has been alive! It should *not* be here. But it is here. Why is it here?"

He paused, adjusting his oar in the *fórcola*. We looked at each other. Did he want us to answer?

"Well," John said. "I guess—"

"—It is here," he said, "but it should not be here. This black lagoon. These canals and waters mean that no city should be here. But one thousand years ago we built it. The Venetians built Venice! Out here on the Grand Canal you will see it for yourself. One thousand years of architectural splendor! You will see it here."

He had what you might call a taste for the dramatic.

"Right," John said. "But how did they build it? Who built it? Where did the labor come from?"

"We built it, of course," he said. "We Venetians built Venice in this black lagoon. Why here?" he asked again. "How did we do it?"

"Well," John ventured again, "it seems to me that—"

"—Out here on the Grand Canal you will see it for yourself. One thousand years of architectural splendor! You will see it here. Wait a moment," he said, sweeping his hands out in front of him. "Wait. There! Venice! You see the different style of architecture here. One thousand years of Venetian history all here on the Grand Canal.

Byzantine. Renaissance. Baroque. Functionalism. Modernism. Post-modernism. Byzantine-Baroque. Baroque-Byzantine. Renaissance-functionalism-modernism. Postmodern-Baroque-modernism. Post-modern-modernism. And Byzantine. It's all here."

"So you regard Venice as a Byzantine city?" John asked.

"This is Venice," the gondolier said. "Venice. It should not be here. But it is here, here in this black lagoon. It is because of this black lagoon that the Venetians built it. This black lagoon protects the city. It is safe here, in these waters. You may think these waters are a problem. *Yes*, they are a problem. But they are not a problem. You see, when the water comes up and floods the houses and shops, the people let the water pass. They get some warning and move every-thing from the first floor to the second floor to let the water pass. The water must pass," he said. "If water not pass, water destroy!"

We turned now onto the Rio San Giovanni Grisostomo, where we'd do a little loop back to the Grand Canal. We passed under a bridge by the same name, and the hearty gondolier called out in his deep voice to warn other boats of our coming.

"You see here," he said. "This was the house of a very wealthy man. It is here because he let the water pass. When the water came, he let it pass. Water must pass," he said again. "If water not pass, water destroy!"

On around we went, the canal narrowing, the houses and shops close on each side, Maria futzing with a decorative golden winged lion along the gunwale, then with the little knob on her seat; John with his long arm around Carmen; and me sitting opposite, star-ring into the murky waters. We came to a corner again and the Teatro Melibran, an important venue for opera during the seven-teenth and eighteenth centuries. At the crossroads with the canal that leads to the piazza, our gondolier called out again as we turned the corner to complete our circle.

"Ah," he said. "Here used to be the great palace of a very rich man! It is still here," he said, "because he let the water pass—"

I know, I thought. Water must pass. If water not pass, water destroy.

In the morning, I would take the early vaporetto to Marco Polo to fly back to Spain, and after a few days more, back home to the American West. My friends would be headed by train to Pisa before returning to Spain, where they would stay on for the rest of the summer. We had the evening for a final hurrah.

Carmen, the intrepid, was on the hunt for a local place for supper, something out of the way and into the breach of real Venetian life. We set out to explore down the Via Garibaldi and into the Arsenale. We happened upon a little place along that wide street, busy with mostly everybody in town, a place between places. Since we were not sure where we were going, Carmen said, "We might as well have one drink." And so we did, a beer and a few snacks, as we settled in among the local people. We roused and toasted to friendship, to the holy interlude between then and after, to this easy moment without cares. What more could anyone want, really, but a moment, just a moment in Venice with his friends? Before long we were afoot again, wandering beyond the Arsenale and into Castello, God knows where, lost really, again, among the winding streets from this plaza to that, all of us feeling suddenly hopeless, except Carmen.

"I'm hungry," Maria complained.

"I don't think we're going the right way," John said.

"We're not going to find anything out here," I whined, certain the universe was bent against us.

"How about here?" Carmen said in her unshakeable optimism, as a little restaurant rose up out of nothing. "Looks like we can have the bigoli with salsa. I want to try that before we leave."

Over supper we played a spelling game—in English, thank goodness, as it's the only language I know. It's so hard to be trapped inside one language when your friends command several more. But do I go around feeling sorry for myself? Of course I do, when even Maria, who is a quarter my age, is fluent in two and working on two more. No wonder she trounced the lot of us at our game. I suppose we might say three hallelujahs in praise of the young and cerebrally fit.

John and Maria turned in, while Carmen and I thought we might make a visit to Harry's Bar. Everybody who is anybody in Venice, so the saying must go, finds the way to Harry's Bar. Hemingway loved the place and wrote about it in his novel *Across the River and into the Trees,* and you can add to the list Orson Welles, Alfred Hitchcock, Peggy Guggenheim, Woody Allen, Princess Aspasia of Greece, and on like that. And so, being nobody at all, Carmen and I found the front doors closed. Closed? It was just after eleven. Not quite the hours I was used to keeping in Spain, where, as John loved to inform me, this is the time most Spaniards are wondering what to have for supper. Carmen and I went on, looking for a clean place to sit. It was stop and go. Stop and go. Stop and go, turning through the streets until we happened upon a bar with tiny bright lights and modern furnishings. It wasn't really my kind of place, but as Carmen likes to say, "We might as well have one drink, no?"

She ordered a grappa and I a sambuca. When the time came for a second round, we each ordered what the other had had. Grappa, a kind of brandy made from pomace (the skins, seeds, and stems of grapes left over from winemaking), has a powerful kick, and this was only the second, maybe third time I'd ever tasted it.

"This grappa is really strong," I said.

"This?" Carmen said. "This? We Galicians drink this from our mother's breasts!"

Oh, glorious, thought I, this really is a fairy city of the heart.

And what about this story? What of Venice? You can't arrive at grand conclusions. You can't capture it in a phrase or sentence, in an image or dance routine. You might do well enough to repeat what others have said. Guy de Maupassant: "Venice! That single word seems to send an exaltation exploding in the soul." Cees Nooteboom: "a paradise of beauty that was driven out of itself because the earth could not endure so much wonder." Diogo Mainardi: "There can be no better place than this."

But even then, everything that has a beginning also has an end, a time when it will no longer be what it is. The universe was born

out of the Big Bang, and it looks like it will expand outward forever until the stuff of it is so spread apart as to be nothing at all.
Before that, long before, our sun will run out of fuel. It will expand
and expand and consume our little earth and all the inner plan-
ets before collapsing into a white dwarf. You and all your precious
things, your photographs and iPhone, your favorite movies and coffee cups, your Ford pickup and backyard garden will vanish into
the oblivion of black space. Not a remnant will remain, not even a
memory of human life, as there will be no one left to remember. But
take heart. One can hardly say this about Venice. Perhaps it is the
one true exception, or rather it is the exception's exception, the city
that was a nation, the swampy mudflat that became a marble island,
the dwarf that is a giant. And it will always be so. You can never
come to the end of Venice, the way you can never come to the end
of Shakespeare or Mozart. So why bother with this great theme? As I
said, its vastness allows everyone to say something, and so, I've gone
ahead and tried to say it: ah, Venice, again.

DEATH IN SEVILLE

Spain, 2009

When I was sixteen, like a lot of young men who want to write, I fell in love with Hemingway. It was his short stories that drew me: "The Snows of Kilimanjaro," "The Short Happy Life of Francis Macomber," and "Big Two-Hearted River," both parts. It helped that my father, when he was a boy growing up in Michigan, had fished the Big Two-Hearted, and then later gave me a wild and natural boyhood in Oregon. Like the protagonist in "Big Two-Hearted River," I loved to fish and as a boy always fished in lakes and rivers near our homes, and I loved to paddle canoes. I loved the simplicity of Hemingway's world, the straight-on style of his writing, the way I thought he was writing about me, the way I thought I would one day write like him. I wondered if Hemingway was not somehow part of me, I so deeply felt him when I read his stories. Certainly, I wanted to be Hemingway.

That was some time ago, and I've moved on, the way you move on from a broken heart or idealism. I've moved on, but I have not forgotten. I carry with me still that little butterfly feeling that came when I leafed through books about Hemingway and looked at photographs of him, which I did, for hours, in the Hemingway Western Studies Center and the library at Boise State University, where I was a student. In my adult life I've come to know the darker parts of him, regard him as something of a sham man, a brawler too, a bully who never quite grew up. But the power of his stories and those images of him stop me still. You know that photograph of Hemingway drinking water from the brim of his hat in Africa. Or the one standing at the prow of the *Pilar* on the Gulf Stream, his pole bent down and away, tucked in against his right hip, the camera behind him, his shirt off, gazing onto the sea. Or in partial shadow on the front porch of his house in Ketchum, Idaho, where he died and near where I, for a time, lived. Do you blame him for killing himself? I hated him for it, especially when I stood before his grave with my best friend, Scott, at age nineteen on a pilgrimage to that cemetery and to the Sun Valley Lodge and the Hemingway Memorial on the Big Wood River. But I don't hate him for it anymore.

I didn't care for his work on bullfighting, but as a boy I thought I should. When I made my first journey through Europe in the spring of 1993, I went on the trail of Hemingway through Paris and Spain. I visited Shakespeare and Company, the Place Contrescarpe, and I gazed up at the windows of his first apartment. I bought a blue beret, and I tried to write in cafés in Paris, as Hemingway did, with a pencil sharpened by my pocketknife. I ordered café au lait and made long lovely sentences in my journal about my solo adventures, and then I made short, clear sentences. It was the best feeling in the world. I tried to drink wine, too, which Hemingway calls "the most civilized thing in the world," at outdoor cafés, and tried to drink heavily in my room each night. But I didn't have a stomach for it, and I still don't. In Spain, it was too early in spring for bullfights, so I walked the empty streets of Pamplona on an empty Sunday morning to gaze at the bust of Hemingway near the bullring. Not this time, I thought, but one day I would find my way to a bullfight.

Seville is hot in summer, unbearably so, and in April you can feel the front end of that heat pushing against you. I had been in Spain for several months now, teaching travel writing in the study abroad program at my university. When my friend John (a professor of

Spanish language and literature) and I entered the bullring, the famed Plaza de Toros de la Real Maestranza de Seville, on that day, April 22, 2009, the sun was against us. We would be sitting on the sunny side of the ring in the high, cheap seats, and the sun would strike us square in the chest. It would not dip below the top of the bullring opposite us until the final bull. The drama of the *corrida de toros*, the modern Spanish bullfight, almost always takes place across the ring from the sunny side because wounded bulls, weakened by loss of blood, their heads slung low, retreat to that crescent of cool shade to make their last stand. Or they may retreat to that shade to give up when their spirit has been broken. What the bullfighter wants, and the crowd wants too, is a bull that does not give up, a bull with a will to live that overwhelms its body's possibility, and so after the sword pierces its body and while the blood is foaming from its nose and mouth, its lungs filling with blood, the bull breathing through this blood, it desires to live, it defends itself from the men in the ring and the sword in its body and the sun bearing down on it and the betrayal of its body that is dying—it will defend itself from itself—its body now a thing apart as the bull shrugs off that body, there in that crescent of shade, before the crowd and the bullfighters, bravely, as if it were not dying, but mastering death by dying.

At John's suggestion, we purchased disposable hats, a piece of rectangular cardstock folded and stapled in the back and fixed with a stretchy chinstrap. It looked silly but was a tremendous relief while facing the sun. And then we had a cold beer, an Estrella Galicia, out on the open-air terrace behind our seats and overlooking the pit where the picadors were mounting their armored horses. We stood there for some time because there was good shade made by the stands, and we liked watching these men prepare to face the bull. I wondered what it was going to be like to see a bull die. On our walk to the bullring, John and I had stopped at a little place on the calle María la Blanca. The barman had a suggestion for us. "Be sure to take a bag," he said in English. "To vomit in. It's disgusting."

Though he had spent many years in Spain, John had never

attended a bullfight. He was doing so today against the preference of his wife, Carmen, a Galician (and also a professor of Spanish language and literature). Bullfighting, she asserts, is not Spanish at all, but rather endemic to specific regions of Spain: here in Andalucia, in Castilla, and also in Navarra. It was Franco who insisted that Spain and the world call bullfighting a Spanish art form. Interesting that in the world of the ring, the term *franco*, which means "frank" or "open," is given to a noble bull. Today the country is divided between those who want bullfighting banned and those who do not. Even the king and queen are divided: he is a bullfighting aficionado; she would rid her kingdom of this cruel spectacle. In July 2010, Catalonia voted to ban bullfighting in the region, following the Canary Islands, which banned it in 1991. Some hail the Catalonian ban as a triumph over animal cruelty. Others argue that it is yet another political posture to rally support for the region's separatist movement, that Catalonians reject everything quintessentially Spanish. So is bullfighting Spanish, or not?

The bullfight is not a contest between a man and a bull, as Hemingway states clearly in *Death in the Afternoon*, his treatise on the subject. It is not a sport and certainly not a blood sport; it is a tragedy. The bull lives only so that it may die in the ring, and when the bull enters the ring, it is going to die. You need not worry yourself with hopes that the bull will triumph over the man. Its life on the campo and under the open sky is over. It did not ask for this, but this will happen. Even if the bull kills the matador and thus "wins," it will be killed, because an experienced bull is far too dangerous to ever enter the ring again. Very rarely, perhaps once in a decade or more, a bull may walk out of the ring alive. This is not to honor the bull so much as to humiliate the matador who was incapable of killing him.

The bullfight consists of three acts, the first two of which prepare the bull for the matador to kill. Act 1: The picadors, mounted bullfighters, "pic" the bull with long lances. They get him to bleed, and weaken his powerful throwing muscles at the top of his shoulders. Act 2: The banderilleros, bullfighters on foot, plant three sets of two harpoons covered in colored paper (banderillas) into the bull's shoulder muscles. Sometimes the matador may place his own banderillas. And act 3: The matador, after a series of passes with the cape (*muleta*), kills the bull with a sword (*estoque*). In a typical bullfight, three matadors each face two bulls. Today the matadors would perform in this order: Antonio Barrera, Juan Bautista, and Luis Bolívar.

Luis Bolívar is a striking man. You can see that, especially compared to the other two matadors performing that day: the Frenchman, Bautista, who is pasty-faced with frumpy hair; and the Sevilleano, Barrera, whose long nose and drooping chin give him the look of John Kerry. You see in Bolívar's face the heroic ruggedness of a feminine beauty: dark eyebrows over dark eyes, a gracile nose into his perfect lips. His cheekbones are high on his face but not angular. Next to him, the other two men look awkward and uncertain of themselves, generally outclassed. I mention this because it seems that beauty matters in matters of the bullring. Hemingway writes about the feminine beauty of the matador in *Death in the Afternoon*. Chicuelo, though he is plump and has no chin and a bad complexion, also has the "long eyelashes of a girl." And Juanito Martin Caro, a "child prodigy," has the "pretty, pretty look of a young girl." So it is not only the beauty of the matador's work with the muleta, his ability to master the bull, but his face too, which also must win the crowd. It's uncertain whether this has any effect on the bull.

The first bull entered the ring charging, its head up scanning the ring to sweep it clean of dangers, charging boldly and powerfully, the smooth wet hide a shimmer of muscle and sun, the horns like partisans, its pizzle a flow of urine so forceful I heard it slap the yellow sand. The bull is so jacked up on adrenaline when it enters the ring, so crazed with a demonic fire, that it is woozy, punch-drunk, almost exhausted. Whatever moves, it will charge and kill. A bull will even charge whatever does not move—the red walls of the ring—and strike it with its horns.

A spontaneous cheer went up from the crowd as the bull came in. It was nearly impossible to resist. I cheered too, having never decided to cheer. It was like seeing the Grand Canyon for the first time and every time after. It was like walking among coastal redwoods; I still cannot believe them. It was like the first time I went backpacking in southeastern Utah and woke to the call of a canyon wren. The bull was beautiful.

This was Barrera's bull, and he killed it in the shade opposite of where I sat with John. It was the first bull and the first killing I witnessed. I had been thinking about this moment for a long time. What would it be like to watch the bull die? Would I be sick, or sickened, as the barman had asserted, or somehow turned away by the spectacle of it? Would I like it? Would I discover an aberrant quality in myself, a darkness in my pleasure at watching the bull die? But when it happened, I felt neither disgust nor pleasure. The killing of the bull felt oddly natural and perfectly strange. It felt as though it had to happen, as though it had happened already. I watched the sword come up in Barrera's hand, a glint of light off the blade as he broached the sun-line at the edge of the crescent of shade, the bull like a cat ready to strike the man in front of him, to clear the ring to make it safe, the blood from the banderillas slick now over his back and making him weak, dizzy, sleepy, so that he wanted to lie down as he had done in the middle of the ring just minutes before, no longer interested in charging the man who faced him. He wanted to lie down, as he had done just days before for days and nights on end out in the campo, the fields of the Spanish countryside, lying in the shade of a live oak, say, chewing his cud and lazing away the day. Or perhaps I misread him, as he had had a taste of his own power moments ago when one of the bullfighters, a banderillero, was caught by a horn and lifted twice off his feet. The crowd cheered as the bullfighter rode the bull's head for a few feet, bobbing up and down violently, then pushed himself off and away to safety. Or maybe there was nothing at all in the bull's mind, just a tired blankness cued by movement as Barrera sighted along the blade and stepped forward to meet the bull. The bull stood there mostly, his head down, the sun battering him in his fatigue as the sword came in, and then he came into it, and it slid neatly into his body at his shoulders as the *muleta* was pulled from Barrera's hand and whirled off and away like a petal on a breeze. The bull with the sword in his back felt a bite of something before the blood came, and as the blood came, so did Barrera's toreros with their capes to wave the bull this way and that as the bull's feet drained of his life under his great weight, his feet dying first, dying before he did, and he went down onto his knees and then onto his belly in the shade and twisted his head as if to look at the thing in his back, and then at the crowd who did nothing to help him, and then at the sky, and then his head went down and he never got up.

Hemingway writes in *Death in the Afternoon:* "What is moral is what you feel good after and what is immoral is what you feel bad after and judged by these moral standards . . . the bullfight is very moral to me because I feel very fine while it is going on and have a feeling of life and death and mortality and immortality, and after it is over I feel very sad but very fine." I think, maybe, I'm not sure, this is what it was like for me too. I did not feel angry or sickened or aggressive, but sad—yes, I felt sad, the way I feel sad when I think about how my dog died that day in Colorado or when I lie next to my German shepherd now and look into her dark eyes and imagine that one day, not so long from now, she will die too. But this is not the sadness of avoidance or denial. When the first bull died in the ring in front of me, I felt privileged and a little embarrassed to witness it, to be part of this most intimate moment in the bull's life. And I wanted to see it again.

The second bull was for Bautista. It was a feeble effort, and twice the crowd whistled and jeered to signal disapproval: once for the bull and once for the Frenchman, the Frenchman because he was heavy on his feet and uninteresting to watch, the bull because he could not stand punishment, because he came in hard at the *muleta* with his head so low that he caught a horn against the sand and all of his power went into the sand so that his light back end came up and up until he was standing on his head in the ring, and then he came down onto his back, rolled to the side, his left front leg caught beneath his tremendous weight so that he could not stand. A bull can badly injure himself in the ring, making him impossible to work with, and this is one way to do it. The bull lay there as if he'd had enough, and Bautista's toreros rushed in to help him up, one pulling on his tail, another at his horn. The crowd whistled and groaned: what a bull, they were saying. What a bull. Bautista didn't have much to work with, and he wasn't much himself, and when he killed with the sword, the bull lay down and would not die. It was not his great spirit that kept him alive; he had already given up. He wanted to die, but he couldn't, like a man who can't make a decision. One of Bautista's toreros came in with the dagger (*puntilla*) to end it. He jabbed the blade in deep just behind the skull, and the bull sank and was dragged out by the mules to be butchered and sold in the market.

Neither of these two bulls, nor the third, fifth, or even the sixth bull, which won Luis Bolívar an ear, carried that beauty and sadness Hemingway writes about, the kind of bull the Spanish call *valiente*, or courageous. The third bull was Bolívar's first, and after the *estoque* went in, it was killed with the *puntilla* in the sun near my seat. I could hear him huffing and grunting as he died. The fifth bull evoked more jeers and whistles for Bautista, who was taking too long, which meant the bull was suffering. When Bautista killed it cleanly, he looked up at the crowd defiantly, as if to say, see, you do me wrong. And now the sixth bull, which won the day for Bolívar, a Colombian, twenty-four years old. This final bull of the corrida went down lightly, not heavily—heeled over and died. There was blood, of course, wet on the bull's back, but it was not obscene or gaudy. Bolívar had been nearly flawless. It was one long piece of choreography, the bullfighter and the bull, as if the bull too knew its part and was willing to play it, willing to die. The *pañuelos* came out in the stands, a fanfare of white kerchiefs, as the audience roused the president to award Bolívar the bull's ear. With the ear in hand, Bolívar made his way about the ring to offer his grace and gratitude to us—his audience, his critics, his patrons—we who had decided that he had done well, that he was worthy. Was he a hero? Flowers came into the ring from admirers, women and men, girls and boys, and then at last the night sky relieved us of the day.

But though the sixth bull won the ear for Bolívar, it was the fourth bull, Barrera's second, that won the honor of that name *valiente*.

The relationship between men and bulls is at least twenty thousand years old, as the most prominent and famous images among the paintings in the caves at Lascaux are four monstrous black bulls, the largest of which is some seventeen feet long. Gilgamesh, in the *Epic of Gilgamesh* (the world's oldest recorded story, dating from the seventh century BCE), defeats the Bull of Heaven, sent by Ishtar to cool his arrogance. Roman soldiers, from the second to the fourth centuries, practiced Mithraism, a religion in devotion to the god Mithra, a god of war among other things, who was born from a stone and slew the great bull. These soldiers made sacrifices to Mithra, and in one of their rituals, inductees stood in a pit beneath a grate to be purified in the blood of a bull slaughtered above them. Much later on the Iberian Peninsula, mounted aristocrats hunted bulls in the countryside with lances. This practice led to bringing bulls in from the country to the city, where such aristocrats were fond of slaying bulls from horseback at festivals in a public arena. The modern Spanish bullfight is attributed to Francisco Romero of Ronda, who developed the technique of killing bulls with the *estoque* after a series of dalliances with the *muleta* in 1726.

But the past is a story of who we were, and we are different now. Despite this difference, the bullfight flourishes in the modern world, as it did in the ancient. Why? I think bullfighting embraces what modernity left behind. Modernism is a wave ridden out from the wreckage of Romanticism, out from the Industrial Revolution, which followed it. As we rode this wave, rode the great promise that technology would solve all our problems, that it would complete us, like religion, like meaningful work, like love, we left the sacred mysteries of the natural world behind. We didn't need nature anymore. Instead of reverence, awe, and love for the mystery of life on earth, we worship steel, oil, and the silicon chip.

In the twenty-first century, it has become increasingly clear that while technology has forced everything to move faster, it has failed to save us time, fix our problems, and make us happier. Once in India, a young student said to me: "Sir! Sir! Americans are very rich. They have everything in the world. But are they truly happy?" The answer is certainly no. But it is not technology itself that is the problem. It is our reliance on it, and our resulting disappointment in it. When it comes to technology, what seemed like magic yesterday is empty and mundane today. Our hunger can never be sated. Technology has not failed us; we have failed it.

In his book *The Sacred and the Profane*, Mircea Eliade writes that "it is only in the modern societies of the West, that nonreligious man [Eliade also uses the term "profane man"] has developed fully." In this world, it is not the universe that makes man, but "man [who] *makes himself*, and he only makes himself completely in proportion as he desacralizes himself and the world." For the modern man, and so for modernity, the "sacred is the prime obstacle to . . . freedom." As this is so, it follows that the modern Spanish bullfight, a highly ritualized ceremony that follows from the religious iconography of Lascaux through the Mithraic mysteries and into the Maestranza here in Seville, should have long ago fallen from popularity and settled into a story of who we used to be. But it has not. The bullfight is alive and well in Spain and in other countries. Why? Eliade goes on to assert that "profane man cannot help preserving some vestiges of the behavior of religious man, though they are emptied of religious meaning. . . . He forms himself by a series of denials and refusals, but he continues to be haunted by the realities that he has refused and denied." Though profane man has desacralized the world of his ancestors, Eliade writes, he holds the sacred in waiting, "ready to be reactualized in his deepest being."

Modern art is an expression not only of the modern world but also of its failure. Think on the fragmentation and confusion of Picasso's cubism, the dark nihilism of Eliot's *The Waste Land*, and Nietzsche's terrifying realization that God is dead. As a modernist himself, Hemingway registers his discontent with the world in his lifelong devotion to bullfighting. He does not consider the bullfight an empty ritual that preserves only vestiges of the sacred; instead he sees it as fully sacred, as an antidote to modernism. When Nietzsche writes, "God is dead. God remains dead. And we have killed him. How shall we comfort ourselves. . . . Who will wipe this blood off us? What water is there for us to clean ourselves? What festivals of atonement, what sacred games shall we have to invent?" Hemingway answers: the sacred ritual of the killing of fighting bulls in the ring.

I am not cruel or titillated by suffering and death. In fact, I was surprised how little the bull suffers and how quickly it dies. But like many people, I have lived much of my life protected from death, insulated from the sight and experience of living beings in their final moments. Engaging it in the ring helped me know in my own body how fragile I am, how fragile my friends and family are, how fragile is the thin envelope of air and water on the earth's surface where life is possible. Life is not possible anywhere else within reach of a human lifespan. We cannot go to another place to live. We have only this one place. And what a beautiful and mysterious place it is.

And if you wish to tell me that there are other ways to learn this lesson, consider this: most livestock these days live short, abject lives covered in their own shit in, say, feedlots in eastern Colorado and West Texas. I consider it more dignified to live free in the Spanish countryside and die in the ring. Or not to live at all. And for my part, I'd rather eat the meat of a bull so killed in the ring than the packaged flesh of a feedlot cow whose life was itself a living death.

Antonio Barrera stepped into the ring for his second bull, the fourth bull of the day. The sun was lower in the sky, about halfway from where it was to where it would be. John and I sat with our strange sun hats on, the heat coming in hard against us, an oppressive force that would not let up for another hour. Through Hemingway, I had imagined a more festive atmosphere: a wool beret, a bota of wine I sprayed expertly and joyously into my mouth, the energy and unity of the crowd in support of the bull and the bullfighter. But Hemingway was Hemingway. Here in Seville, I was nobody, we were all nobody, even as we were about to witness this final moment of the bull's life. The tragedy of the bullfight was unfolding again before me, for this, the fourth time, and I was missing it with inattention, the way you miss parts of a football game buying a hot dog or talking with your friends as I talked with John. I felt lazy and soporific, dulled and emblazoned by the sun. I wanted the whole affair to end so I could find relief from this terrible heat. And then the sword went in.

Aside from the graceful way Barrera moved—he seemed not quite planted on the ground as the *muleta* whirled about him like a dancer's skirt—he was barely interesting. With Bautista, something was at least stirring in the crowd: some measure of discontent. Like the others, Bautista (perhaps I have done him wrong) is a professional killer of bulls. He faces the bull and his fear each time in the ring, the way Hemingway faced the blank page. I don't think it is a fear of dying but a fear of failing to face fear, of disappointing the crowd, of not killing cleanly and so causing the bull to suffer, of losing a place among his brothers, of not finding the moment, the perfect moment when the universe coalesces and everything falls into place like tumblers in a lock, and knowing that moment as *the moment*, and thus not missing it. Yet even missing it in the ring feels better than not going into the ring at all. In Seville, Bautista was raw, so the audience experienced something of the rough edges that prove a matador is also a man. We could see part of his process, the working out of the problems of the bull, as though we were part of the working out of it, like holding up Hemingway's drafts next to the final story.

What woke me from my strange lethargy was that Barrera's sharp calls to the bull, which echoed in the ring as if he were in some far-off place, stopped. I came to attention to watch him ready for the kill. He stood sidelong to the bull with his feet together, sighted down the blade, stood up on his toes, went back down onto his heels, and then turned to face the bull with his chest bared, his one knee bent in an arc. And when the sword went in, it went in. First it was in Barrera's hand, and then it was inside the bull. That bull was so black and muscled, so powerful and hard, it looked impossible to penetrate, but the sword went right in.

The bull swung his great head, hooking one way and then the other as Barrera's toreros came in fast with the capes to draw him out and away, out and away, as Barrera himself, exposed now and vulnerable to those deadly horns, made himself a target, but an impenetrable target impervious to the bull's violent tosses of his head, hooking and working the air to clear off the two and half feet of steel deep in his body. He went down. The bull went down onto his belly, panting hard, huffing, the men moving variously in front of him, waiting, the blood now pooling up over his back where it rushed up the hollow along the blade and came red to the surface to pour over his back, sticky and wet, and his head went down too. The crowd gave a rousing cheer and the clapping rose and settled and it was over.

We waited a moment, a little space of silence in honor of the bull's life. The toreros moved in. The dead bull lifted his head. And then the bull came up undead onto his hind legs, his head still down in his death near the yellow sand red with his blood, and he stood that way like a dog at play as a tremolo of voices rose in the crowd as the bull now rose too, onto his feet, standing again on his four feet, swaying a little, the blood pouring out from the *muerte*, the place the sword went in, and we all felt something then; we all became someone in the low murmuring of our voices that became gasps and then heroic cheers rising and rising as the bull's power and desire to live crested as its life was leaving it. Here was that moment for the bull, as it was for Barrera and for us, the sharing of the art between the man and the bull, the resacralizing of the world. Was he a hero? The bull was walking blind, blood now pouring from its nose and mouth, its soul wandering back and forth between worlds as its feet seemed no longer attached to the ground, swaying from side to side in a lightness, a heaviness, a tree in the wind. He took a few steps forward, then a few steps to the side, and died on his feet, the ground coming away from him as he lifted to go, and then fell over dead.

The people cheered.

BUYING A RUG

Morocco, 1993

In those days, what you knew was different from what you know now. The world was a soft place with many pillows, and people were kind and generous and looked after strangers and rescued kittens from the trees. The rivers coming out of the mountains brought down the great snowfalls of winter and watered the plains in spring, softly, happily, bright running waters all fevered with the organic materials of life, the star stuff to make the wild wildebeest and the elephants and baboons and the birds of migration and the first woman and the first man who walked among them and gave them names. Grasses, long and green and wonderful, grew up over the shining hills that rolled on across an Eden born out of a green mind. A tender mind. A virginal mind. If you travel innocently at first, even blindly, the traveling will change that, because it is only by traveling that you can awaken, that you can learn to love. The passing country through a train window south from Cordoba to Algeciras reflects those essential questions—what? why? who?—until finally you see the image of your own face, your lips and mouth, your nose and ears, your sideburns long to your jawline, your eyes, not a reflection in the window only, mind you, but the eyes of who you used to be. It's easy to wonder, so you ask. Is that me? Or, rather, was this me? And then the "you" that is you becomes "I," so you call it out, remembering that line from e. e. cummings that everyone remembers in moments like this, the line that I would one day know but did not know just then:

> (now the ears of my ears awake and
> now the eyes of my eyes are opened)

I came to leave the shelter of friendship in Cordoba on March 16, 1993. My friend, an old pal from the second grade in southern Oregon, had taken up house with a Cordoban woman. They would eventually marry and shuck out a little boy, who would then waddle across the kitchen floor and stare at his own reflection in the sliding door leading out into the back yard. That boy will have his moment soon enough; this one is mine.

"I'll be right back," I said. "I have to make the crossing into Morocco. Have a look around. I want to be able to say I've been to the continent where man was born."

I asked my old friend, why not come along? But no, he had English classes to teach, a choir to sing in, a woman to love. I didn't, so I went alone, intending to return very soon. So long, friends. So long, great river, Guadalquivir. So long to the beauty of the Mezquita, and so long to the gaudy cathedral stuffed inside. So long to the oranges of Andalucía along the city streets leading to the Avenida de America, where a train, like a great basilisk, lay in wait for me. And running out from under the cavern of the station, the train rode me south toward the sea.

At twenty-three, I had yet to find a rhythm for my life, a pattern on which I could write my story. I went looking for it, indeed, and these trains through landscapes I did not know, these ferries across foreign waters frightened me, and comforted me too. I didn't know why, but I wanted to keep moving, and whenever I came to a stop, I began to feel a little off. A modest agitation rose up, an annoyance that grew into an urgency until I found myself either rearranging all the furniture in my rooms or packing my bags for the road.

"Stay on the road," advises the thirteenth-century Sufi poet Yunus Emre, "until you arrive."

At the port in Algeciras, I met Bob and his lover, Ron. Bob wore a gray felt bowler and a smart wool sports coat with black jeans. Bespectacled and slight, he was thin to almost underfed, and he was stiff, though he spoke with a pleasingly soft voice: "Hi. I'm Bob." Ron was shorter, more businesslike, even a little preppy. He also wore a jacket but without the squared shoulders, along with black jeans, dress shoes with those little leather tassels, a red scarf. His hair was neatly arranged, though cut so short there wasn't much arranging to be done. Handsome boys, both of them. Think of them as Talking Heads meets Vampire Weekend.

"Headed to Ceuta today, or on down to Tetouan?" Bob asked as we stood at the rail looking out on the strait. "Or are you headed farther on?"

"I don't know. Just going. Should I go to Tetouan?"

"Yeah, you should definitely not stop in Ceuta. Cross the border. Get into Morocco proper." At the edge of his hat, the breeze off the sea tousled his curls. Then he said, "Why don't you travel with us? We can share a taxi."

"Yeah?"

"Yeah," Bob said.

Ron nodded but didn't say anything.

"Thank you. That would be most helpful."

"Safety in numbers, you know," Bob said. "We're headed into Morocco for about a month."

"I'll be only a day, maybe two," I said. "Friends in Spain are waiting for me, and I'd really like to travel up north. Just need to pop over for a look."

"Well, we can travel together for a day then," Bob said.

I suppose another reason I was crossing into Morocco, if even for a day, was that one of my heroes, British novelist and travel writer Bruce Chatwin, had traveled in these parts, had sought out nomadic peoples during a journey he made into Sudan (OK, really far away, but same continent), and into Mauritania (a bit closer, but a stretch all the same), where on February 20, 1970, he wrote in his notebook, "One of the worst nights I have ever spent anywhere at any time," and then a few days later rallied with, "The happiness that is to be found sleeping under tents is unbelievable." And since Chatwin himself had followed in the footsteps of his own hero, travel writer Robert Byron, whose book *The Road to Oxiana* is widely considered the crown jewel among travel books, I had taken it upon myself to carry on the tradition and follow in Chatwin's footsteps, if only in my small, private way. Chatwin's story into Africa, as he tells it, began one morning in his early twenties, when he was working as an art expert at Sotheby's. He woke up blind. His doctor told him it was from looking too closely at paintings. He decided to look at some "long horizons" and chose Africa. Traveling in the Sudan with a camel driver named Mahmoud, who makes Bear Grylls look like a JV cheerleader, he went on a hunt for rock art in the desert. On finding it, "red ochre pin men scrawled on the overhang of a rock," he understood his former convictions to be true: that the cities of the West are "sad and alien" and the "pretensions of the 'art world' idiotic." So he quit his job to wander in the desert. Among the Nemadi in Mauritania, an ancient, toothless woman smiled at him, and he then came to believe that human nature is fundamentally good and that this goodness will arise not in the city but in a return to our original state, a nomadic life in the desert, or, if you will, to Adam and Eve in the garden.

I didn't bother to explain all this to my new friends, Bob and Ron. Instead I watched the sun ascending over a sparkling sea. The day was breaking cleanly. It was good, standing this way at the railing without concerns for anything, and Bob and Ron alongside me for companionship and protection as we had agreed, and so we passed together into the unknown. A little door opened in that moment, and Bob offered a bit more of himself.

"We're performance artists."

"Honestly?"

"Honestly," he said. "In Chicago."

"What does that mean exactly? What kind of performance?"

"Well. Let me describe one of our shows," he said. "We do this one show where the stage is black. Everything is black, really, except us. As the piece opens, the curtain is down. Some low music plays, something ominous. We like to change it from show to show. But instrumental only. As the curtain comes up, the audience sees Ron hanging from a rope by his feet. He's naked. And upside down, of course. So you can see his white body against the black backdrop. He can't hang there for too long, you know, so the next part moves along pretty quickly."

"Uh-huh."

"At this point, the audience hears the music shift, change. You know that piece by Neil Diamond, 'Girl, You'll Be a Woman Soon'?"

It just so happens that instead of church, I grew up with the music of Neil Diamond playing on Sundays, especially his 1972 album *Hot August Night*, recorded live at the Greek Theater in Los Angeles. It played on the Panasonic reel-to-reel stereo my dad bought when he was in Vietnam. So, yes, I did know that song. And I'm not too proud to admit that I rather liked it, especially as a recall of my childhood spiritual training.

"Yeah," I said. "I know that song."

"It's a schmaltzy song," he said. "Very schmaltzy. Anyway, that song comes up and up and up as Ron hangs there. Then, when the volume is near its fullest expression, I step onto the stage. I'm naked too, except I wear a gold chain around my waist. And I carry a long feather duster. But it's more like a giant leaf you'd see a slave fanning a pharaoh or something, or like a peacock's tail feathers. More like a giant peacock's tail. The male peacock with its feathers standing in for an exaggerated phallus. You see what I mean?"

"I think so."

"So I walk across the stage very slowly, almost like I'm performing a dance. I was trained in ballet . . . Anyway, as the song plays, 'Girl, you'll be a woman soon / Please come take my hand . . . Soon you'll need a man,' I start to beat Ron with the feathers. I swing them against him, beating him as hard as I can with the feathers, only they're feathers and so no matter how hard I swing he isn't hurt. And I'm screaming while I do this, really screaming as loud as I can to challenge that song, 'Girl, you'll be a woman soon . . .' and eventually the feathers, from the force of my swings, break somewhere at the base above my hands."

He paused then, waiting for a response.

"And then?" I asked.

"Oh," Bob said. "Well, that's it. That's the end of the piece."

"The curtain comes down?"

"Right, the curtain comes down so I can take Ron off the rope and get him upright. He's starting to get a little dizzy by now. So I help him down off the rope, and then we change costumes and go on with our show, which usually includes six or seven short pieces like that."

Ron nodded but didn't say anything.

"Sounds interesting," I said.

"Maybe you can catch one of our shows if you're ever in Chicago."

"I'd like that."

The ferry landed in Ceuta, a city of some seventy-five thousand, and a Spanish territory, a holdout from the old days (1640), from the give-and-take, the push-and-pull that cycled on between the Muslims of North Africa and the Christians, specifically Roman Catholics, of Iberia. Both Ulysses and Hercules traveled through Ceuta, but it was Hercules who fashioned the Strait of Gibraltar, through which we had just passed. One of his twelve labors was to fetch the cattle of Geryon far to the west, and when he came to the great Atlas Mountain between what is now Spain and North Africa, he broke through it, thus opening a passage between the Atlantic Ocean and the Mediterranean Sea. The Pillars of Hercules, then, are the points on opposite shores of the strait, the Rock of Gibraltar on the Iberian side, and on the African side, though disputed, Monte Hacho in Ceuta. The Pillars stood as a gate at the western limit of the known world, a gate beyond which, Plato claimed, lay the mythic city of Atlantis. To travel beyond the Pillars was a reckless endeavor, sure to result in loss and death, even the story of which would never be known. So they bear a warning: *Nec plus ultra*, or "Nothing farther beyond." The Pillars became a powerful symbol and were adopted by Charles V, Holy Roman emperor and king of Spain during the early exploration of the Americas, for his impresa. He modified the warning to read *Plus ultra*, or "farther beyond," an invitation, or a compulsion perhaps, to explore and conquer.

I walked with Bob and Ron from the ferry port straight to the border of Morocco. We passed through several checkpoints, offering our passports each time, until the hot, dry dust of North Africa blew in over us like a christening. We had arrived. As it turned out, the border was a rather dull-looking place. A flat plain stretching this way and that. People wandering about in all directions. A few taxis waiting for passengers. And then there was Ahmad. Later I would learn that the name Ahmad means something like "most highly adored" and is a variation of the name Muhammad, the name of the prophet. But for now, Ahmad seemed more like a fly buzzing in our ears.

"Ah, hello, hello, Americans," he said. "Come this way, please. I am your guide. I take you where you want to go. I will take you to a good place. You need a hotel? I know a hotel. You need something nice to eat? I know a place. You need something to smoke, eh? Something real nice? I know something. Come with me. This way, please."

"I don't think so," Bob said.

"Come," Ahmad said. "You can trust me, of course. I am your guide. I will take you where you want to go."

Ahmad, who looked to be in his late twenties, wore jeans with white socks and black slip-on shoes, a black boiled wool overcoat and a dark collared shirt beneath. His hair, tightly curled against his head, accentuated his broad flat nose, and one, perhaps two of his front teeth were missing. He ran his tongue through the gap there, speaking to us as fast as he could. He wore a little mustache.

"I am Ahmad," he said. "You tell me your names so we can be friends. Then I will guide you where you want to go."

"I don't think so," Bob said.

"Come. It will be good for you," Ahmad said.

"How much?" Bob asked, almost reversing his position.

Ron nodded, but didn't speak.

Ahmad looked at me. "He wants to know how much. How much do you think?"

I ventured a guess. "One hundred."

"One hundred dirham," Ahmad said. "Hmm. That is not much for you in dollars, is it? And you?" he asked Bob.

"Two hundred," Bob said.

"No," Ahmad said. "Not one hundred. Not two hundred. It will cost you nothing. I will be your guide. No cost."

"No cost?" Bob said. "Come on. I don't think so. We'll be all right on our own," and he marched off ahead.

Ron and I followed him, leaving Ahmad behind. I looked back to see him standing there, and he wore a sour, lonely look on his face. Then, as if by magic, Ahmad appeared before us.

"Now, fellas," he said. "I am your guide. I will show you everything. No cost."

"Leave us alone," Bob said.

"No cost at all. Maybe you can't believe it. But it is true," Ahmad insisted.

We kept on walking, headed for the row of taxis. Ahmad came up behind us again. "Now, fellas. You will need a guide like me. So why not choose me? I will show you everything. I will take you where you want to go. Please, follow me. This way."

Bob turned sharply away from Ahmad, and Ron and I followed him. It became a funny little game in which everyone was following Bob.

"Leave us alone," Bob said.

Ahmad came up behind us once more, running this time, and snatched Bob's passport from his hand.

"He just took my passport," Bob said.

"Motherfucker," Ron said, his first words. "Go after him. Let's go."

But Ahmad turned an arc in front of us and came jogging back. He handed the passport to Bob.

"Hey, it is a joke," he said, a little breathless. "I am only kidding. Come. I am your guide. This way. Here is a taxi for you. Let's go into town, and I will show you a nice place to sleep. A good restaurant. It is Ramadan, you know. I will not eat. But you may eat. I am a good man. I returned your passport, eh? I will show you the town. You will like it. Just here," he said holding open the door of a taxi. "It is the best thing for you. Please do not delay," he said. "The taxi is waiting. Please get in."

"No cost, huh?" Bob said.

"That is my word," Ahmad said. "No cost. Now please. Get in."

So we did.

Tetouan is a desert town, but it is also a river town set close to the sea and backed by the Rif Mountains, where the Berber tribes have roamed since the first man and the first woman walked north out of the shining deserts of Ethiopia. Like many towns and cities on the edge of the great historical conflict between Christians and Muslims, Tetouan was built and destroyed several times, beginning with its first inception in the third century BCE. After the Reconquista in 1492, the city became a refuge for both Muslims and Jews expelled from that star of Moorish Spain, Granada. A bit later, in the seventeenth century, Morocco's famed King Moulay Ismail Ibn Sharif built Tetouan's defensive walls. His fame extends not from this minor achievement, however, but from two others: (1) he holds the world record for fathering children, which stands at 888 (not all with the same woman); and (2) his cruelty earned him the nickname "the bloodthirsty," as he is said to have adorned the walls of Meknes, his capital city, with ten thousand heads of his slain enemies. Enemies are one thing, and nearly forgivable, but apparently he went about lopping off the heads of his servants and workers too, with the greatest of ease. What an asshole.

Though Tetouan is not a border town, it thrives with lowlifes and hustlers, touts, many of whom, like Ahmad, present themselves as guides but actually work for a number of restaurants and shops, namely rug shops. The 1991 Gulf War savaged the tourist economy in Morocco, so guys like Ahmad, and the merchants he works for, became especially desperate. But what you don't know, you don't know until, of course, you know it, which is almost always after you need to know it. I was green and innocent, and so, like a dry leaf from an almond tree in a heavy spring wind, I was swept into North Africa and into the waiting hands of Ahmad.

As we sped down the highway along the Alboran Sea, Ahmad pointed out the features of the country that he thought fellas like us would enjoy. "Look, a camel!" he said. And sure as shit, there was a camel. "You see all the sand of the desert," he said. And we did see it, lying about everywhere as it had since the beginning. "There is a man driving a cart with a donkey," he said. And so it was.

"Hey, Ahmad," I said. "What hotel do you recommend?"

"Hotel? Yes, I am taking you to the finest hotel. I know the way. I will talk to this driver and he will take us there. Please do not worry. I am your guide."

"I understand," I said. "But which hotel? Which hotel is your favorite?"

"Ah, which hotel. Personally, I recommend the Hotel Iberia," he said. "It is the finest in town. Also very cheap."

Bob was turning pages in his guidebook. He nodded to Ron and whispered, "It's OK. I see it here on this page."

"You mean it is the finest and also cheap? Or that it is the finest of the cheap hotels?" I asked.

"Very smart question," he said. "You are very clever. But you do not need to worry, my friend. I will arrange it all for you. You will be very comfortable." And then he pointed out the window again. "Look," he said, "another camel."

Ahmad left us at the Hotel Iberia, situated at the city center on the Place Moulay el-Medhi with a promise to return in one hour. "I will take you on a tour of the city," he said. "No cost." Our room was a spare monstrosity with eight beds covered with clean white linens. A few white curtains hung from the ceiling to cordon off sections of the room for more privacy. Bob and Ron took up a far corner but chose against cordoning, and I took the bed closest to the door.

"I don't know if you noticed," Bob said without warning, "but we're a couple."

"I had noticed."

"And is it all right with you if we sleep together?" he asked.

"Of course."

"I need a nap," Ron said, as if the word sleep were the thing itself.

We heard a knock.

"Ahmad," Bob said, opening the door. "You said one hour. It's only been twenty minutes."

"Yes, I know," Ahmad said. "But soon I must do some things for my grandmother. So I am in a very great hurry. Shall we go now?"

"Where are we going?"

"I will show you the city, of course," Ahmad said. "Please bring your valuables with you."

Bob looked back at Ron.

"I need a nap," Ron said.

"I'll go," I said. "Let's have a look around."

"All right, Ron. Why don't you rest here," Bob said, and then turned to me. "Let's go."

The sky had grayed over, and the city center looked drab and forgotten with its collection of palms and quiet streets. Ahmad led us into the medina. He walked at a furious pace.

"Please keep up," he said. "I will show you the old city, and we will see the palace where the king will stay when he visits Tetouan. He is King Hassan II, a great and powerful king. There it is," he said triumphantly. "We are passing it now. You see, this is the palace. You see how wonderful it is? All right. That is enough. Come this way. Please keep up."

We wound through the maze of streets, the whitewashed buildings looking not white but gray under that gray sky, until we came to the market where fish and eel lay on open tables among a few fresh tomatoes, and the spice stalls with their many sacks of colored spices set against doors swung open and hung with plastic schlock for sale, and vegetables at other stalls, root vegetables and onions and other hardy stock, and iron bedframes and shoes and bags, and along through a section of sewing shops, where men, sitting on rugs and wearing rubber boots, made *thawbs* (traditional ankle-length garments) by hand, and then we arrived at the mosque.

"Here, we have arrived," he said. "This is the Great Mosque. Please have a look through the door, but do not step inside. And do not take a photo. It is forbidden."

We peered in through the iron door, and a few people peered back at us.

"That is enough," Ahmad said. "Follow me. We will go now to the roof for a special panorama of the city. No cost."

Down a few streets and up a few streets we walked at a furious pace.

"Here," he said.

We entered a door and arrived inside a dark little courtyard that smelled of manure.

"Donkey parking," Ahmad said. "This way, please."

We ascended a flight of stairs to the roof. There the thickening fog and low hung clouds gave the scene a feeling of despair: an ending, perhaps, but not a beginning.

"Please look out onto the city. You see the beautiful mountains and the white houses going up the mountainside there. What a nice scene. Don't you think so? All right. That is enough. This way."

Ahmad led us across the roof and through another door, down a flight of steps and into a reception. Two large men met us there, one with a tray set with tumblers of mint tea.

"I must leave you now," Ahmad said. "These men will serve you this delicious tea. Please enjoy as much as you can. I will be back very soon. Do not worry. I am your guide. I will be back to show you again to your hotel. Please drink this tea." And he hurried out through the door.

A man came out from behind the counter. His face was pitted from what must have been a Herculean bout with teenage acne, and he wore a trim little black mustache.

"Ah, welcome, Americans," he said, in a tired sort of way. "I am Fahd, and here is my shop. Here you will buy a beautiful rug to take home with you to America. Many beautiful rugs are here. But first we will have tea together."

I looked at Bob. Bob looked at me.

"Please," Fahd said. "No cost."

Bob and I both reached for a glass of tea. Fahd then selected a glass for himself.

"Please sit here," he said, showing us to a low bench with decorative pillows. "Now, how was your journey?"

But before either of us could answer, he brought out a black ledger book.

"Have a look inside this book," Fahd said. "You will notice the many fine guests who have come away with beautiful rugs. It is entered here that Miss Yumiko Tanaka of Japan has purchased a rug for 2,100 American dollars. You see it is entered here. And here is Miss Alice Maywether, who is from Britain, and she has paid 750 dollars for a very nice rug. And one more if you notice, Mr. John Dagner, probably American, who is here written to have paid 4,000 dollars for three fine rugs, which he is said to take home to his business partners. So you see, many people like to buy a rug from me."

He reached for his tea.

"Please don't hesitate to turn the page and have a look some more," he said.

I did, turning several pages to notice the names and the prices they paid. "Thank you," I said, closing the book.

"Very well," Fahd said. "And now you will buy a rug of your own. Please, this way."

Fahd led us up a flight of stairs into a showroom, with the two large men trailing behind. Once we were all inside, one of them closed the door, and they stood as sentinels on either side. Another Goliath was waiting in the room, and Fahd took a seat in the corner on a little stool across from us, where we sat on little stools. The walls were hung with rugs of many sizes and colors, beautiful things, all, and the floor could not be seen for the rugs. They were rolled open and piled in huge stacks, each stack about four feet high. Goliath began to lay rugs out in the center of the floor to the tune of his master's voice.

"These rugs were made by mountain peoples," Fahd said. "They are the nomads. Very far into the mountains, they make these rugs and bring them to me to sell. When you buy it, you help the mountain peoples."

He meant the Berber tribes of the nearby Rif Mountains, the people who hold ancestral claim over this land and who are said to be descendants of Oranian and Caspian Man, dating back ten to fifteen thousand years. When the Romans controlled much of North Africa, the Berbers maintained their autonomy, secreted away in their mountain fastnesses. They were the people who invaded Iberia in 711 and built the great mosques in Cordoba, Seville, and Granada. Later, under two separate dynasties, the Berbers ruled the region (from the mid-ninth century until the early thirteenth), but they have mostly lived outside the rule of the state, and the name they give themselves, Imazighen, means "free and noble people."

Their home, the Rif Mountains, which rise to just over eight thousand feet, are lush and well watered. Woodlands of cedar, fir, and juniper, as well as oaks (both cork and live oak), offer a sanctuary for some birds, especially storks, and also fox and boar. But overhunting has been devastating for wildlife in Morocco, and the great Barbary lion, which the Romans used in amphitheaters and the kings of Morocco put to use devouring their enemies, has been extinct for fifty years. The Rif Mountains are now better suited to cultivating hash, also called kif, a skill at which the Berbers have grown rather adept. Weaving and selling rugs to tourists and for export is a good business, but with a ready drug market across the strait, kif is better, an industry valued at about $2 billion a year.

"You see I have many types and kinds," Fahd said. "These rugs here are very nice in the living room of the American house. You will enjoy them for many years. Now, which of these rugs do you like best?"

"I don't really care for any of them," I said. "I like them, but I don't want one."

Fahd nodded to his man, and he laid out more rugs on top of those already in the center of the room. The pile grew up from the floor.

"Now these here are a weave of silks and wools, and you can see they are very colorful. Very nice for your American house," Fahd said. "Or if you like, please have two, and give one to your most beloved friend. Now please tell me, which rugs do you like?"

I said nothing. Bob said nothing.

Fahd nodded again to his man. More rugs came out and the pile grew and grew.

"Now is the moment," Fahd said. "We will go through them again. My assistant will roll the rugs back up from the pile, and you must choose your favorites. Please," he said, "which do you like?"

I imagined Bob and I had an unspoken pact. We would choose nothing and very soon walk out to meet Ahmad in the reception area.

"I like that one," Bob said. "Yes, and those two there."

"Very good, sir," Fahd said. "But these are not rugs. These are blankets."

"I like them," Bob said.

"All right. Any others?"

"Yes," Bob said. "Those small ones there."

"Those are not rugs, but samples only, please," Fahd said. "You must choose a rug."

"All right," Bob said. "But I like those best."

Fahd nodded to his man, who put the samples aside with Bob's blankets. "Now you, sir," he said, looking at me. "Please make your selection."

I did not want to make a selection, as I was certain I didn't have enough money for a rug. And I didn't know how I would I carry it anyway.

"Please," Fahd said. "The time is growing late. Your guide will be here soon."

"All right," I said. "How about those three there." I chose three nearly identical rugs that Fahd had indicated were wool and silk, very colorful. They differed from each other, as far as I could see, only in color, and slightly in pattern. I did like them, these rugs, and I began to imagine having one as a remembrance of my journey.

"Very well," Fahd said. "Now please sir, you come with me."

Fahd led me back down the stairs into a room adjacent to the reception, while his man gathered up the rugs. Bob was left behind with the other two men, who stood at the door.

"Where is my friend?" I asked.

"Do not worry. He is very fine. Now, please, you have chosen these three rugs, very nice each of them. Please choose the one you enjoy the most. Meanwhile, perhaps you would like more tea."

"Yes, all right," I said. "I mean, no tea. But, this one? How much?"

"This one, yes. This rug is $850."

"I'm sorry," I said. "These rugs are much too expensive for me. I really don't have enough money." I stood up to leave.

"No, no, no. Please give a moment, sir. These other two are much cheaper. Which one do you want to know about?"

His man pulled the first rug away and presented the remaining two.

"I don't think they are any different," I said.

"This does not matter," Fahd said. "They are much less money. And very affordable for you."

"All right. That one."

"This one," Fahd said. "This rug is $395."

"No," I said. "Much too expensive. I can spend about $50. No more."

I am not, nor have ever been, nor will ever likely be, very good at this sort of thing. I was not trying to get a better deal; I really didn't have the money. If I had had more money, I probably would have spent it, but not because I am reckless (in fact I am frugal). It's just that I have a hard time facing down authority like this, especially spontaneously. Often, in countries where such negotiations are common, I avoid shopping altogether.

"Well, we are in luck," he said. "You cannot pay this price, but the next rug is even cheaper. Our most value."

"How much?"

"This rug is $295," Fahd said. "That is the best price for you."

In those days, airline tickets and money were still mostly paper, so I carried all the money I had for the next few months of traveling in a pouch around my neck beneath my clothes: about $2,000 in travelers' checks, and my flight ticket back home. I inventoried my remaining resources in my mind. No, I couldn't do it. I'd rather go to this museum and that museum and eat. "No. Sorry," I said. "I just don't have enough money. And it is time for me to go."

"No," Fahd said. "Just a moment more. Now. Here is a small paper." He produced a scrap of paper from his pocket. "On this paper, you will write your price." He handed me the paper and a little pencil.

I wrote, "$50," and handed it to him.

He sighed heavily when he saw the sum. "Look what you buy," Fahd said. "Look what you buy. That is much too little. Now, you write here, not $50, not $295, but between. You write your best price. Please."

Again I wrote, "$50."

Fahd stood up, angry this time. "Look. Look," he shouted. "You must not be so unkind. Look what you buy. Excellent quality. Made by the mountain peoples. Wonderful for your home in America. You are very rich, and I am very poor. My country is a poor country. Please," he said, waving his hands in the air, and then returning to his seat. "Please," he said. "Please write your price."

This time I wrote, "$100."

"Now, this is better," Fahd said. "But it is not enough. Once more, please," he said. "Please try one more time. Try your best. We are very close now."

Again I wrote, "$100."

Fahd looked at the paper, and a long sigh came from his weary face. "All right, sir," he said. "I understand. You are a good boy. You can pay $100. Yes, I will accept your offer." He motioned to his man, who rolled up the carpet. "Now, we take traveler's checks, and cash, of course. We can take US dollars or Moroccan currency. And we can ship the rug for you to America. Thank you very much for your business, sir. Perhaps more tea? No? All right, sir. Please come, this way," and he led me back to the reception.

The rug I had purchased, I would later learn, is a kilim, a flat weave suitable as a wall hanging or perhaps a furniture or bed covering. In traditional cultures of the region, and farther north and east, such rugs are essential to everyday life. They serve as a shelter from wind and windborne sand, as a table or a bed laid out on the ground, as a social space for discussion, as a cradle for babies, as a funeral pall, and as a space for prayer. While selling rugs in Morocco is men's business, their creation is rooted in the female world. In his wonderful book *Kilim: History and Symbols,* Dario Valcarenghi describes the weaving of kilims as a nine-thousand-year-old tradition that has been passed down from mother to daughter. It is the women who make life, so it is the women who weave rugs. Weaving is a reenactment of the process of birth, which "comes out of the union of two opposites": on the loom, the warp and weft; in the womb, the sperm and egg. When the weaver finishes her work, she "cuts the threads that link it to the loom, and while doing this, pronounces a formula of blessings that is the same as the one used by the midwife when she severs the umbilical cord of a newborn child."

This meeting of opposites is rooted in the great archetypes Jung finds bubbling up from the collective unconscious: night and day, death and birth, masculine and feminine. "If the meeting of opposites does not take place," Valcarenghi explains, "nothing is created, for each element is defined by its opposite and takes its meaning from it." On the loom then are two threads: the warp, which runs vertically and is stretched taut; and the weft, which undulates horizontally and is intertwined with the warp. "To produce the textile," writes Valcarenghi, "it is necessary for these two threads to be bound, otherwise each will remain a fragile and fluttering potentiality." Here in North Africa, Valcarenghi asserts, the warp is associated with the sky, and the weft with the earth. As in mythologies all over the world, the sky, and thus the rigid, taut warp, is male (the sky father), while the earth, in all its undulations, is female (the earth mother). To weave is to unite the male and female into a human community and to unite the sky and earth into a world in which we might live.

Valcarenghi makes a distinction between the female world of the kilim and knotted rugs, like the wall-to-wall carpet in many American homes, which he considers male. While the kilim requires the meeting of opposites, warp and weft, a knotted rug is made by tying threads to the woven warp and weft, thereby creating a third opposite. "The knotting," writes Valcarenghi, "introduces a third element into the original duality of the two directions of the kilim. . . . Two is a *feminine receptive* number and three is a *masculine penetrative* number, since the former embraces a totality and the latter prepares a new opposition." He goes on to assert that knotted rugs are made from a fixed pattern and therefore can be copied, but the pattern changes to accommodate changes in culture and society. The kilim "was transmitted orally from mother to daughter," so both the art of weaving and the pattern woven into a kilim are symbolic and unconscious. Valcarenghi regards these patterns as a symbolic language, a language "evocative of ideas, convictions and states of mind that were deeply rooted in the collective unconscious of the women who wove them." While knotted rugs are a sign of the times, the kilim is ancient and universal. As kilims were used and wore out, the patterns were transmitted from mother to daughter and from rug to rug, like DNA. If the pattern in a kilim is indeed a symbolic language, then the weaver is engaged in an "unconscious inner dialogue" with her foremothers "stretching back nine thousand years."

Color was important too in the kilim, especially red, as the first uses of color by paleo peoples was red ochre, which was associated with a belief in the afterlife. Mircea Eliade writes that in the Paleolithic period "there is evidence for the use more or less everywhere of red ochre, a ritual substitute for blood, symbols of life, as a testimony to the belief in an existence after death."

What did the patterns on my rug mean? Valcarenghi cites a fourteenth-century Middle Eastern expression: "Everyone can pull his own kilim out of the water." In other words, everyone can recover their own lost identity or everyone can dig out their own truth from the unconscious. So if Valcarenghi is right, and Jung and Eliade are right, perhaps whatever attracted me to my rug is rooted deep inside me, and if I could understand the language of the rug, I might come to know myself a little better. Or perhaps, like a horoscope, the patterns in a kilim are general and universal, so each one can apply to most anyone at all.

My rug is made up of a series of long bands of pattern drawn across the width. Among them is a long wavy black band, repeated thirteen times, possibly the symbol for running water. Running water is the symbol for life, say the scholars. Pretty general. Moving on, Valcarenghi writes about the "the body of the goddess," a symbol of a female figure with legs and arms spread, often stylized to look more like a geometric shape. The goddess, or mother goddess, is a hermaphrodite, as she possesses the power to create both male and female. She also possesses the power to take life, hence her association with the forces of nature beyond human control: vultures, lions, wolves, bulls. According to Valcarenghi, in the pattern of the kilim, the image of the bull is often posited inside the image of the mother goddess. The bull possesses a "deep ambivalence." It is "male for its sexual vigor, the abundance of its semen, and the strength of its body," and it is "female for its roundish curves, its color of the earth and its horns," which link it to the moon, the night, and nature's fecundity. The essence of the bull is this dualism, asserts Valcarenghi, so in the ancient world, the "religions of the great mother were founded on the cult of the bull." In an early ritual, initiates stood in a grated pit while a bull was sacrificed above them. The warm blood that rained down over them was "a symbol of energy and life," writes Valcarenghi, "a dual symbol: male as the origin of physical strength and vitality, female as the cyclic flow linked with birth."

Looking at my rug, it is easy to associate two slightly different bands with the great mother and the bull, but then also I see here the wolf's mouth, or what is sometimes known as the wolf's track. This symbol, in all its variety, is common among nomadic tribes who regard the wolf as both a spiritual force and an enemy to their sheep, goat, and cattle herds. To weave the wolf's mouth into a rug is to help ward off wolf attack. And I could recognize the bird symbol, too, and find in the scholars' interpretations such various and general meanings as to be nearly meaningless: bad luck and good luck; happiness, joy, and love; power and strength; impending news; and the soul of the dead. Emre, who was a shepherd as well as a Sufi, writes of death, "The bird of life has flown off," and "We took off, became birds, and flew, Thank God!"

When I arrived at the reception desk, Bob was there with Ahmad, and Fahd's men now stood on either side of the front entrance. Bob held nothing in his hands. Fahd glanced at him with disgust but then turned to me with great enthusiasm.

"Here our friend has purchased a very fine rug for a very fine price," Fahd said. "He has done well. Please, sir, write your entry into my ledger. I will wrap your fine rug in brown paper. Now, of course, we will ship to any place in the world. If you leave your rug with us, for you, we will ship it to America. What would you like to do?"

"I'll take it with me," I said, opening the ledger. Inside I wrote: John Smith, $100.

"Ahh," Fahd said, winking at me. "You will carry your rug with you. A very wise boy. It has been a pleasure," he said. "I have enjoyed your company and patronage. Please, Ahmad, take care of this fine boy. He has done very well."

One of the men opened the door and showed us our way into the street.

"What did you pay?" Ahmad asked.

"One hundred dollars."

"Yes, very good! You have done well. Very good. As Fahd said. It is a good price."

The kilim, because of its tight weave, requires more work than a knotted rug, so it is more expensive, perhaps somewhere in the range of three dollars per square foot in Morocco. The rug I bought was no more than twenty square feet, so a fair price, at the upper end, was about sixty dollars. The same rug in the United States would indeed go for the kinds of prices Fahd had recorded in his ledger.

"Well," Ahmad said. "Now I will take you to your hotel. When the time is near, I will return and we will go to a very nice restaurant. You will hear me knock at the door. All right? Come this way, my friends."

Later we heard a knock at the door.

"Friends," Ahmad said. "I will take you to a very nice restaurant. Come with me."

Ron had come around after his nap and was dressed, washed, ready to go. We followed Ahmad through town like puppies. He led us on dark streets and across narrow alleyways. Where we were, I did not know. I tried to keep track, marking buildings and other odd-looking structures in my mind, trying to see the streets as if from above, on a map. But a few minutes into this maze, I was lost. Bob was lost too, and Ron was without a response. We were completely in the hands of Ahmad.

"Just this way, my friends. Just here."

We stopped in front of a little restaurant and went inside. The interior was dark and cluttered with bric-a-brac, but it looked clean and well cared for. It was full of people, too, all men, and every head turned when we walked in.

"These are my friends," Ahmad announced. "They need a nice table and some good food. Please, this way," he said. "Please sit here and I will have the chef bring you his best. OK? Do not worry. I have arranged it for you."

The meal unfolded as a series of courses, beginning with a lentil-based soup, probably *harira*, with flatbread and a sad-looking salad, which Ahmad warned us against eating. "No," he said. "You will become ill. Please do not take this dish." Then on to a lovely fish, which Ahmad assured us came from the sea that morning. And then a sample, which Ahmad insisted on. "Yes, you will like to have the story of eating the *bastaila*. Please try this small bite. No cost. It is a specialty here, but mostly you find it more south." *Bastaila*, I would later discover, is a rich pigeon pie. And then a pastry for dessert, which reminded me of the Spanish churro. No one else was eating, just me, Bob, and Ron.

"Come, gentlemen," Ahmad said. "We must go now, as the Ramadan is about to be broken for these gentlemen here. The restaurant is for them now and not for you. Please come with me."

We went out into the Moroccan night, following Ahmad through the streets. I recognized this and that, and then realized we were just a few streets down from the hotel.

"Now," Ahmad said, "you will like to try the local smoke. It is very nice after a good meal. I know a place where you may buy the best kif in town. We will sample several kinds, everything you want, and then you may buy what you like to carry. This way."

I stood there on the street corner as Ahmad led Bob and Ron away.

"Come, my friend," Ahmad called to me. "This way. It is the best thing for you."

"I'm going back to the hotel."

"Come, my friend," Ahmad said, and hurried back to where I waited under the dim streetlight. "Will you not come?"

"No," I said. "I am not a smoker. I'll just go back to the hotel."

"OK, my friend. OK. I understand you now. Please go back to the hotel. It isn't far. Do you know the way? It is just there and there, and then to your left side. You will find it very easily."

"I know the way."

Deep into the night Bob and Ron returned to the room. I had locked the door, so they awakened me with their knocking.

"My god, Ron," Bob exclaimed, as they burst in. "I didn't think we would get out of there." Then to me, "You wouldn't believe it. You wouldn't believe it."

But I did believe it. What happened at the border, what happened in the rug shop, and what had been happening all day with Ahmad also happened in the kif dealer's home.

"We kept telling them, no, we didn't want to buy that much," Bob said. "No. No. But each time they would not listen, and they would not let us out the door. And we had smoked a lot, so we felt obligated, but we didn't want that much. And that fellow at the door would not let us out."

"And Ahmad?" I asked.

"He had gone to help his grandmother," Ron said.

"Yes," Bob said. "It took hours. First we were smoking happily with these guys, and then they wanted us to buy, god knows how much that was, but they wanted about $1,000. Finally we consented to buy $100. But we had to buy to get out, so once we did, they opened the door for us. That's when Ahmad appeared again."

"What a coincidence," I said. "Where is he now?"

"No telling," Bob said. "He left us at the door downstairs."

We heard a knock at the door.

"Oh, Jesus," Bob said.

The knock came again. "My friends," Ahmad said through the closed door. "It is me, Ahmad. Your guide. Please answer, please."

Bob opened the door.

"Yes," Ahmad said. "It is me. Your guide. Did you enjoy your day in Tetouan? Yes, of course you did. You received a nice tour of the city, a good dinner. This gentleman," he pointed to me, "bought a fine rug for a very nice price. You received this accommodation in the best hotel, and then a nice smoke. Now, what are you willing to give?"

Bob rolled his eyes. "Look, man," he said. "We've paid enough."

"I have given you a very nice service. Now you must pay."

"You told us no cost," said Bob.

"At first, yes, there was no cost, but now there is some cost."

"Get lost, man," Bob said.

"I cannot go to my family without my wage," he said. "My grandmother needs medicine. My sister must eat. I must buy shoes. You see what I mean. What are you willing to pay?"

"Unbelievable," Bob said.

"Please believe, my friends. I must have my wage."

"What have you got?" Bob said, turning to Ron and me.

We pooled our cash. About 300 dirham, which was about $35.

"Here," Bob said.

"This is not good," Ahmad said. "I must have twice this money."

"It's all we have," Bob said. "Now please go."

Ahmad threw his hands into the air. His kind face became dark and stormy. He stood in the doorway a moment. What was he going to do? He waited. He stormed. He seemed to be about to burst. Then he turned and went out. We closed the door and locked it.

As the sun got up, so did I. Bob and Ron lay together on the far bed with their heads on one pillow, their legs entwined. I did not wake them, and I did not say goodbye. I went quietly downstairs into the lobby, then out into the street to hail a taxi for the border.

"How much?" I asked.

"Eighty."

"To Ceuta?"

"Eighty."

"I paid only twenty to get here."

"Private taxi," he said. "Eighty."

"Twenty."

He motioned me to get in. We picked up four other men, and when we arrived at Ceuta, I paid him thirty. He smiled and thanked me.

Now the border. I passed through a gate and showed my passport.

"This way," a fellow told me.

I went that way to another Moroccan checkpoint and showed my passport once more.

"This way," that fellow told me. "The window, please."

I went to the window, showed my passport, received my stamp, and passed through one more checkpoint.

Several feet beyond that, a man accosted me and demanded my passport.

"I just showed my passport several times," I said. "I have my stamp."

"Give me your passport," he said.

"I have already shown it several times."

"I am a policeman," he said.

"Let me see your badge."

"I am a policeman!"

I showed him my passport, and he snatched it from my hand. I snatched it back.

He took hold of my arm and pushed me in front of two uniformed guards. They looked at me and shrugged.

"I am sorry," I said. "I did not—"

"You shut your mouth, boy," he said.

He forced me through a small door in the checkpoint station. Inside was a desk and a chair.

"You smoke?" he asked. "You have something inside? Let me see your bag."

"I am sorry," I said again. "I did not mean to be disrespectful."

He searched my backpack. He looked into my plastic grocery sack, which I had carried since Cordoba. He pulled out a sealed container of warm yogurt. It dripped onto the floor.

"Must have sprung a leak," I said.

He dropped the yogurt into the sack, threw my passport on the desk, and walked out. I gathered my things and followed him through the door. I was back in Spain.

On the train to Cordoba, I watched the blue sky over the country-side from the train window, the long ruffled rivers coming down into the sea, and the people the way you want Spaniards to be, old-faced with well-worn hands and tired eyes across the dust of their long history, a history bound up with the people across the strait.

The green hills rolled on. We passed through Cortes de la Frontera, a village that fell below a great stone mountain draped in long green sweeps of grass and water running through it. I saw there an old man with his long walking cane bringing in a great band of goats, his dogs moving slow along his side, walking slow himself, looking up and out across his valley, the walls of his world fallen away across a sea of grass and sky.

FOUR MOUNTAINS

United Kingdom and Ireland, 2007

Mount Snowdon, Wales (1,085 meters / 3,560 feet)

And so that morning of June 27, 2007, in heavy rain and fog, I thought I might climb Mount Snowdon alone. It's the highest mountain in Wales. The waitress at Pete's Eats in Llanberis, where I breakfasted on a monster omelet, open faced, with chips, told me only professionals climb Snowdon in this kind of weather. And a kind old woman at a shop where I bought fruit, cheese, and bread for the trail said, "What? You're going up Snowdon? In this weather?" We looked out together at the rain slashing sideways at the windows.

"Why? Don't people climb Snowdon in this weather?"

"Only if they're mad."

Therefore, I stepped out the door, squared off with the rain, and up I went, up the Llanberis Path, the most direct, least technical of the several routes to the summit.

Wordsworth climbed this mountain too and wrote an account in his epic poem, *The Prelude*. He went at night with a companion, and a shepherd as his guide, intent on seeing the sunrise from the summit. If I understand his poem, Wordsworth makes an astonishing discovery on that ascent. He comes to this great truth: "The highest bliss / That flesh can know" is "to hold fit converse with the spiritual world." Perhaps you're thinking this isn't news at all, but there is a great difference in the wisdom that comes by experience and the wisdom that comes by way of musty books. To know, as others have said, you must make the journey yourself. For Wordsworth the climb becomes a pilgrimage, and he works out a kind of thesis for his life. The moment of discovery, he relates, "fell like a flash" before him. He looked up into the night sky to find "the Moon hung naked in a firmament / Of azure without cloud, and at [his] feet / Rested a silent sea of hoary mist." It's a beautiful moment, a beautiful passage, and on reading it, any wistful wanderer like myself cannot but ask: if it happened for Wordsworth on this sacred mountain, why can't it happen for me?

But I had come to the United Kingdom for more practical reasons: (1) to attend a writers' conference at Bangor University; (2) to travel with an old friend from my native Oregon; and (3) for sheep. I know, I know—there are all the various jokes and whatnot. But for me, sheep are serious business. I had spent some time traveling with shepherds in Idaho intent on writing about their lives, and so I thought the next step in my inquiry was to explore the pastoral landscapes of Great Britain. I had financial support too, a grant from Texas Tech University, where I teach. If I had had any sense at all, I would have roused to this good fortune. Isn't it every writer's dream to be handed a substantial budget and told, "Go find something to write about"? But truth is, I was racked with guilt. What did I mean by "explore"? Where was my inquiry headed? Why sheep, for god's sake? Quite possibly nothing at all would emerge from my journey, and then I'd have to answer to the state of Texas for my irresponsible behavior. I was rather used to failure, but so far I had mostly done it with my own money.

I rounded an elbow on the Llanberis Path and passed a country house at the foot of the mountain. Here I came to a sign that told me not to expect toilets, shelter, or a café at the summit, luxuries I had no reason to expect until I learned I could not expect them. A little farther on, another sign appeared: "This is sheep country. Keep your dog on a lead." Perhaps the state of Texas would get good value for its money after all. Thus emboldened, like Wordsworth "I panted up / With eager pace, and no less eager thoughts," the black slugs, hideous and strange, making a gastropodinal minefield in front of me. Incidentally, it turns out that black slugs are not only black, but various shades of that color, which I understand to mean gray, and they can also be white. If you want to cull the population in your garden, the two best methods are, according to my source, dousing them with salt, or boiling them in a saucepan on your kitchen stove.

The rain let up, and I felt like the day might go my way. I picked up the pace and shed my Gore-Tex rain shell, strapping it happily to my Osprey daypack. My boots were comfortable and, so far, dry, and I could see ahead that I was gaining on two figures in the distance. I felt hale and fit as I overtook them, two young women in sporty outdoor apparel. I passed on the left and said, "Good morning," to which they enthusiastically offered the same. I suppose I might have slowed and walked with them, but did I want company on my climb? Not really. At least I didn't think I did. I pressed onward and up, passing a few scattered sheep, toward the heavy cloudbank settled in over the mountain. A huge boulder appeared out in front of me. My map told the story of a local legend: if you spend the night near the boulder you will experience a transformation—you wake up either a poet or a lunatic.

Thinking it better to avoid both, I developed a steady cadence as I humped up the mountain, and soon became so preoccupied thinking god knows what that I didn't notice the railroad tracks along the route until I passed under them, and then farther on, under them again, where at last I reached the ceiling of the sky. Apparently people don't always climb this mountain but instead hop the train to the summit. I couldn't imagine a Wordsworthian epiphany arising out of that kind of voluptuousness, but here, as I paused beneath the stone overpass, it began to rain again, and I wondered if the train wouldn't happen by and stop for me. The temperature fell and the wind burned my exposed ears. Visibility was only fifty feet, perhaps even thirty, here in the misty clouds.

What if, in my blindness, I walked off the western face and plunged to my gory death? Unlikely, and yet I thought about turning back. Then I thought about thinking about turning back: would I think about turning back if I were climbing with my old friend? No. We'd press on through the storm. I put on my toboggan cap, then my rain shell, and pulled the Gore-Tex hood over my head.

I had not felt lonely until now, and when it came it surprised me. I was alone on the back of the greatest mountain in Wales suffering impossible weather, and no one in the world really knew where I was. A million miles from home, I was hungry and tired and bereft. Because no one knew me, and there was no one here to know me, I thought I could be anyone in anywhen, and oddly the idea of wandering out of my old life made me happy. I wasn't happy exactly, but happy that I was lonely. I thought of Bashō and the three conditions for his haiku: *sabi* (loneliness), *shiori* (tenderness), and *hosomi* (slenderness). I thought maybe I had them all, and when I reached the summit, I hoped to find waiting for me a sort of grail, an answer to a question I had not asked. Who could accomplish such a knight's errand but me? And Wordsworth, of course.

Then I heard voices. Lots of voices. Were they the songs of guiding angels descending with the rain? No, for out of the mist came a colorful band of several dozen schoolchildren, laughing and shouting and splashing in the rain. A couple of smiling teachers brought up the rear. "Cheers," one of them said, as they passed on by. So much for heroics. I ate six Fig Newtons, then stepped out into the rain and muscled up the way. I could hardly see anything at all, but I found that as I walked deeper into the mist, a little more of the trail ahead was revealed to me, and in this way I reached the top of the mountain.

At the summit stone I now understood the sign below announcing that there were no services at the top. Not because there were no services at the top, but because the services at the top were under renovation. A dozen men scurried about concrete foundations, and several excavators tore into the mountain's skin, making a horrendous racket. I stood there a moment in the sharp wind, the surrounding peaks of Snowdonia obscured from my view, and noted how utterly anticlimactic it felt. I wondered if I would have found the summit more enchanting had I climbed the mountain with my friend. As it was, the universal mystery did not reveal itself to me the way it had for Wordsworth, and I imagined no length of waiting around, alone and battered by the bitter wind, would change this fact. What was the problem, anyway? Were these not conditions ripe for a miracle? Were such miracles even possible? Here in the yeasty heights, I had to come face to face with the possibility that the great poet was full of shit. Then a thought rose up in me: If not here, why not there? Why not climb another great mountain with my old friend when he arrived in Dublin? What is the highest mountain in Ireland, anyway? In fact, why not climb the greatest mountains in England, Scotland, Ireland, and Wales? Perhaps Wordsworth had not led me astray after all. I offered the summit a final nod, knowing I'd likely never return, and started back down the mountain.

Mount Carrantuohil, Ireland (1,039 meters / 3,409 feet)
Bashō traveled with a companion, Sora. Samuel Johnson explored the Hebrides with James Boswell. Bruce Chatwin claimed to have traveled alone, but he lied—he almost always went with a friend. Peter Matthiessen accompanied George Schaller into the Himalayas. And of course Wordsworth and Coleridge made regular walking tours in the Lake District. This tradition of traveling with a companion inspired me, and it was in Matthiessen's book *The Snow Leopard* that I read: "The Roshi was pleased that there would be but two of us—this seemed to him a condition of true pilgrimage." If making a solitary ascent of Snowdon was to bear me no fruit, perhaps hill walking with a friend would. Besides, I was tired of traveling alone and tired of being lonely. To my good fortune, my old friend Scott Dewing had agreed to meet me in Dublin.

Scott and I had grown up together, passing through those affected high school years and on through college. It was a kind of miracle—more so than Wordsworth's inspiration in the face of natural beauty—that after twenty-three years my friendship with Scott was still intact. No. Better than intact. It was flourishing, which was far more than I could say for the numerous friends whose lives I had passed into and out of over the years. Certainly we had our differences. Scott was married with two daughters; I had been married and now wasn't. (We were each best man at the other's wedding.) Scott had put on fifty unnecessary pounds and lost his hair; I had grown my hair long and kept fairly fit. Scott had moved from northwest Oregon to southwest Oregon, with a few flights into foreign lands; I had moved from northwest Oregon to almost every state in the West and hit twenty-four countries along the way. I admired his steadiness; he admired my wanderlust. I sometimes longed for his family life; he sometimes longed for my solitude. He could still kick my ass, but I was sure I could outrun him. Yet we both still loved books and good writing, outdoor and indoor adventures, and long walks on the beach. Even as months, sometimes years, passed between visits, we always seemed to pick up where we left off. After high school, Scott and I had planned to make a journey together through Peru, but college and lovers and making a living took precedence, and we left that dream behind. Now, at long last, such a journey was imminent. I took this as a sign of good fortune, and after a long day of wandering Dublin in the rain, Scott and I boarded the train for Killarney Town to climb Carrantuohil, the highest peak in Ireland.

From Cronin's Yard, the path leads up the Gaddagh River to the Devil's Ladder, a steep scree-filled gully eroded by the thousands of hill walkers who make this trek each year. The sun broke through the clouds as Scott and I walked through Hag's Glen and between the brilliant waters of Lough Callee and Lough Gouragh. We felt good and talked about old times, the mountain sheep grazing the green green grass.

At the Ladder, I pulled easily away from Scott, scrambling over huge boulders, slick in the rain, as we rose up dramatically off the valley floor. I was passing other hill walkers with ease, and I felt fit and fast and wanted to go faster. Instead, I stopped shy of half-way to wait for my companion. Twenty years ago, Scott and I were fairly competitive, and a situation like this would usually awaken his anger. He'd fume and sputter to catch up to me, throw his pack down where I waited, and curse the weather or the terrain or his shoes. He wasn't used to losing. He was bigger, stronger, and faster than me, but over the long haul, I usually beat him. Now it mattered not at all. Scott's life was full and complete, and he devoted himself daily to his family and his work as a teacher and computer administrator. As I was single again, I filled some of my idle hours with running and cycling and wandering just to stave off loneliness. My fitness wasn't a sign of anything, really, except time spent alone.

"How you feelin', man?" Scott said. He put his big hand on my shoulder.

"I'm feelin' great. You?"

"Haven't felt this good in years. Look at that! Aw, man."

We looked back down the Ladder, where the green valley drew a line to the horizon. This would likely be the only grand view we'd get, as the top of Carrantuohil was nearly always occluded by heavy clouds and mist.

"Don't feel like you have to wait on me," Scott said. "I'll make my way up at my own pace."

"No, man," I said. "Let's walk it together."

The plot to climb the four highest mountains in England, Scotland, Ireland, and Wales rose out of our friendship and our search for a purpose. I had thought to climb Snowdon in Wales and Scafell Pike in England because these were the mountains of the great pastoral poets Wordsworth and Coleridge, but the notion to climb them all, and climb them together, came out of some deeper need to get things done. Much of my friendship with Scott revolved around getting things done—we skied the closed Forest Service roads deep into the Cascades; we trained and completed a triathlon at age sixteen; we created a course for ourselves in Egyptology when our high school failed to inspire; we ran the steep, winding trail to the top of 620-foot Multnomah Falls, the second highest waterfall in the United States; we paddled canoes up and down the great Columbia. Some of this was youthful exuberance, but we also made a concerted effort to lead each other forward, to imagine heroic labors because there seemed to be no one to imagine them for us. One day we realized, quite by accident, that those labors had made us the best of friends. Now here we were again, two decades later, up to our old tricks.

It started to rain, not much, but enough so that we both put on our rain gear. We climbed and rested and talked our way to Christ's Saddle, and then on up to the great iron cross on the summit. It was busy at the top, hill walkers everywhere talking and eating and laughing. Scott asked the fellow next to us if he would take our picture together near the cross. As it had been for me on Snowdon, we couldn't see a thing through the clouds. We found a rock shelter safe from the wind and spread out our lunch: cheese and hard salami, bread, fruit, and canned oysters. Aristotle is no friend of mine, but I do know that in his *Nicomachean Ethics* he devotes a number of pages to friendship, stating that "friends are the only refuge" and that "without friends no one would choose to live." I certainly felt that now, as here on Carrantuohil I wasn't anticipating the revelation of the universal mystery but rather the long, slow hike down engaged in conversation with my old friend, and, later, gorging on meat and Guinness at a Killarney pub. A much better option than epiphany. I reached for the oysters then, and a ray of sunlight broke over my hand. Blue sky cracked the mountain peak as the clouds parted and rolled down into the valley. The bustle at the summit went still, and everyone everywhere stood up. There was Ireland! The Slieve Mish Mountains on the Dingle Peninsula. The Galty Mountains to the east in Tipperary. Kenmare Bay to the southwest, and Inch and Rossbeigh Strand to the northwest. Cameras buzzed and snapped, but Scott and I just stood there looking out. This is a scene for poets, I thought, and to be shared among friends.

Later, showered and happy and empty, Scott and I asked the slender beauty at the desk of the Neptune's Hostel where we might find a good meal and a good beer.

"The Laurels," she said. "That's the place you want."

"How do we get there?" Scott asked.

"All right, then," she said. "You go out onto the front street there, that's New Street. Take a left. Then right on High Street. You can't miss it." Then she paused as if channeling the muse. "It will just hit you," she said, "like fate."

Ben Nevis, Scotland (1,344 meters / 4,409 feet)
In Fort William, over wild boar burgers and Guinness at the Grog & Gruel, I couldn't think of anything else to complain about, so I complained about my good fortune.

"I don't know. Is this research?" I said. "I mean, how can I spend this grant money on climbing these mountains?"

"Dude," Scott said. "This is what you do. Would you rather be in a library somewhere reading some archive?"

"No way."

"See, you gotta let that go. You're collecting data. It's just that your data is experience."

"Yeah, yeah, I know," I said. "But will the university president buy that? I mean, I'm enjoying this. I can't imagine doing anything else right now. Administrations don't cotton to fun."

"Christ," Scott said. "This is the best money the state of Texas has ever spent. Look at it this way—you're supposed to be learning, right? Gaining knowledge and using that knowledge to write and teach?"

"Right."

"So, experience as data—at least in my view—leaps over the whole tedious stage called 'research' and directly to knowledge. You don't have to research anything. Experience is knowledge. That's the difference between research in the humanities and research in the sciences. Your school is getting good value for its money, much better value than a scientist who goes on and on spending money for decades, data set after data set only to conclude that people have sex because they're attracted to each other."

"Right, but—"

"No buts, man," Scott said. "You could write a whole fuckin' paper on this difference, don't you think? But who would want to? It'd be called something like"—and with that, he worked out a proper title to appease my overindulgent guilt—" 'Differential Data Gathering Methodologies between the Sciences and the Humanities, or How to Use Your Research Funding to Vacation in Europe.' "

"That's genius," I said. "That ought to do it."

"Right. Plus you went to that conference, read your work, made contacts, and gave your school a good name."

"Yeah."

"And then you'll use these experiences to write your shepherd book."

"True."

"And you'll share this journey with your students, not to mention your colleagues, who always benefit when their teachers actually live a life, rather than sit at home and watch reality TV."

"Indeed."

"And other pieces will come out of it too. I mean, maybe you'll write about this."

"Maybe."

"So give it a rest," he said. "Plus, look at it this way: the grant won't even pay for beer, right? So here you are again spending your own damn money to bring all this knowledge back to your school. I find that almost criminal."

Ben Nevis, the highest peak in Scotland, and in all of the UK and Ireland, was just out our door from the Calluna Hostel. After a night of reading melodramatic poetry about the mountain—

> Oh! for a sight of Ben Nevis!
> Methinks I see him now,
> As the morning sunlight crimsons
> The snow-wreath on his brow . . .

—followed by a little Burns and Sir Walter Scott, then a three-hour commitment to Mel Gibson's *Braveheart* (we were bent on Scottish immersion, after all), we walked the several kilometers to the trail-head and started up toward the Red Burn. We'd come to learn that a popular challenge in the UK was to climb Snowdon, Ben Nevis, and England's Scafell Pike all within twenty-four hours. I boasted that I would climb all of them too, plus Carrantuohil, in twenty-four days.

We came up out of the alder and Scots pine, the violets, heathers, and primrose at the bottom of the glen, and into deer grass, bog asphodel, butterworts, and sundews at Halfway Lochan. The mountain, as usual, was shrouded in mist. Likely all we would see at the summit were other people, hundreds of people streaming up the mountain track. (About a hundred thousand people reach the summit each year.) And sheep, which were everywhere on the green hillsides. I stopped often to snap photographs.

"More pictures of sheep, huh?" Scott said. "That'll show those bastards."

Few friendships weather the great, ordinary life transitions: youth to adulthood, single life to married life, student-idealist to pragmatic citizen. How ours did, I'll never know. Perhaps it was the way Scott and I helped raise each other. We both had powerful, emotionally distant fathers who instructed primarily by way of pragmatism and criticism. My father's style was to put me in an oar boat on a big river in the American West and push me off into the swirling current. "Don't hit any rocks," he'd call after me. "I paid good money for that boat." That was one way, and a pretty good one too, but it didn't cover all the ground. Scott had an older brother, but they weren't so close in those days, and I had grown up with two sisters. There were those hallmarks of Western male society—athletics, the frat house, the military—but either they were insufficient, or we skipped them altogether. So there were holes in our journey to manhood, and we turned to each other to fill them.

A boy becomes a man only "through ritual and effort—only through the 'active intervention of older men,'" writes Robert Bly in *Iron John*. He cannot make the transition from being under the care and protection of women (his mother, primarily) to joining the society of men (his father, primarily) without help. And he requires the help of older men. "Having no soul union with other men can be the most damaging wound of all," asserts Bly. Back in the day, the men would enter the mother's house with spears, snatch up the boy, and take him by force to the edge of the village. There the boy would be instructed by other initiated men, his father among them, and on returning home, he would indeed be a man, with a man's responsibilities. Without this kind of ceremony and without such strong, emotionally open older men to show the way, a son will have what Bly calls "father hunger" all his life. I have felt this father hunger and felt it most deeply when Scott and I were rounding out our high school years. It's not that our fathers did nothing or tried not at all, but that they didn't go far enough. At the threshold of manhood, it was Scott who was there for me, just as I was there for him.

When Scott and I were sixteen, my father suggested, in the way that he did, that we take the drift boat and run the upper John Day River to Clarno. Perhaps he knew what he was doing after all, kicking us out of the house to work off a little baby fat. Scott and I drove out to eastern Oregon with food and gear for three days, along with a little contraband: a gallon of cheap wine, a half case of beer, a fifth of Jack Daniels. That first night on the river, after having run several small class II rapids and enduring the cold fall winds and rain, we grilled elk burgers on the fire and topped our glasses with JD. The sky cleared for just that night, and standing there under the simple stars, the hunger in my belly near insatiable, we raised a toast to brotherhood. Though I recognize it only now, these many years later, it was that moment that stands as my initiation ceremony, and it was Scott who was there to share it with me.

Ben Nevis stands a thousand feet higher than all other mountains in the UK and Ireland, and our climb up it didn't want to end. We climbed up and up, crossing a snowfield near the summit. Soon we could see a series of humps on the arc of the mountain's back, humps that were the many rock shelters at trail's end. Once again, as if the landlord were looking out for us, the clouds broke and the sun shone through. We walked the final steps bathed in light, and as it was so, we had no old complaints, no new desires.

Scafell Pike, England (978 meters / 3,209 feet)

Wordsworth and Coleridge were like brothers for a time, and they famously lived in proximity in England's Lake District composing their greatest poems with the other's favor and guidance. Dorothy was there too, Wordsworth's beloved sister, and the three walked miles and miles together through the hills and glens. The height of their friendship was also the height of their poetic industry. Coleridge wrote "The Rime of the Ancyent Marinere," and Wordsworth was already at work on the poem that became his epic, *The Prelude*. They published a volume together, *Lyrical Ballads*, which was largely a failure then but is a staple of Romantic poetry now. On a walk to Keswick, near England's highest mountain, Scafell Pike, Coleridge exclaimed, in typical Romantic bombast: "O my God! and the Black Crags close under the snowy mountains, whose snows were pinkish with the setting sun and the reflections from the sandy rich Clouds that floated over some and rested upon others! It was to me a vision of fair Country." I had never been to the Lake District, so I anticipated fair country as well, not to mention—O my God!—my deepest immersion yet in all things pastoral, all things Romantic, all things sheep. Well, not *all* things sheep.

We spent a few nights in Edinburgh, where Scott and I explored the pastoral paintings in the National Gallery, toured the Writers' Museum, and viewed the work of that intrepid walker, Richard Long at the National Gallery of Modern Art, and where we adventured with a drunk witch from Portland named Sabrina.

Then we struck south for Wordsworth-land to climb Scafell Pike, the last mountain on the list. Scott was nearing the end of his journey, while I would travel on for several more weeks. My sense of security had become so dependent on my companion I could hardly imagine what I'd do after he left.

It was raining, of course, when in Grasmere Scott and I boarded a bus for Keswick, then on to Seathwaite, which was not a town, but rather the end of the road. We passed through the gates of a sheep outfit, where the shepherds kicked their dogs and beat the ewes into a pen, to find unfolding before us a system of trails ascending the hoary crags. We walked easily and steadily in the light rain, up Grains Gill and along Seathwaite Fell. Soon we would make a turn up Ruddy Gill and then onto the Esk Hause trail to the summit. Though Scafell Pike was the lowest of the four mountains, the climb challenged us more, with trails running every direction through the wilds, and the rough going over misty boulder fields.

Wordsworth had his Mount Snowdon, but it was Coleridge who scrambled up Scafell, not the mountain we were climbing, but the one next to it with nearly the same name. Some think of Scafell and Scafell Pike as the same mountain, but each has a distinct summit, the latter fourteen meters higher. At the top of Scafell, Coleridge, never without pen and ink, worked on a letter to his beloved Sara Hutchinson, the sister of Wordsworth's wife, Mary (not to be confused with Coleridge's wife, also named Sara). That done, Coleridge thought he could see a route to the summit of Scafell Pike (which apparently he thought was Bowfell, farther to the east), the mountain local shepherds believed was the highest in the land. He had no map, no compass, no guide or guidebook. He relied only on his poetic sense. The going was hard, and he found the ridge between the two mountains too much for him. Abandoning Scafell Pike, he started back down, dropping over vertical ledges onto narrow shelves of rock. He passed the carcass of a sheep, "quite rotten," which had fallen to its death. Not an altogether good sign. Soon he reached an impossible ledge, impossible for him anyway, and there he was, crag-fast—he could go neither up nor down. "My limbs were all a tremble—," he wrote later to Sara Hutchinson: "I lay upon my Back to rest myself, and was beginning according to my Custom, to laugh at myself for a Madman, when the sight of the Crags above me on each side, and the impetuous Clouds just over them, posting so luridly and so rapidly northward, overawed me. I lay in a state of almost prophetic Trance and Delight—" Somehow, perhaps with Providence on his side, he discovered a great crack (known today as Fat Man's Agony), which he thought might just be the only way down. He moved his rucksack to his side, and down he went, stemming his way to the bottom. Clouds closed in around him, and the rain fell. He hustled down the mountain toward Eskdale, where he took shelter from the storm in a sheepfold. From the enthusiasm in his notebook and letters, one must conclude this treacherous climb was the highlight of his 1802 solo tour of the Lakes.

Scott and I crossed over the murmuring brook of Grains Gill, where we paused on the footbridge for photos. I carried in my pack a few bars of the famed Kendal Mint Cake, the soft, sugary energy bar that Hillary and Norgay took to the summit of Everest. I broke one open and shared it out. From here we could see a good way in both directions—down the gill and up into where we were going. The rain came on, and we took the time to put on our rain gear. A little farther up the trail, we stopped again and took off our rain gear—this time for the last time. Though clouds hung heavy over the mountain peaks, it wouldn't rain again for a couple days. Up we climbed into the clouds, where the moist air wetted our hair and clothes. Sun fell across the broad green backs of the hills in patches, and I wondered if I'd ever seen anything so beautiful. I thought probably I had.

We crossed a great boulder field where the sheep would not go, skipping from stone to stone in our boots. At the top of Broad Crag we descended onto the tongue between them, the crag and mighty Scafell Pike. So here it was, our final ascent. We noticed a few other climbers in bright colors among the rocks winding slowly up the mountain, but compared to Ben Nevis and Carrantuohil, we had the place mostly to ourselves. I broke off a couple more pieces of mint cake, and with that cool, sweet courage, we climbed to the top. There wasn't much to it, really, at least from this side, and we met with no dastardly threat to our health or heels. The mist and heavy clouds allowed us no grand view across the Lake District, so we found a proper seat among the boulders to spread our lunch.

I wondered if, like Coleridge after listening to Wordsworth read from his great epic, I might not be overwhelmed at this juncture, at the completion of this journey with my old friend, by "thoughts all too deep for words!—," and then might fall delicately into a reverie, part trance and part delight. But no—for thence erupted from my lips, without my consent, a string of hopeful words:

"You gonna eat that?" I asked, indicating the last bit of hard salami.

"Nope," Scott said.

And that was it; there was nothing more, only the shorter, faster grind back down the mountain, a happy, sunny ride through the countryside on the second level of an open-air bus, and, in the evening, food and beer without end.

In Ambleside, the morning of Scott's departure, we walked together from the big hostel on the lake to the bus stop. We had hardly slept at all, as the hostel was overrun with a belligerent rugby team, shouting drunken obscenities and vomiting in the hallways. Scott would take the early bus to Windermere and then catch the train south to London. I felt a terrible anxiety welling within, and I didn't think it was lack of sleep. Before Scott's arrival, I had emboldened myself to travel alone (not the first time, certainly) and made my way through Wales and up Mount Snowdon. But something in me had shifted, and now I was flooded with questions. What in god's name would I do with myself after Scott's departure? When would we see each other again? Would we ever make another journey? What if one of us kicked off without warning and this was really, really the end? What does one say in a moment of such finality? I still had a couple weeks to travel before I went home, and now who would I talk to over good food and beer? Who would help me plan the route and take up the idle hours of the day? Who would hold my confidence, my hesitations, my deep expostulations, and return them with a generous reply? Who would watch my stuff on the train when I got up to take a piss? We had grown together across these mountaintops—I could feel it—and now this sudden separation knocked about my heart. I was struck by a sense of fear and emptiness. I wanted to express my brotherly love, to say something lasting and profound that we'd never forget. The bus pulled in, just like that, and in that hurried way that people take their leave when consumed with the details of schedules and connections, we shook hands and he was gone.

What else could I do but go a-walking? In the wake of my great friend, I took up my pack, provisioned just so with water and mint cake, and made a turn through town and out toward Lily Tarn. I followed trails I did not know, out beyond Ivy Crag and Loughrigg Fell, walking, walking, walking to shrug off my loneliness. I passed Rydal Cave and Rydal Water until I arrived at the Wordsworths' fond old home, the house and beautiful gardens, the poet's library and study, then through the trees and back around toward Ambleside, I wandered. Posting over those footpaths, the Lake District felt more alien to me than ever, more so even than the first day when Scott and I arrived. I hardly recognized myself or anything at all: no bird, no flower, no tree, no face looked to me familiar. Where were the birds I knew, the great falcons and hawks of my native land, the western meadowlark and mountain bluebird, the blue heron and sandhill crane? Where were the Douglas fir and rhododendron, vine and bigleaf maple, the wild blueberries, serviceberries, Oregon grape, and trillium? There were no beaver or black bear, no elk or mule deer or coyote. I was utterly lost and bereft, and the sun was falling in its arc. Like Bashō, I wanted to sit down on my hat and weep to forget all time, but I steeled my constitution against it and pressed on. I wandered and wandered, lonely as a cloud through the fields and fells near Ambleside until, later, at the threshold of the dining room, a radiant Taiwanese approached me with her three friends. She said, in perfect British English, "Hello. I'm Xiaolin. Won't you come out for a walk?"

LES FEMMES BELLES
AVEC MERCI

Scotland, 2007

If there is no end to Paris, there is no beginning to Edinburgh. Its ramparts reach out from the center at Edinburgh Castle as far as a man can walk in a day, as far as he can roam in a year, as far as light may course beyond the sun; you will not find a wall to separate it from the world. Edinburgh is a free and open country. Nothing can contain it—no badge or definition or family crest, no rule or government or martial law. It is a growing, folding, dividing thing, and the moment you try to pin it down, it becomes something else. Did not Werner Heisenberg develop his great principle while having a pint at a street café in Edinburgh? "Ah-ha!" he famously said, as he lifted the glass to his lips. "When I try to take the measure of Edinburgh it changes to become not Edinburgh. But that *not* Edinburgh *is* Edinburgh still. Therefore, I cannot know both Edinburgh and Edinburgh at the same time. This is why," he reasoned, "when I measure the position of a photon of light, I cannot know its velocity. And when I measure its velocity, I cannot know its position. Beautiful. I will call this phenomenon, yes, the Edinburgh Principle." He later swapped the city with his own name to give himself credit. Didn't he? But no matter. Edinburgh is still and has always been Edinburgh, even as it is not Edinburgh, and light in all its velocity and positions will illuminate the stone walls of its castle forever.

Now that I've got that bit of romantic exaggeration out of my system, let me tell a story about Edinburgh and an American witch who, like a black cat, happened across my path while I was traveling in Scotland with my old friend, Scott. On our way north to climb Ben Nevis, the highest mountain in Scotland, we thought it wise to stop off to see The City that so many people dither on about. I'm not much for cities. At least not in the way some women I've known claim to be from the city, of the city, and for the city, and that any wonderful city will do. Oh, you know, the shopping, the restaurants, the museums and galleries, the people watching. It's all so wonderful to be in a city. Are you kidding, I protest. Cities are dirty and ugly and they smell bad. People pissing in alleyways and sleeping in doorways and eating from dumpsters. Cats and rats and pigeons eating each other and shitting on everything. Meanwhile, the people with money are locked away in little rooms on floors in high buildings afraid to go outside for the pollution and crime and high prices. What's good about a city?

Then as I stepped off the train in Edinburgh, the weather turned around. Edinburgh, I sighed. It's not so bad.

So there we were, my pal Scott and I, checking into the Edinburgh Backpackers Hostel, just a short hop from the train station, up the winding slope of Cockburn Street leading on to the Royal Mile. The cheaper prices are for larger rooms with more beds, and since this was an adventure, we took two beds in a room with eight. Who knew what we might find there, who we might meet. Aye, there's the rub. So we shouldered our packs, the signature of the American traveler in Europe, and climbed the stairs looking for the door that fit our key.

"Hello," she said. "I'm Sabrina."

"Hello," Scott said, reaching out his hand.

"Nice to meet you," I said, reaching out mine.

She had taken the bottom bunk across from us and had most of the contents of her two bags spread out over every square inch of the mattress. Long, black hair, a little clumpy and stringy, a pleasant face, warm smile, a little plump, but a nice-looking girl all the same, and dressed in long black flowing robes, or maybe it was a dress, or maybe it was several massive silky shirts, one piled on top of the other—it was hard to tell. It was the kind of arrangement you find on larger women trying to hide what's under it, so it seemed. She seemed a little fantastic, or just overtired, maybe a little at loose ends. And yet we both noticed something familiar about her too, something comforting, something downright homey.

"Where are you from?" Scott asked.

"Portland."

"What?" I said.

"Oregon?" Scott said.

"Yeah," she said. "Oregon."

"We're from Portland too," Scott said.

"Or at least we used to be," I added.

"That's right," Scott said. "Went to high school there."

"Whaddaya know," she said. "Well, nice to meet you."

And after other pleasantries, she said, "So, you boys are just out on a little journey?"

"Exactly," Scott said. "How about you?"

"Yep, same here. I'm married," she offered, "and on this trip I'm traveling alone. My man is back in Portland. He's a musician. Part of a band. And he's always traveling with the band. We live very independently, but we're close too. Of course."

"Of course," Scott said, thinking of his own marriage.

"But," she said, and we all heard the drum roll in the background, "I have a license to cuddle."

A little space of silence forced its way into the room.

"My husband has given me a license to cuddle," she explained, as if a license to cuddle was an object she brought with her in her luggage, a little doll or a wooden box or a trinket of some kind. "The rules are, you know, no sex with other guys, or girls for that matter, but it's OK to cuddle."

"It's OK to cuddle," Scott said, as if she had hypnotized him.

"Right," she said. "Nothing wrong with a little cuddling, so long as it doesn't slip over the edge into sex. That's what we've agreed."

"That's great," I said. "Sounds very clear between you."

"It is. And it's so wonderful to be able to cuddle."

"And can he cuddle too?" I asked.

"Of course he can," she said. "Otherwise it wouldn't be fair. But I don't think he does, not much anyway. Me? I like to cuddle."

"You like to cuddle," Scott said, and now I knew she had hypnotized him.

"That's right. I like to cuddle."

Our conversation turned to other subjects, none of them very interesting after this, until the urge to get out and walk around took over, and Scott suggested we all meet up later for a drink.

"Great idea," she said. "I bet we'll see each other back here this afternoon or evening, and then we can go out and find a drink together. No problem. I'd like that."

"All right then," I said. "See you around."

"But if we don't meet up, boys, don't worry about me."

"If we don't meet up, we won't worry about you," Scott said.

"All right," I said. "Sounds good."

"See you around, boys."

Back in the world, the first order of business was to have a look at Edinburgh Castle. Not the inside—we'd make that tourist commitment in the morning—but the view of the castle from the outside, the featured image of the city. We followed Cockburn Street back the way we had come and out onto Waverly Bridge, spanning the train tracks. The castle rose up in front of us, the site where in just a few weeks the Royal Edinburgh Military Tattoo would kick off the fantastic Edinburgh Festival.

Staring onto the strange and beautiful stone walls of the castle, visions of *Braveheart* flashed in my head, and Sabrina somehow appeared in there too, abracadabra. In my mind, she took on a most pleasing form. Her body and face and hair and lips morphed into my private vision of perfection: Uma Thurman as Venus rising from a bivalve in *The Adventures of Baron Munchausen,* or any number of gorgeous porn stars that none of us has ever seen. I heard her voice in my head, her tantalizing words wafting like a vapor in the air, like a smoke, like a cloud in the shape of a camel or a weasel, her hot, sweet breath in my ear: "I like to cuddle. I *like* to cuddle. I like to *cuddle.*" Well, I thought to myself, this isn't so bad. In fact, maybe a license to cuddle is good. Maybe it's for the best. Maybe a long, successful marriage is dependent on such nonthreatening freedoms like cuddling, so that neither party feels controlled or owned by the other. Maybe cuddling is a way to relieve sexual tension and whatever other kind of tension, to take a married woman or a married man to the brink of bliss without plunging over, so that the choice to remain monogamous is offered once again, willingly, not by force of law, and then accepted, a husband privately renewing his vows to his wife and a wife privately renewing her vows to her husband by cuddling with someone else. Or maybe Sabrina and her man were on the rocks, and this is how they were dealing with it.

Not two years ago, I had met Thomas, a Cuddlemaster from Germany. He facilitated cuddle parties, wherein a group of people in their nightgowns gathered in a neutral space to cuddle. There were certain rules, of course, put forth by the originators, Reid Mihalko and Marcia Baczynski. They claim that cuddle parties are about "compassion, affection, and touch." They claim it's a movement, a movement that takes place in those more liberal European countries and stateside in places like California and Colorado, certainly not Texas. You can read all about it at their website: cuddleparty.com.

"Well, look at that," Scott said. "Jimmy Chung's."

For just a few pounds, Jimmy Chung's offered an all-you-can-eat Chinese buffet. If we planned our day right, we could catch the tail end of the lunch hour (when the price was at its lowest), stuff ourselves for an hour or so, and that was dinner. It allowed us more money for beer. We agreed to come back after we had walked around for a while.

"You think that's her real name?" I asked. "Sabrina?"

"Nope," Scott said. "I think she made it up. She's a witch. That's her witch name."

"Just what I was thinking."

"Yeah, she's a witch," he said. "For sure. Black hair. Black clothes. Black cat. Black magic. The whole thing."

"There are quite a few witches in Oregon," I said. "Well, you remember that night out in the gorge."

"I certainly do," Scott said.

"Jesus," I said. "That was nearly twenty years ago."

"No," Scott said. "That *was* twenty years ago."

I meant that fall night back in high school on the eastern fringe of Portland when Scott and I joined forces with our pal Brad to buy a little beer from the local grocery. Since Brad worked at the neighborhood grocery, he went ahead and carried twelve 25-ounce cans of Foster's Lager through the checkout stand. The checker, who knew Brad, of course, asked for his ID. Brad handed it over as a line formed behind him. The checker said, "Hmm. You must be about seventeen?" Brad nodded that this was true. "OK," he said, and rang up the sale.

Triumphant, we drove out the Columbia Gorge toward Crown Point in the wild abandon of our youth to find a secret location overlooking the great river to the Pacific to drink beer. Three underage dudes drinking imported beer on the rim of one of the greatest rivers in the world—it can't get much better than that. We discovered a little dirt road off the highway that led into the darkness. We decided to park and walk it, down the side of the gorge and through the dark trees, which occluded all light. We walked and drank, drank and walked, until we came to a little clearing where the moonlight shone through.

The TV news had been reporting for months, years really, that some weird shit was going on in our woods. Farmers had been waking up to missing cows, sheep, and goats, and sometimes they found pieces of them scattered in their fields. People were saying it was black magic, animal sacrifice, ceremonies to the underworld. Whatever.

"Hmm," Brad said. "What's this?" We all felt something strange and squishy underfoot. "This might be a dead sheep," I said. "No,"

Scott said. "This *is* a dead sheep." Then in the haze of that spooky light we spotted a platform in the trees, a wide table, an altar or something. "What's that?" Brad said. "Yeah, what's that?" I said. "That's an altar or something," Scott said. "You know. That's where they killed this dead sheep we're standing on." And then we turned and ran like hell.

"That was a good night," Scott said, scanning Edinburgh, plotting our next move.

"Yeah. A good night," I said. "And we probably just met the chick who sacrificed that sheep."

"Naw," Scott said. "You ever hear of an evil witch who likes to cuddle? She's Sabrina, the good witch."

"Good point."

We traveled on, Scott and me, under the shield of our former youth, exploring the streets and shops and pubs of this gorgeous city.

Tucked away in Lady Stair's Close, we explored the Writers' Museum, featuring Sir Walter Scott, Robert Burns, and Robert Louis Stevenson. There really wasn't much to it: a few handwritten manuscripts, some musty books, a pair of spectacles. I was about to give up on it when I came across a few lines by Stevenson, a passage pulled from his travel writing:

> O toiling hands of mortals! O wearied feet, travelling ye know
> not whither! Soon, soon, it seems to you, you must come forth
> on some conspicuous hilltop, and but a little way further, against
> the setting sun, descry the spires of El Dorado. Little do ye know
> your own blessedness; for to travel hopefully is a better thing
> than to arrive, and the true success is to labour.

Those words were so gorgeous and stirring they returned me at once to my youth, to the wild energy of that dark night in the gorge, the exhilaration of running up the steep dirt road through the trees from the terror of black magic, an open can of Foster's in my hand, my friends close beside me, and really doing it, taking it all in, straining at the edge of experience, our lungs burning and our legs growing woozy from going uphill as we reached the little brown Volkswagen Rabbit, the ship I commanded in those days, where it appeared suddenly out of the night, and we leapt in and drove back down the winding canyon road to the pizza shop where our classmates usually gathered, laughing hysterically all the way, to tell the story of our adventure.

Stevenson's travels determined his life, transformed the way he thought, transformed the way he wrote. In the essay that contains the passage above, "El Dorado," he heralds a life of continuous unfolding. We live happily, he writes, on "an ascending scale," with "one thing leading to another in an endless series." And happily, we cannot know what that next thing is until it unfolds. We are blind to our futures. Will I reach my goal or not? Irrelevant, Stevenson asserts. It is not the attainment of the goal that makes us "spiritually rich" but having a goal to attain. What matters is not how we end but how we begin. In fact, says Stevenson, "we shall never reach the goal; it is even more than probable that there is no such place." Thank goodness there is no such place, "no end . . . to making books or experiments, or to travel," so that we may go on discovering and rediscovering all our lives. "Desire and curiosity are the two eyes through which [a man] sees the world in the most enchanted colours: it is they that make women beautiful or fossils interesting."

And so in the close rooms and passageways of the little museum, I claimed that same path for myself, because nothing feels better than knocking about the world in awe of the faithful, the changing, the fantastic.

After that, we took our turn through the National Gallery of Scotland, a slow meander through the paintings. My growing love for all things pastoral alerted me to *Shepherd Boys in the Roman Campagna* by Martinus Rorbye (1835), *The Sheepfold* by Alexander Mann (1905), *Pastoral* by Sir James Guthrie (1885), and, finally, *Wandering Shadows* by Peter Graham (1878). The latter painting, oil on canvas, is a muscular landscape of the Scottish highlands, looking up a glen against the flowing water of a broad creek. The shoulders of two huge mountains, one bespeckled in sunlight where a sidestream flows into the main, the other, farther off, in the darkness, ringed by misty clouds that swirl and cradle it, an impending storm. The mountain faces are rocky and hard, and in the sunlight they appear a deep fold, like a gyrus in the brain. Below, among the quiet bones of the earth, are a few sheep, five all told. Two lie together, sheltered by a monolith, as another looks on. One grazes farther off. And the last, maybe a lamb, is lying with its front legs over the edge of a stone. You can see a figure approaching the creek where the waters tumble over a stone obstruction—the shepherd, of course. But then, perhaps the shepherd has gone home, leaving his sheep to the weather. The figure's left arm is raised up, as if he is fishing—it's a fisherman, perhaps, among the ewes. What will he catch in those waters? Perhaps he has fished here before, yet each time he dips a line, he cannot know what might happen.

Well, we whiled away the rest of the day, ducked into Jimmy Chung's for our early supper, and then swaggered out drunk on grease and MSG.

"I could use a beer," Scott said.

"That's the whole point," I said.

We found a little place and ordered up two pints. Then another two. Maybe one more round, and it wasn't long before the sun was down and the streets darkened and the city whispered its history to the dingle stars. We certainly were not drunk, but we'd had a few and decided to turn in for the night. Now, here is where the story really begins.

We had almost made it to our hostel when we happened by another little place called the Arcade, just across the street and a little down from Fleshmarket Close. It looked inviting. Scott stopped at the door.

"Just one more," Scott said. "Whaddaya say?"

We were in Scotland, after all, and there was no telling when we would travel together again. So I said, "Why not?"

In we went, and no sooner had we come through the door when we hear a familiar voice. "Hiya, boys," Sabrina said.

"Sabrina," Scott said. "What a surprise!"

Sabrina, despite that moment of lucidity, was under the spell of some great quantity of alcohol and a certain Spaniard, on whose lap she was now sitting. She had only just come up for air, and as we pressed our way to the bar, she went back down, fishing for his tongue with hers.

"Goodness," I said. "Now that's the way to cuddle."

"It certainly is," Scott said, and ordered us a couple of pints.

"You lads know her?" asked a stubby little man to our left. He was balding, wore jeans and a T-shirt, maybe in his late forties, and looked a couple days out from a shave. Maybe a couple days out from a bath.

"We met only recently," Scott said.

"So you're Americans," he said. "The accent. I'm Jordie," and he stuck out his hand.

A fellow as friendly as this wants something, especially this time of night in a small pub next to a blitzed American witch sucking face with a Spaniard. We shook hands with him anyway.

Our beers came up, and Scott nodded and raised his glass. We made a little toast to the unexpected, as Jordie made a little argument against us.

"Now look," he said. "You bloody Americans are a belligerent lot. Going into Iraq the way you did. A bloody belligerent lot. And I don't mean just the invasion. You've been going about the world doing it for decades. Decades."

"I see," Scott said.

"You certainly do," Jordie said. "A belligerent lot, going into Iraq the way you did."

I wondered if he'd forgotten the violent history of his own country—not just Scotland and its wars with England and the like, but, well, you might remember the British Empire, an empire based on belligerence and bullying and theft and on which once upon a time the sun never set. Not to mention that it was the British Empire that cobbled together a few cultures who had long been at odds into the thing we now call Iraq. It was not, in those days, a country, but rather the Brits' idea of mopping up their own mess.

"We're just here for a pint," Scott said.

"Well, you're gonna get more than that, lads," Jordie said. "Which brings me to the truth: the people in Iraq don't want you there. Anyone can see that. My countrymen don't want you there either. And my countrymen don't want to be there themselves. It's you Americans who got us into this war. You bloody Americans. And it's that cowboy Bush who muscled Blair into following. That little fop has no stones of his own."

"Really," Scott said.

"Really," Jordie said. "And if we pull out, if the British pull back, you're fucked. You're fucking fucked. Ya see, it tells the world that you done wrong. That you shouldn't have gone in in the first place. So you need us, see. In fact," he said, "you need us more than we need you."

"I see," Scott said. "We need you more than you need us."

"That's right," Jordie said. "And I'll tell you another thing—"

Then we heard a sound from Sabrina, whose cuddling had increased in pace and vigor. It seemed she was about to tip slightly over the edge into some kind of preliminary stage of sexual arousal, what with the moaning and all. She was still inside the limits of her licensure, Scott and I agreed, but it was clear that there wasn't much wiggle room anymore.

"Fuck me," Jordie said, his lips all shiny from his beer. "That chick is ripe. She's really coming on now. Tell you what, fellas. I'm gonna shag her. I'm gonna fuckin' shag her."

A redundancy, I thought, for sure.

Sabrina made another little moan, and then she lifted her head up from the Spaniard's mouth and hopped off his lap, no worse for wear. She moved in between Scott and me, sorta forced her way in, rubbing up against us a little. I could smell her breath. Yep. Really, really drunk.

"You boys have a good day?" she asked us.

"I'm gonna shag 'er," Jordie said in a dark little whisper. "I'm gonna fuckin' shag 'er."

"I had a really great day," Sabrina said.

I could feel the heat of her against me, and she leaned in a little too close, a little too much: not sensually, really; rather, she needed help standing up.

"Well? Did you?" she said.

"We did," Scott said. "A very fine day."

"Ooohhhh," she said. "That's nice." Then she stumbled off to the water closet.

"That's right, lads," Jordie said. "I'm gonna shag 'er. Now where was I?"

"You bloody Americans . . . ," Scott said.

"Right, you bloody Americans need us more than we need you. We don't need you at all. We don't give a damn about you. But you need us."

"OK," Scott said. "Whatever you say."

"Bloody Americans," Jordie said.

Now, Scott is a big man, a good six feet two, carrying 230 pounds. He could squish little Jordie between his fingers. But Jordie seemed not to notice his disadvantage because he was drunk too, and he probably had something else there hidden in his jacket. A sharp blade? A Ruger .357 mag? A wounded heart left over from his mother's sexual betrayal of his father, which caused him at the tender age of nine to blame himself for their divorce? It was hard to tell.

"I'm gonna shag 'er," Jordie said, watching Sabrina as she returned from the pissoir. "Hi, love," he said to her. "You gonna ride down with me tomorrow like we said?"

"That would be really great," Sabrina said. "Really great. I don't wanna buy a train ticket, you know. Not a lot of money left. I'd appreciate the ride."

"That's right, love," he said. "You'll appreciate the ride. Lads," he said, now turning to Scott and me, "I gotta make a delivery down in Manchester tomorrow, and this bitch here is gonna ride down with me. Now that's how you get things done, lads."

"Yeah," Sabrina said. "He's got to make a delivery down there."

"That's right, love. Got some biz-nuss down there. And you're gonna ride down with me, aren't you? Won't cost you much at all."

"Oh, good," Sabrina said. "I don't have much money left."

"Not much at all," Jordie said.

Things seemed to be spinning out of control for Sabrina. Here she was, an American witch in Edinburgh with a license to cuddle, drunk off her head, and she had a Spaniard all worked up on the stool over there and Jordie the drug dealer ready to drag her into Fleshmarket Close and lift up her skirt.

"You on your way back to your room?" Scott asked Sabrina.

"You boys going that way?" she asked.

"We are," Scott said.

"I'll walk with you," she said. "Two nice boys like you."

"All right, we'll walk with you," Scott said. "Let's go."

"Not just yet," Sabrina said. "How about one last round?"

"We're done here," Scott said. "We're headed back to the room. If you want to come with us, come with us now."

I appreciated this move in Scott. It was obvious Sabrina needed a little help. If we could get her out of that bar, it would probably be better for her in the long run.

"Not just yet," Sabrina said again, and hopped back on top of the Spaniard. Then Jordie started in again. What else was he to do?

"That's right, lads," he said. "I'm gonna take that bitch down in Manchester. I'm gonna shag 'er."

"Nice talking to you," Scott said.

"Leaving so soon?" Jordie said.

"That's right," Scott said. "You enjoy your evening."

"Nice talking to you lads," Jordie said. "You take care out there. You never know what can happen."

Scott turned to coax Sabrina down off the bar stool, but abracadabra, she and the Spaniard were gone.

Outside in the night air, Scott worried over her safety. "Man," he said. "She's gonna end up raped and murdered in some alley somewhere."

"God. Horrible," I said. "Maybe we can look around a little for her. She can't have gone far."

"Yeah, let's have look," Scott said.

Making our way back to the hostel, we cased Jackson's Close and then Fleshmarket Close as we passed by. Nothing.

"She's a grown woman," Scott said. "I mean, what can we do? Are we now responsible for her? What if we'd never met her? I mean, she is a grown woman. Doesn't she know what she's doing?"

"She is," I agreed. "And maybe she does. Of course, she's drunk. That's a problem. I don't know, man. I doubt we'll find her."

"Right," Scott said. "Let's head back."

At the hostel, we got ready for bed, and the four Chinese women sharing the room with us were doing the same. I climbed into the top bunk, and Scott sat down on the lower bunk.

"Don't forget I'm down here," Scott said. "Don't be firing off any rounds up there."

"I'll do my best."

"I sure hope she's OK."

"Yeah," I said, looking over at Sabrina's empty bed.

Scott went across the room to the light switch and indicated to our four roommates that he wanted to shut out the light. They nodded it was OK, and the room went dark.

Just then, Sabrina walked in and flicked on the lights. "Hi, boys," she said.

"Good to see you're all right," Scott said.

"Oh, you don't have to worry about me."

"Well, we did," Scott told her.

She came in close, leaning in against the upper bunk, where I sat now with my legs hanging down. Scott stood there beside her. She was drunk, of course, but it appeared that she could manage it. She leaned in and took up my left foot in her hands, and began to work it over. She pressed my foot in against her chest.

"This," she said, finding a particular pressure point, "is your liver."

"No," Scott said. "That's his foot."

"Very funny," she said. "No. It's his liver," and she pressed in on the place, and it felt really nice.

"I can tell you one thing," Scott said, exercising his signature humor. "His liver is in better shape than yours."

"Very funny," she said, leaning in on my foot, pressing it between her heavy breasts. "Very funny."

She worked my foot a bit, and suddenly I felt happy and relaxed. But I resisted.

"We've got an early day," I said. "Right, Scott? Off to bed now?"

"Yep, that's right," he said.

"All right, boys," she said. "I'm pretty tired too."

"I'm sure you are," I said.

"Yeah, and you're gonna have a headache in the morning," Scott said.

"Whatever."

Scott and I settled into bed, and Sabrina went out to the facilities, came back, turned out the light, and settled into bed herself. Our Chinese roommates were either asleep or pretending to be asleep, who could say. The room was still, very still, and I was just dropping off when Sabrina got up wearing her nightclothes, some kind of long gown, and came by our bunk. I could see her down there pacing at the foot of the bed in the darkness. She walked in little circles, around and around, back and forth. Around and around. Her pace seemed to quicken, until she took hold of the end of the bunk and climbed in on top of me.

"I just wanna cuddle," she said into my ear.

I have to admit here a certain rise in my interest, as she was a warm and pleasant presence, stretched out fully on top of me, her curves palpable along my body. She sorta worked her way in and pressed in against my pelvis and put her nose against my chest and kissed me.

"What are you doing?" I said, rather lazily.

"I don't know," she said. "Just cuddle with me. That's all I want."

The Chinese woman closest to us leaped out of bed in terror and hurried over to climb in with one of her friends at the farthest reaches of the room.

"Sabrina," I said. "We really do have an early morning train."

"I just wanna cuddle."

"I know, but I've got to get some sleep."

"Really, I just wanna cuddle," she said again.

"I'm sorry," I said. "I do have to get some sleep, and this is a very public room."

"Oh gosh, oh god," she said. "I'm so sorry. I'm so sorry. I hope I haven't offended you."

"Oh, no, no," I said. "No."

"I'm so sorry."

"No, don't worry about it."

"Oh gosh," she said, and hurried down over the end of the bed and left the room.

Scott took hold of the edge of the upper bunk and pulled himself up, just as I leaned over to hang down: our faces met in the darkness.

"You're killing me, bro," Scott said. "Can I come up there and cuddle with you?" And we laughed and laughed.

Scott and I rose early and made our way out into the city. Sabrina was there in her bed now, sleeping heavily, reestablishing the balance of the four humors, and it was doubtful that we would ever see her again. We walked up to the head of the Royal Mile, where you could get an early coffee at the corner shop. As we sat there together with those lovely lattes, the Edinburghness of Edinburgh spread out before us, a world of possibility opened with the rising sun.

"I wonder what's going to happen next?" I said.

"I do too," he said. "I do too."

In Inverness, Scott and I had just come to a sort of stopping place in our conversation about relationships and marriage, and so naturally, after the food and the beers at Bella Italia, Scotland's version of the Olive Garden, Scott, the best man at my wedding—which, five years later, had ended in a divorce—got up and headed north to the facilities.

He'd just confessed the hardships and struggles he and his wife,

Kacey, had passed through, empathized with my plight, and acknowledged that it could have easily been him. (And her, of course.) But you know, they had the children, and maybe that helped bind them together in a way childless couples are not bound together, and they had the house on some beautiful acreage in southern Oregon, and yes, they also loved each other, and so they worked through the garbage to come out on the other side. "There is nothing stable in the world," Keats writes. "Uproar is your only music."

"Now things are better than ever," Scott said. And then, "You're not going to have children, are you?"

"I'm gonna have a vasectomy."

"Really? Well, it's not too awful bad," Scott said, rubbing his balding head. "You can't drive home on your own, but a long weekend will see you through recovery. Except you have to wait awhile afterwards before you can use it." Then he left for the loo.

That's when Tia, the hostess at the restaurant, came to my rescue. She arrested my descent into a minor depression, the kind that usually follows such a grave conversation, especially after your buddy gets up for a piss and you're left sitting alone in Inverness, Macbeth's happy town, fiddling with your fork or napkin or whatever.

"Where are you from?" she asked.

She was the most gorgeous creature I'd seen all day. Shoulder-length black hair, kinda ratty and witchy, huge dark eyes like Bambi blinking at that raging forest fire, a long graceful line down the length of her tight black trousers, and the most unexpectedly perfect chest. She spoke in a dark smoker's voice, which, unbeknownst to me until then, kinda turned me on.

"From?" I said, always at odds about how to answer that question. "I live in Texas, but I'm not a Texan. I grew up in Oregon. But I wasn't born there." Slow down, I thought, that's enough.

"Oregon," she said. "That's a beautiful place, isn't it? And what are you doing here? Just traveling?"

"Yeah," I said. "Just a summer journey. I'm here with an old friend, and we're seeing the country, climbing some mountains."

"How long are you here?"

She spoke with an accent, not heavy, but certainly not Scottish. When Scott and I walked in the door earlier, she said, "Buona Sera," which made me hope that she was Italian, because I had never really recovered from that Italian romance I'd had—her name was Daniela—while backpacking through Europe fifteen years earlier.

"We're here just for the night," I said. "We're heading to the Lake District to climb a mountain."

"That's not long," she said, "one night."

"So, if you had one night in Inverness, where would you spend it?" I asked.

"In my bed," she said.

"What?"

"In my bed," she said again.

But I still wasn't convinced I'd heard her correctly, and I was a little startled, a little hopeful, a little weirdly surprised, so I nodded and said, "Aahhh."

Scott arrived at the table then, and she scooted away back to work. As we were settling the bill, she returned again, and this time slipped me a scrap of paper with her name and mobile phone number.

"Tia," I said.

"If you want, maybe we can have a drink later," she said, bobbing her head from side to side.

"Dude," Scott told me, as we drank a bottle of wine at our hostel, "if you don't call that number tonight, you're fuckin' crazy."

"Inverness," I mused. "This is really a great town. The best place we've been yet!"

"Call that number right now."

"But I'm not sure I heard what I heard. C'mon. Who says that?"

"That's what she said, all right. And she was hot, hot, like Africa hot."

"Yeah, but c'mon. There's something else. I mean, who says that?"

"Obviously, she does," Scott said. He filled the glasses, and we drank. "She's probably a guy," he said, and we laughed at that.

Then something soft and easy leaked in, and there was a quiet moment between us as we looked across the rooftops onto the city. Scott said, "Yeah, but you have to remember that if she is a guy, this guy is a person too."

"What?"

"You know, if you get into a situation, I mean, and you reach down there and find out she's a guy. I mean, she's a human being too. Or he is. And you have to treat her like a person, not like some freak."

"She's not a guy," I said. "Plus, who says I'll be doing any reaching?"

"C'mon," Scott said. "'In my bed'? You'll be doing some reaching. C'mon. This bottle is empty. Let's go get a beer."

So out we went onto the town and, conveniently, we walked right by Bella Italia. And there she was standing out in front smoking a cigarette.

This was a curious position to be in. Was I going to cross the street and make good on the offer that Tia, this perfect stranger in a foreign town, had made me? I am not a whore. I'm a respectable professional guy. I'm a divorced man who might have become a father but won't. I'm good counsel when my friends come knocking. I'm domestic; I bake bread, brew beer, mend fences and socks, keep a tidy house, fix leaky faucets, and pull the weeds that come up. I'm a spiritual seeker of sorts. I'm a scholar, or so I think. I'm a writer. I'm an avid outdoorsman. I keep myself physically and mentally and emotionally and spiritually fit. But am I not also a man? And doesn't a man have needs? Desires? Aspirations of the body? Doesn't a woman? And so isn't it natural for two creatures to spot each other across the watering hole, display their intentions, and steal away to meet among the secret trees? Was I going over there? Of course I was.

"OK, I'm going over there."

"All right. I'm going back to hostel," Scott said. "Don't forget we have an early train tomorrow. Have fun. Be careful. Use protection."

"Hello," Tia said. "You don't smoke, do you?"

"No," I said. "That's right."

"Thought not. I have to wait here for a few minutes until my manager lets me go. But you want to get a drink, right?"

"That sounds good."

Minutes later we crossed the street and walked into Johnny Foxes, an Irish pub on the frontage of River Ness. Yes, that's right, the river that flows from the famous Loch Ness through Inverness and six miles down to Moray Firth. You know that there is no Loch Ness monster, right? But apparently the Firth is swimming with bottlenose dolphins.

She ordered a Bailey's on ice and ordered me a Guinness, both good Irish icons, and we sat in a booth near the window.

"You ever been to the festival in Edinburgh?" she asked.

"No," I said. "I keep hearing about it. Perhaps I should go. But I'm going to miss it, I think. We'll be gone before it starts up."

"I'm going up there in a couple weeks," she said. "I'm very excited. They have a drag show up there. All kinds of transvestites and transgendered people will be there. It will be the first time for me, so I'm very excited."

I nodded in agreement. "Sounds great," I said. And then, of course, Scott's voice came into my head—"She's probably a guy." But I had attended a drag show in the town where I live, The Kinsey Sicks. Best show I'd seen in years. I laughed and laughed. There was nothing odd about going to the festival for a drag show, was there? Perhaps it was the way she said the word "transgendered" that got up my back. Spooked me a little. Now I saw something in her face that I had not seen before, some squareness in her jaw, some firmer construction in her complexion, some yang in her yin. She winked at me and bobbed her head back and forth.

"Where are you from?" I asked.

"Me? Well, I'm from Jordan. Amman actually. I grew up there. But my mom is Scottish. So I moved here, but it's so cold and rainy here. And people are not open-minded. I love the hot weather, you know," she said. "Luuuv the sun. I love to lay out in the sun and tan myself. Yes. But my doctor told me I could not be in the sun too much right now because of the hair removal treatment. Ooh, it hurts so much," she said. "It's like this burning pain every time. But I have to do it. It's like this," she said, and she pressed the back of her index finger into my arm. "It takes a little area like this, and it hurts so terribly."

"You're having a hair removal treatment?" I asked, as if I were the most dim-witted creature on earth.

"Yes. I'm removing the hair from all my body," she said. "You know," and she clicked her tongue three times against the roof of her mouth, "everywhere, including the secret places. The genitals." She whispered it. "And everywhere else too of course. Ooh, it hurts so much. But it's my dream."

So then, gentle reader, how long do you think it took me to see the picture clearly? But no, I was not yet convinced. After all, lots of women have hair removal treatments. The technology by which hair is removed was developed to cater primarily to women, was it not? The market for such treatments relies on women, does it not? No. There was nothing surprising about a Jordanian woman in Inverness undergoing a hair removal treatment.

"So you don't like it here in Inverness?" I asked.

"It's beautiful here if you like the rain and the clouds and the water," she said. "But I love the sun. I ache for the sun and to sun myself and tan my body. Oh, I love it too much. But here it is so dark and depressing to me. The worst part is not that, however," she said. "No. It's that people are not open-minded. So many people here are so critical and afraid. Maybe in a place like Glasgow or Edinburgh I would love it. I grew up in a city, you know. I love the city life. And people have so much experience and have seen so many things. Not like here in Inverness. These are country people who live in a very small world."

Have you not noticed, reader, how my little questions led to a great deal of unsolicited information?

"I have a friend," she said. "This friend is a transgendered person. She belongs to a very small group of us here in Inverness. Too few of us, really. And one night she came here to this pub, this very pub, with a man she had met, a man who was very excited to meet her." And she bobbed her head back and forth and clicked her tongue again. "They were sitting at the table over there, and talking, just like we are taking now. And then another man, a local man, a very ugly man who knew about my friend, walked right up and said: 'This woman is a guy. Don't you know that, you fool. You're talking to a guy!' Ooh, was she so mortified and embarrassed. So angry too. You can only imagine it. So now I am very curious about my rights under the law. How I am protected, and what I can do. You see, it is very hard for a transgendered person to live happily in Inverness."

I took up my glass and drank several swallows of the lovely Guinness. The air around us was delicate, and I was filled with the milk of human kindness. "So," I said, "*you're* a transgendered person."

"Oh yes," she said. "I am. But it has been such a long journey for me. Since I was fifteen, I knew I was a woman. And at that time, I started my journey. It took some time for my psychologist to confirm that I am sound in my mind. That I am not crazy. No. I am a very happy and stable person. Yes. And that took about one year. It was such a long year. After that I began my hormone therapy. Then I had my breast implants in Jordan." She removed the shirt she wore over her tank top to show me. She sat up very straight, her shoulders squared back.

Nice work, I thought. Lovely indeed.

"Yes, and in less than one year I will achieve my life's dream. I will be completely a woman."

Perhaps you are thinking what I'm thinking now, that line by Lady Macbeth: "Come, you spirits that tend on mortal thoughts, unsex me here!"

"You will have the surgery," I said.

"Right. That is the most important and delicate of all the transformations," she said. "I will have the surgery. It's not possible to find a doctor for this in Jordan. At least it is very dangerous, and maybe impossible. I had to come here to the UK to reach my dreams."

"I see."

She drank off the last of the Bailey's over ice. She looked at me, harder now, and a measure of tension rose between us. She had just entrusted me with the most fundamental part of her being, and as it was held in trust this way, she waited to see whether I would violate it. I think she knew that I would not. I think she also knew that I was no longer attracted to her *romantically*, and that tension fell away too. Something shifted between us. Was this friendship or fellowship? Neighborliness or cordiality? Or was it something else? Something without a name?

"That sounds wonderful," I said. "I mean, that you will be able to reach your dream. Most people don't, you know."

"Yes, of course it is," she said. "It is. It is so wonderful. I am so excited by it. And you see it's not this way with all transgendered people, because I can so easily pass as a woman, right? You didn't know, right? Some of my friends however will never be able to pass as a woman like me, but somehow I can do it. They will be forever stuck in between, and that is a very hard life for them. Yes. People will always look at them strangely, except other transgendered people. People will always hate them, and some people even feel violence toward them. Toward us. But for me, after I have the surgery, I think I will be completely a woman, and that is my dream since I was only fifteen."

Dear reader, do you remember your *Macbeth*? How strangely that play is consumed with lines devoted to gender—can you imagine it? Meeting Tia here in the very town where black Macbeth murders his king and steals the throne? For example, there are these obvious lines given to Banquo, who addresses the witches: "You should be women, / And yet your beards forbid me to interpret / That you are so." That aside, do not forget that Lady Macbeth challenges Macbeth's manhood when he first refuses to murder his king. "I dare do all that may become a man; / Who dares do more is none," he tells her. "When you durst do it, then you were a man," she tells him. Of course he does do it, and, in doing so, is not a man at all. I mean that the murder reduces him, as he foretells, and he becomes something else, a beast really, the rugged Russian bear, the armed rhinoceros, the Hyrcan tiger. When Lady Macbeth finishes her rant, she claims that at least she possesses a man's murderous powers—that she could dash the brains out of even her own child. To which Macbeth exclaims: "Bring forth men-children only, / For thy undaunted mettle should compose / Nothing but males." Well, we know they both get it wrong. A man is not so murderous, at least not *only* so murderous. Indeed, Duncan, on greeting his thanes after the war, is more motherly than fatherly, like a woman giving birth to these noble sons of Scotland: "Welcome hither. / I have begun to plant thee, and will labor / To make thee full of growing." Did you notice the pun on the word "labor," and that "growing" is about fecundity in the garden, about pregnancy? Later MacDuff redeems all men when he reveals his wounded heart. On hearing that his entire family, his wife and children, have been murdered by Macbeth, Malcolm tells him, "Dispute it like a man." To which he responds, "I shall do so; but I must also feel it as a man."

If Shakespeare wasn't Christian (for who can say what genius is), at least his plays live in a Christian world. And the Christian world, despite its protests and its present fear and paranoia on issues of gender and same-sex marriage, is a world founded on the "androgyny of primordial man," as Eliade explains in the first volume of his *A History of Religious Ideas.* In Genesis, Eve is created of Adam, woman is formed of man, which points toward a relatively widespread belief (not to mention the origin of the incest taboo) that "human perfection, identified in the mythical ancestor, comprises a unity that is at the same time a *totality*," writes Eliade. "We should note," he continues, "that human androgyny has as its model divine bisexuality, a concept shared by a number of cultures." In this spirit, it is the androgynous person who is whole, not the man alone or the woman, or even the man and woman in holy union. Androgyny is holy union. As you won't be stymied by another leap of faith, let's quote the *Tao Te Ching*:

> Know the male,
> Yet keep to the female;
> Receive the world in your arms.

Inverness is home to an odd curfew law. At midnight the doors of all drinking establishments close. The drinking goes on inside for several more hours, of course, but the doors are locked tight. You must enter your place of choice before midnight, and when you decide to step out, there is no stepping back in.

"I need a fag," Tia said.

"All right," I said. "I'll go out with you."

"We won't be able to come back in," she said.

"That's all right."

I stood with her on the patio near the riverfront while she smoked. "It was lovely talking with you," she said. "I hope you have good travels."

"And you," I said. "Good luck in your journey. And take care of yourself."

"Yes, of course."

"I'm headed this way," I said, motioning upriver.

"I'm headed that way," she said, motioning downriver.

And from here, gentle reader, our scene becomes so filled with mist, it's impossible to know what happened next.*

---

*Much of the final line of this essay is borrowed from, and used in honor of, Yugoslavian writer Dubravka Ugresic's fine short story "A Hot Dog in a Warm Bun."

INTO THE HORNSTRANDIR

Iceland, 2013

Who has gone farthest? for I would go farther
— Walt Whitman, "Excelsior"

In Hesteyri, a collection of summer cabins near the mouth of Hesteyrarfjordur, the leftovers of a failed fishing and farming effort a century ago, Scott and I met an older couple coming out of the Hornstrandir as we were headed into it. British, presumably married, in their early sixties, visibly shaken, their faces pulled down as if they had just slipped past death. They both wore rain gear, despite the clear sky overhead and the bright sun pitching off the water.

"You've certainly got a good day to start," the man said to me.

"We do," I acknowledged. "A great day."

He stared at me then, waiting, saying nothing, and, in saying nothing, he begged me to ask. It was clear he had a story to tell and wanted to tell it, a story about something he and his wife had passed through, and he looked annoyed that the world had not noticed. Whatever drama had unfolded out there, whatever terrors they had faced, whatever joys, the world had gone spinning on, and with maybe the exception of some few people back home, nobody cared.

"We didn't have a good start," he finally offered. "The weather came in. Terrible rain. Terrible wind. A fog in the passes. We couldn't see anything."

"We couldn't see anything," the woman repeated, coming up behind him.

"That's right," he said, shaking his head. "We couldn't see anything. I thought we'd never find our way out. It was so empty. So desolate. We were lost for some while. We couldn't see anything."

To consider that kind of isolation, that kind of fear, he let a silence build between us again, standing there at the waterline of that gorgeous fjord, the boat we came in on bobbing on the gentle waves, dockside. A moment in time, a little moment passing as the breezy clouds formed and broke apart, and the waters came into their bluey blueness, and the birds sang in the palace of summer, buzzing with summer insects.

"C'mon," the woman said to him, making a move for the boat, which was headed back to Ísafjörður. "Let's get the hell out of here."

There wasn't much for Scott and me to do but adjust our packs and set out, walking up the long track along the fjord into whatever weather, whatever darkness, or light, awaited us. We had come too far to turn back now. It was nearly 4 p.m., a late start, but at this latitude, it wasn't going to get dark. We had all night to get to our first camp.

Scott and I planned to walk the Royal Horn, a popular route through Iceland's remote Hornstrandir Peninsula. The boat had dropped us at Hesteyri inside the first of five fjords in a greater fjord, Jökulfirðir. Day one would take us over a high mountain pass and down the other side into the bay of Haelavik, facing north onto the Greenland Sea, a distance of sixteen kilometers. Day two (fifteen kilometers), we'd walk the beach to the foot of another high pass, descend on the other side, and then climb again, up and over, descending into the bay of Hornvik at Höfn, where sits a ranger station and one of the great seabird cliffs of the world, Hornbjarg. On the third day (fifteen kilometers), we'd climb over our final high pass and descend into another great fjord, Veiðileysufjörður, where the boat would pick us up on the fourth day.

Going out for a walk this way, four days stretched out before you, your little gear stowed in your pack—your food and stove and tent

and bag, a map and GPS—you feel the long reach of the cities pushing at you, the discourteous thrum of traffic and industry, the foul
air and the noise of the dispossessed; you feel it pushing at you, driving you to the perimeters of the world, where you have only a thin
edge to walk, a precarious strip of quiet and solitude coupled with
the kindnesses of a few other walkers. The Industrial Revolution
has made the walking tour a nightmare: it has made all roads into
high-speed corridors of goods and services and death. It is more
and more difficult to find a good place to walk, alone or with an old
friend, as I am now, and you often have to travel very far to find it.

This was not so when Wordsworth, in a fit of youthful delin-
quency, left the comfort of his studies to roam on foot through the
Alps. Or when Stevenson led a donkey through the Cevennes. Or
when the greatest American walkers set out—Thoreau, yes, and
Whitman, the poet of the public road, or Lewis and Clark, who also
journeyed on horseback and in boats. In those days, nothing moved
faster than a horse, so all roads were foot roads too. But these days,
to travel on foot, it's best to seek out the places at the edges of other
places where the wild country is, where now all walkers must go.

Walking up Hesteyrarfjordur, Scott and I angled out toward a bright
snowfield where the British volunteer ranger at the landing had
told us to go, picking our way through steepening fields of boulders
and using our trekking poles for support. We did not find a path
so much as a lightly worn discoloration of the rock, an occasional
bootprint in a chance pot of sandy soil, a dirty sightline across a
snowfield, a string of great rock cairns drawing out the way. Over
the wider, flatter passages along the treeless rimtop of the fjord,
the defeated snowpack formed streams that fell away into the sea
far below. We crossed sometimes by skipping from stone to stone,
and at other times by stopping to change our shoes for sandals and
wading the frigid, fast-moving runnels. This, so Icelanders claim, is
the cleanest water on the earth, so we drank freely without filter or
compunction.

We rose to the final push of our first mountain pass, Kjaransvikurskard, just below Geldingafell (598 meters high). At the base of it, Scott and I stopped. The way up was covered in snow and much steeper than we were prepared for, as we wore only simple low-top walking shoes, which had no hard edges. Already our feet were bruised by the hard stones of the path. The snow arced above our heads, breaking over the broad back of the mountain saddle into that permanent blue, a ramp into the sky.

"Which way do we go?" I asked.

"We go up," Scott said, and up he went, kicking a stairway into the snow with his light shoes and pressing up with his legs under his heavy pack. I watched him rise a few steps ahead before I followed up behind. Though others had gone before us this season, the sunstrike on the exposed snowface had erased all traces. It was as if we were the first people on earth to ascend here.

The way was slow going, and with the weight on our backs, a slip, a moment's hesitation, or a failing in the courage of the legs would send us tumbling down the mountainside. We would likely survive such a fall if we rolled well and somehow avoided a cracked skull, but it would certainly ruin the day. We beat out a rhythm as we went: kick, kick, step; kick, kick, step; kick, kick, step. To look up was to risk losing my balance, so I mostly kept my head down. Kick, kick, step; kick, kick, step. Listening to the sound of my buddy above me in the interstices of my own climbing, I moved up ever more slowly, hoping my little shoes would keep their place in the snow—kick, kick, step— until that comforting presence above me seemed to draw away and then vanish. I went on, feeling a strange emptiness bind up my heart, and then I looked up to see Scott press on over the top and out of sight. The slope curved away from me now, and the ground flattened out beneath my feet, but it was here, as my lot began to improve, that I felt a twinge in my right leg, a weakness at the next step. Was the leg going to give? Was my knee going to buckle? Was this a message from the muscles and bones of my body or from the temperature of my courage? I did, in that moment, imagine falling, the twinge in my leg leading me to a little break at the joint, a giving way, as the weight of the pack pulled me back, my head landing me upside down as my feet came over into the sky, and then, in my mind, the view from some other place of my now broken body at the bottom where the snow turned to rock, exposing the bones of the mountain. But I did not fall. I pressed and stepped, pressed and stepped, pushing that pack up the slope, until I found myself standing on relatively flat ground next to my old pal, Scott. We paused to look out onto the fjord far below, a blue line that widened into Jökulfirðir, and on around Snæfjallaströnd to Ísafjörður, where we had started earlier that day. Our walk into the Hornstrandir had just begun.

What causes loneliness?—especially the loneliness while traveling in foreign lands that skips or catches in the breath and then sinks the heart from a high place of exaltation to the darkness of fear and loss. What is it? As a younger man discovering the wild landscapes of North America—the Frank Church Wilderness in Idaho, the canyons of southeastern Utah, the endless boreal forests and lakes of northern Saskatchewan—nature was a balm to me. It was in wild places that I felt closer to the divine, as close as I could, anyway. I am not a Christian, and though I believe in prophets, I do not believe in a loving god, nor do I believe in a religion that persecutes and executes and burns in the name of a loving god. Still, out in those vast wildernesses, I felt the presence of something greater than myself, and that something, I felt, knew me. I wanted to believe in that something when I was in other places too, but I never found any evidence to support it. None. No sign or symbol or voice out of the whirlwind. Just silence. Enduring, empty, black silence. Prayer, I learned, is an impish wish, a childish fantasy, as selfish as two opposing football teams on bended knee, each with the same ardent belief that God is on *their* side. The older I get, the more certain I am that there is no "spirit in the woods," as Wordsworth asserts. There is no hand of god to guide me. Everything does not happen for a reason; rather, given enough time, everything will happen for no reason at all. The older I get, the more I am convinced of the utter indifference of nature to human wishing and human suffering. And at some point in my travels, I came to feel that that indifference was beautiful, that beauty is an aesthetic of bleakness, of the black emptiness of cosmic space. In imagining tumbling to my death in the Hornstrandir, I did not look to god in nature to comfort me or save me. My only refuge was the beauty of these empty lands and traveling in the company of my old friend.

We descended. Down the other side of the mountain pass we went, walking now at a good pace, the northern sun waning in its arc but not falling, a colder air coming in over us. We sweated and beamed and delighted in the power of our legs, the ease soon to come to us, for we could now see all the way to our camp, the shining waters of Haelavik facing the Greenland Sea. I began to think of the rum we had brought along and the vodka, spirits that might lift our spirits in this cold, desolate, beautiful place where now we darkly walked. The valley made a series of great benches carved by a long-forgotten glacier, and as we came off one and then another, more great benches were revealed to us. After an hour of walking, Alfsfell (584 meters) rising above us on the east and Fannalagarfjall (618 meters) on the west, it appeared we were no closer to the bottom.

"Shit, man," Scott said. "Isn't it just right there? We've been walking awhile."

"We have," I said. "And it is right there. I can see it."

"Got to be," Scott said. "But it isn't getting any closer. And I'm wrecked."

"Yeah," I said. "I'm ready to stop too."

Strange how light worked in that country under evening summer sun, that this series of benches, from our point of view, made our camp look refreshingly near, but it was instead painfully far. Perhaps the angle of our sightline allowed these long benches to appear stacked, one on top of the next, and, foreshortened this way, gave us a pleasurable false hope.

We pressed on, our quads and knees and feet bearing the weight and jounce of our walking, and the hard, stony ground came up under us, battering the bruising in our feet. The path got clearer now, and in some places it became a trail, and we walked it out from cairn to cairn all the way to the sea. The beach sound roared in against us, with that fresh sea air, and at the first wide grassy place where other walkers had camped before, we threw down our packs and shucked off our shoes. First order of business: a slug of spirits to toast our long good day.

Now in this lower light of evening—it was past ten—the sun moved sidelong behind a headland, and the temperature sank. We put on another layer, set up the tent, and sat in the lee of it to cook a simple meal of tuna pasta with onion and broccoli, crisp bread, and chocolate digestive biscuits. While we ate, two figures emerged from a tent we spotted away on the hill. They stood into the wind held in each other's arms, seemingly impervious to the bracing cold. A postcard you might send home.

"Damn," Scott said, crawling into his bag inside the tent. "I'm beat."

"Nice to have a clear night, though," I said. "Happy it's not raining."

"True," Scott said. "True. I'm beat, but good thing is, I'm dropping weight. I got to be. We got worked today."

"Right. You got to be. I'm probably dropping a few pounds too."

"Did I tell you I'm down to about 230 now?"

In high school and in his early twenties, Scott had been a talented athlete: football, basketball, track, and rugby. But a few years ago, he hit an all-time low by hitting an all-time high of 265 pounds. His gut spilled over his buckle, and his face became fleshy and soft. It looked like he was headed for more weight, too, and the many problems that come with it: diabetes, heart disease, immobility, and chronic joint pain, not to mention sexual dysfunction leading to a general distaste for life. But something awakened in him, and he put himself on an exercise regimen and started eating better food. This wasn't a flash weight-loss gimmick, which always results in a frustrating loss/gain cycle: the weight he'd lost would stay lost. Over the past year, a major motivation for him was making this trip. He ramped up his regimen to get into good walking shape.

"Damn, 230," I said. "Would you say this trip saved your life?"

"Shit, yeah," Scott said, "it saved my life. It gave me something to work for, a goal. I needed that. My long-term target weight is 195, and a couple years ago that felt impossible. But I'm going to hit it."

"That's fantastic."

"Yeah," he said. "I'm feeling fucking fantastic, and fucking fantastically too." He paused. "But lucky for you, Caswell, sleeping next to you so many nights in this tent, my libido is at an all-time low."

Morning came to the Hornstrandir, and I crawled from the tent for a piss. The shore was white with driftwood, a great logjam of giant trees built up on the beach—mostly larch, fir, spruce, and poplar—speckled with colorful fishing floats that had come in out of the sea. Where did all this wood come from, as Iceland is mostly devoid of trees? Out of the forests of Siberia, one of my sources indicates, carried down by those great rivers that flow into the Arctic Ocean: the Lena, Ob, and Yenisei. Traveling four hundred to a thousand kilometers per year, such logs remain at sea for a minimum of five years. The salt water cures the wood, toughening it, so the longer it remains adrift, the tougher it is. The early settlers of Iceland (mostly Norse traders and raiders) used driftwood for building shelters and homes, boats, furniture, bowls, barrels, and boxes, and for making charcoal. Driftwood belonged to the owner of the land and was often branded like livestock. The Icelandic sagas include stories of disputes and negotiation over driftwood caches. And of particular note, during the Middle Ages, my source tells me, witch burning was based not so much on an abundance of witches as on an abundance of wood, especially driftwood. When the wood supply was sufficient, witches seemed to show up everywhere, just waiting to be burned.

I returned to the tent to join Scott for coffee and a simple breakfast of muesli cooked in water, which we choked down with honey. The sky looked fairly steady, though overcast and gray. We broke camp, loaded our packs, and set out on our way.

Auden proclaimed the Westfjords the most beautiful part of Iceland, and the Hornstrandir must be its crown jewel. It was the last region to be settled in Iceland, and the few hardy farmers and fishermen who tried to make a go of it were gone by the 1950s. Winter travel was too difficult, as access was (and still is) only by boat, and the short growing season, coupled with a slow recovery after grazing, made keeping livestock a zero-sum game. In the fjords, seasonal polar ice made fishing dangerous and unsustainable. In 1975, Iceland declared the region a 58,000-hectare nature reserve and national monument, thereby protecting some of the world's greatest seabird cliffs and habitat for marine mammals, and offering a last refuge to Iceland's only endemic mammal, the arctic fox. Elsewhere in Iceland, foxes are hunted and killed as vermin. Once, not so long ago, in the colder world of our grandparents, an occasional polar bear drifted to these shores from Greenland on pack ice, but even as the guns of the sheep ranchers are gone from the Hornstrandir, climate change makes it unlikely that the island will ever see another.

The Hornstrandir is part of a great basalt plateau dramatically inscribed by fjords and bays and short valleys, eroded by glaciers. The plateau rises 400 meters from the sea at Adalvik in the west and up to 700 meters in the east at Hornvik, where we were going; though to look at it, you see not the plateau that has long since eroded away but a vast and wild landscape of rugged and misty mountains. The bedrock here is 14 million years old. Cirques, amphitheater-like valley heads, are a characteristic of this region. Climatic features include prevailing northeast winds, a mean annual temperature of about 3.5 degrees Celsius, and annual precipitation of roughly 1,250–1,350 millimeters. Polar winds push onto the northern coast, which is just some 300 kilometers from Greenland.

During the Last Glacial Maximum (18,000–20,000 years before present), the Hornstrandir was largely covered by an ice cap, which extended some 6–10 kilometers beyond the coastline. The highest points of the plateau, however, were buried not under glaciers but rather under perennial snow, or firn, an intermediate stage between snow and glacier. Such high points in the Hornstradir were dotted with nunataks (exposed ridges or rock features surrounded by firn) and ice-free slopes between glaciers and the plateau edge. After some 10,000 years, during which glaciers advanced and retreated, changing the landscape dramatically, the Hornstradir's deglaciation ended by about 9,500 years ago. The remnant glacier, Drangajökull, is the only glacier in Iceland that is not currently in retreat. With its volcanic and glacial activity, Iceland, and subsequently the Westfjords, must be a world center for rheology, the study of the flow of matter. To the human eye, such mountainous landscapes are fixed, but across immense spans of time, they move. Mountains do walk, as the ancient Buddhist masters have always known. "If you doubt mountains' walking," writes the thirteenth-century Zen master Dogen, "you do not know your own walking."

Walking the shoreline that morning, we made our way along the easy breakers as they came, pushing us up the beach. As the water drew back out to sea, so did we, so that we walked a little wave pattern along the waves, along the wrack line, mindlessly, really, angling down onto the harder black sand where the surf was soon to be, and then back up into the drier, loose sand where the waves pushed us. There was no path on this section of the Hornstrandir and barely a path anywhere in the whole of it, certainly not out through the basaltic boulder fields, which kept no footprints and resisted wear, and not the clean white fields of snow, the paths over which were momentary. A good path is not made to walk but made by walking, as Antonio Machado has written. And a path made by walking is the keeper of all walkers' dreams, those who go upon it now, those who will go upon it, and those who have gone before. You have to be very careful walking in a landscape like this, careful that you do not tread upon another's story. Rather, you walk along-side it, paying homage as you pass, paying homage as you make a story of your own, the outcome of which cannot be known while walking. You do not ask or strive for knowing, or strive for meaning. You just walk, as walking itself is the meaning for which you strive. If someone asks you what you learned out there, it is best to answer that you learned nothing at all. You just walked, and that is enough. You walked, and by walking, you became part of the place you walked, part of it, so that a place that was not a place to you before you walked it becomes now inseparable from your identity. It becomes part of who you are, part of your body and part of your mind, and, as such, your mind becomes another wild place in which to walk. You walk out along the edges of the world, just as you walk along the edges of your thoughts and so, thereby, into the strangest country. The real journey is inward, the thought of which you must keep very quiet, else those threatened by such ideas will invest considerable energy to unhinge you. I have never made a first ascent of a great peak or a first descent of an impossible river or sought the knife-edge between life and death. Such adventuring, while it may make fascinating news, has become all too routine. Everest, for example, that peak of human desire, isn't a journey anymore; it's a commercial industry, where you pay and then get in line to do what everyone else is doing. The real journey, I think, is not in feats of derring-do, but in paying attention to a place, to the outward details, the sights and sounds and weathers, and to the inward details, to exploring the deep and quiet places of the mind and of the heart. Then, once home, the greater adventure is in making beautiful sentences. "The gaiety of language" is our master, writes Wallace Stevens.

The quiet beach that morning led on toward a distant headland dropping sharply into the sea, and beyond it, a massive cirque running up to the sky, white with snow. The way looked shut, and which way we were to go seemed then impossible to know. I looked down at my feet and noticed fox tracks in the sand, two sets—one going out and one coming back. The set going out appeared to be running, as the prints were deeper, more distantly spaced, the animal going along the sea at a charge; the other, coming back, a quiet saunter, a morning wanderer, out for a look around. Perhaps they had passed here at different times. Or was this the same fox twice, with different intentions? I stopped as Scott came up behind me. "Nice," he said, and then we two stood in silence on that silent beach, our own footprints leading to the camp we left behind. Every road leads in two directions: where you've been and where you are going. And since where you've been is not possible to get to, we had no choice but to walk on.

I checked the map as we approached a complex of small houses, apparently a private inholding, likely an old farm that the family never gave up. The sun warmed through the misty clouds, and a worn sweep of path led us between the buildings. At the edge of an outbuilding, three young arctic foxes rolled and played in the northern sun breaking through the clouds. Little brown things, fuzzy and round with little pointed ears and black eyes. All three ran for the cover of the front porch to let us pass. "Nice," I said. We walked on.

As we walked on we began to realize the great cirque out ahead was our path, the first of two mountain passes for the day. I could now see the trail switching back across what looked like an impossible climb. The great, scooped bowl covered in snow where only mountain goats—and maybe the foolish—might go. We rose up off the beach, up and up along the trail. Not so bad, really. The way was clear and easy to follow, narrow and exposed, with nothing to stop your fall, but easy walking if you paid attention. We climbed steadily, not talking at all. I was grateful then for my trekking poles: I had purchased them in Ísafjörður, and now they steadied me. And I was happier still for my Arborwear undershirt, black canopy jacket, and tech shorts, which I wore over a light pair of knee-length black wool tights. On colder days, like this one, I pulled my long black ski socks up, so they met my tights at the knee. So dashingly dressed, with my long locks having fallen from under my cap and waving about my face, and my eyes, surely, reflecting an "innocent good-fellowship," I looked the spittin' image of Little Lord Fauntleroy.

We came up over the top of the pass called Skalarkambur and down the other side. As we went, the way became lost to us through the boulder fields, and we found it again, then lost it once more. The cairn in the distance pointed the general direction, but we could not stay on the path. It was here now under our feet and then out over there as we walked beside it, so faint and light, it wandered through the landscape. Like the waves on the beach, always shifting, or like a photon of light, which according to Heisenberg is not in any one place at any one time but rather shows a probability to be here or over there. Judging by the faintness of the path, the impact we might have on this landscape was so minimal, so light, as to be nearly nothing. We were like ghosts, walking a ghost trail through the black fields of stony rocks. "O you and I who never have existed," writes the Icelandic poet Steinn Steinarr, "One instant, like a shadow on a wall, / Appears the image we were destined for."

A snowfield appeared before us, and we crossed it, following the dirty bootprints of other walkers. It was near impossible for me to keep from kicking snow into my low-top walking shoes. I paused again and again to finger it out, my socks growing ever wetter. I soon learned that if I walked more carefully, more slowly and deliberately, making a wide step like a bowlegged cowboy, I could keep my feet dry. We walked mostly in silence, Scott and I, as it was too difficult to talk and negotiate the snow and boulders, and the weather, which came in tight against us. It misted a good mist, and we pulled our hoods over to keep our heads dry.

Walking these treacherous paths, I came to think about the early Icelanders who traveled here, how they negotiated these passes in search of good ground to plant or a grassy swale where they could graze their sheep. Did they find the divine in these mountains and seas, or did they feel, as I do, that beauty arises from its absence? Perhaps such settlers did not cross this particular pass at all; perhaps it is a crossing for walkers who walk for no reason other than to walk.

Unlike so many modern nations, Iceland was uninhabited in the ninth century when settlement really took off, except for a few stray Irish monks, who (god bless 'em) found Europe too crowded for their taste. Thus, the nation has no dark history of supplanting a people already here, unless you consider the millions of birds and fish and marine mammals taken to feed a growing population. The Norse people who sailed out from mainland Europe in longboats, carrying their sheep, goats, cattle, and gods—especially Thor— must have thirsted deeply for something new, for someplace new where they might establish a civilization of their own. Theirs were largely economic pressures, as most of the good farmland on the continent was already occupied, and some few nobles fled the policies of the tyrannical king, Harald Fairhair (850–932). Yet to choose that option, to set sail on a dark and mysterious sea in a relatively small boat, must have required a measure of courage or desperation or even madness. The passage from Norway to eastern Iceland took about seven days, if the weather was good. A stop in the Faroes would extend the duration, as would an onward journey to western Iceland and present-day Reykjavik, where today nearly two-thirds of all Icelandic people live. Often the weather was not good and the crossing was treacherous. Imagine the number of boats and people gone down to a watery grave in the North Atlantic.

In 1000 CE, Iceland named Christianity its official religion, so the Norse gods went quietly underground. Such a choice, I think, offers a key insight into the way Icelanders came to regard this land, a land I heard Icelandic novelist Auður Ava Ólafsdóttir characterize as "this mysterious black island." Perhaps Iceland was just too dark and cold for too much of the year, too bleak and too empty to go on for long without the comforting illusion of a loving god. To ward off that awful loneliness of winter, nature had to be animated, and conveniently, Christianity was franchising in the neighborhood. This is also the choice most of humanity has made, adopting the supposed comfort of religious doctrine, which promises some sort of everlasting life to stave off the cold, bleak bleakness of an indifferent universe.

To find a sentient creature that might have lived otherwise, we have to go back further, beyond the settlement of Iceland (and off Iceland altogether, into mainland Europe), as far back as forty thousand years ago, when Neanderthals lived alongside modern humans. Neanderthals were robust human beings with great barrel chests, stout bones, and an impressive musculature. They were able to withstand cold and were well suited to carrying heavy loads. One researcher estimates that Neanderthals would have been able to bench-press three hundred to five hundred pounds. And they were incomparable walkers, walkers of the most exquisite type, whose livelihood and daily life shaped their physical bodies. The average Neanderthal, a recent study finds, could keep pace with the best of our greatest athletes, with Pelé, Steve Prefontaine, and Jim Thorpe. Their heavy brow ridge, large and powerful lower jaw with retracted chin, and relatively large nose and nostrils gave them the appearance of that iconic apelike brute we associate with Stone Age humans.

Despite appearances, Neanderthals were little different from modern humans, little different from us. In fact, a number of researchers, especially Svante Pääbo, head of the Department of Evolutionary Genetics at Leipzig's Max Planck Institute for Evolutionary Anthropology, have begun to overturn the image of Neanderthals as mindless brutes. Like modern humans, Neanderthals likely did possess the power of language, or at least of communication; they developed complex tool-making processes and may have adorned their bodies with hematite, or red ochre pigment. And they buried their dead, suggesting belief in an afterlife. It was once thought that modern humans drove Neanderthals to extinction by outcompeting them and possibly killing them. But Pääbo's work has shown that the two species were so similar that they interbred, and since modern humans outnumbered Neanderthals ten to one, we absorbed them. The evidence is in us, as Europeans carry Neanderthal genes today.

However, there is a key difference between modern humans and Neanderthals. Unlike us, Neanderthals did not make much art. For a long time, it was thought that they were not capable of art, but we now know that "Neanderthals were capable of symbolic expression," evolutionary anthropologist Steven Churchill told me. "They were occasionally making items of personal adornment. Even though they weren't making much art, it wasn't because they weren't capable of doing so." Nor were they plagued by restlessness, or whatever it was that pushed modern humans onto the seas to colonize distant continents and islands, else Neanderthals might have peopled

Iceland long ago. In Elizabeth Kolbert's book *The Sixth Extinction,* Pääbo says

> It's only fully modern humans who start this thing of venturing out on the ocean where you don't see land. Part of that is technology, of course. . . . But there is also . . . some madness there. . . . How many people must have sailed out and vanished on the Pacific before you found Easter Island? I mean, it's ridiculous. And why do you do that? Is it for the glory? For immortality? For curiosity? And now we go to Mars. We never stop.

Neanderthals did not do that. They did not venture out onto the hostile seas, and they did not make art. Why? Or rather, why not? Perhaps one reason is that Neanderthals were nomadic, a hunting-gathering culture. The choice for such cultures, as Jacob Bronowski affirms in *The Ascent of Man,* is "starve or move." So they moved, but they moved not out into the unknown, not into the vast seas of the North Atlantic, but during specific times of year along tested pathways where they knew food, plants, and animals were certain to be found. And such moving makes civilization impossible. What you can carry is limited, and you would not make things you could not carry, nor would you develop the ability to make them. Nomads, asserts Bronowski, do not even make memorials, for "nothing is memorable. Nomads have no memorials, even to the dead. . . . The only mounds that they build are to mark the way." So what "happens to the old when they cannot cross the last river?" Bronowski asks. "Nothing. They stay behind to die. . . . The man accepts the nomad custom; he has come to the end of his journey, and there is no place at the end." In this way, for nomads, "the adventure leads nowhere. The summer pastures themselves will only be a stopping place. . . . There is no promised land."*

The story of the Promised Land, the seminal record of which

---

*Bronowski is writing here specifically about the Bahktiari tribes of Persia, who were and are nomadic pastoralists, hence the reference to summer pastures. I have taken some liberty with Bronowski's work to liken some of the cultural characteristics of these modern pastoral nomads to Neanderthals, who would not have kept sheep and goat herds but would have hunted wild game herds wherever they found themselves.

is the Bible, is the story of a nomadic people transitioning to an agrarian economy, a transition modern humans would complete, but Neanderthals would not. Abel, the keeper of sheep, is murdered, leaving the world to his murderer, his brother, Cain, who is a tiller of the fields, a farmer. The Bible is a book about the birth of civilization through the development of agriculture and then the buying and selling of land. It is the myth that parallels the story of the meeting of modern humans and Neanderthals.

Without art, then, without a capacity or a need for metaphor, Neanderthals lived not by the gaiety of language but perhaps by the gaiety of light and warmth, food and sex and companionship, the physical and immediate comforts and pleasures of the body. I don't mean they had these pleasures all the time—they did not—but they lived for them, as these might have been the chief goods of Neanderthal life. Without the capacity for metaphor, was it not easier for Neanderthals than it is for us to live in an indifferent universe? If you consult *Gilgamesh*, the oldest recorded story in the world, you find the selfish and narcissistic worship of individual power, which leads to such a fear of death that the protagonist, Gilgamesh, king of one of the world's first cities, embarks on a journey of folly: a search for immortality. He fails in his quest, of course. Perhaps, unlike modern humans, who are still daily embarking on the journey of Gilgamesh, Neanderthals lived simply, without agitation or worry over life and death, simply in the torrent of the body's pleasures, however brief. In an indifferent universe, perhaps it is easier to be mostly indifferent yourself.

Scott and I reached the bottom of Reykjavik fjord into Hornvik and pressed on around Einbui to Höfn camp. At one point we used fixed ropes to help us over a steep hump of rock along the beach and walked a little foot trail overlooking a sharp precipice falling away into the sea. Seabirds—puffins, black guillemots, and arctic terns—spun along the sea cliff below us.

Höfn was a busy place. The Icelandic ranger was in his cabin, and a few large groups of twelve to sixteen people were camped on the flat. We counted some twenty tents. We found services here too: a

WC with flush toilets, a couple of pit toilets, and a sink tapping water from a spring.

We pitched our camp against inevitable rain, cooked again in the door of the tent, and drank off the edge of our sore muscles and aching joints. An arctic fox made a pass to test us for handouts. The sign near the spring reported that feeding foxes is all right, but please no sweets.

"I'm tired," Scott said.

"Me too. But maybe we should walk around the horn to see the birds?"

"Birds?" Scott said. "All I've seen for days is birds."

"Yeah, but this is supposed to be one of the greatest seabird cliffs in all the world."

"Maybe so," Scott said, "as dramatic as that is. But I can't. I'm all broken."

"Same here, but we should probably do it. I doubt we'll make it back here again."

"Probably not," Scott said. "In fact, I'm surprised I made it here this time. I bet you were sitting around in your house wondering who would be stupid enough to think this was a good idea. Cold. Wind. Rain. Birds shitting on you from the sky. You were looking for someone stupid enough to say: Yeah, okay, Caswell. I'll walk all over Iceland with you. You were asking that question, and the answer you came up with was me."

"That's right. And here you are."

"Yeah, here I am, and now I'm all broken. I can hardly stand up I'm so sore. And my little toe is mangled and purple. How am I going to walk out on this?" he asked, inspecting the puffy little sausage.

"Yeah, that doesn't look good, but that's why we should make the walk out there to the horn," I said. "It'll loosen us up."

"No, we shouldn't. We should sit here and drink. And besides, I'm not as dumb as I used to be. I'm coming to understand, after thirty years of friendship, that you're just a little bit fucking crazy."

"Am I?"

"Yeah, just a little bit. Just enough."

"You're right," I said. "Let's stay put. I've seen plenty of birds today. And yesterday. And the day before that. Why didn't we grab that deck of cards from the ferry terminal? We could have another game of Dirty Oyster."

"Shit," Scott said. "Why didn't you think of that? Dumb shit."

"I don't know. Probably nobody will ever use those cards again. They'll just sit there in the terminal going to waste."

"Yeah, cuz nobody else is dumb enough to read the ferry schedule the way we did and get stuck in that place for seven hours."

"Here," I said. "Let's pour out a bit more," and I emptied the vodka bottle into Scott's cup. "That's the end of that one."

"Good thing we're not staying on another week. We're out of alcohol."

"No," I said. "We have a bit more rum."

We sat up awhile longer, drinking off our sorrows, until the sky came down to squat on the flat, and the rain popped against the tent fly.

"Well," Scott said after we'd crawled into the safety of the tent, "I'm going to sleep."

"Sleep?" I said. "A bit early, isn't it? I mean, it's like 8:30."

"Yeah, it is. But you know what? At 9:30 it will still be light. And at 10:30 and at 11:30, it'll still be light. So what does it matter what time it is?"

"Good point."

"Yeah, it is a good point," Scott said. "And besides that, you know what?"

"What?"

"I'm going to sleep cuz there's nothing to fucking do."

It rained most of the night. I woke again and again to the rain, a light mist, a heavy thrumming, a break to an opening of sky. And by the morning hour, it lifted, and we crawled from the tent to a world soaked in cloud and mist. The mountains we would soon cross, there to our south, were occluded by cloud, and white runnels poured off the face and into the great wetland below. I felt sore and stiff from all the walking, from hauling my pack. And we had another hard day ahead of us.

"It's all wet out here," Scott said, because someone had to say it for us both. "And I'm all wrecked inside."

I made coffee, and we cooked up the muesli, added our honey, and ate and talked about the day. As we packed our wet tent, the ranger walked up. His name was Jon, he told us, Jon Bjornsson, and in these parts, we later came to know, he was legend. He might have been sixty-five, perhaps older, a toque on his head with a tassel, a light jacket, and cotton pants tucked into his knee-high rubber boots. His face was bright, open—this rain was nothing to him— and these dark clouds were pushing a mounting storm. He bore the countenance of a man who'd lived his life outdoors, an easy, wiry look, hard as nails.

"Good morning, gentlemen," he said. "You are heading out today?"

"We are," I said.

"That is very good. It is best to get an early start. There will be heavy rain in the afternoon. It is best to be on the other side."

"We'll be on our way shortly," I said.

"Very good," he said. "You are taking the boat then, in the morning? I will be joining you on the boat."

"Oh, great," I said.

"Yes, I must go to a funeral in Reykjavik. It's a sad story, you know. But Icelandic funerals, there is a lot of alcohol. So it won't be too bad."

"What time will you start up the trail today?"

"I will go in the morning."

"In the morning?"

"Yes. You see, I am very fast."

I nodded. "And you probably know the way."

"Yes, I know the way. I could walk all of it backwards." He smiled. "Well, you best be getting on. This here is the most direct trail. Easiest for you. I will see you in the morning."

We loaded our packs and set out, walking the easiest route for us and ascending a high bench above the flat, crossed and cut by flowing waters. The mists hovering above us set down on the back of the mountain, and the higher we climbed, the closer we came to the clouds. That strange border between outside and inside the clouds drew near, and when we walked in, visibility collapsed to fifty meters, maybe less. Shambling along through the mists, we crossed several snowfields, which were so bright in the dark air we had to put on our sunglasses. In some places we did not know if we were on the route or not, and then a cairn came into view at the limit of our sight, so we went that way. Arriving at that cairn, we followed a dirty footpath through the snow, trusting that in time we'd see another cairn, which we did, just as we began to question where to go. It would be so easy, walking those paths, to become disoriented and wander lost in the misty boulder fields. The GPS would show us the general way, but if we were delayed and its batteries ran down with no sun to charge it, what then? Crawl into some deep hole in the rock for shelter and wait for a clearer day? These cairns, one after the other, appeared before us when we needed them most, like a sign or sentinel. Still, what separated me from a complete loss of bearings was not the wish or belief in a guide from another world but the permeable membrane of companionship, a friend who would put out a hand in the dark.

We walked on, and on, until our path turned sharply up, the final hump to the saddle of the pass. We ascended, pushing up the pathway to the top, 515 vertical meters from our camp. At the summit pass the wind pushed and beat us, coming cold out of the mist and dark. At my feet I discovered fox droppings set down in a little X on a stone in our path and, next to it, a collection of tiny white flowers, bending in the summit wind.

Walking is difficult, I have learned, not so much because we are weak but because it re-creates the original pain of birth and the inevitable separation from the mother. It's dying that comes easy. Each time you set out on a walk, you must sever your ties to home. You don't know—not really—when you'll be back, or even if you'll get back at all, because you don't know what might befall you on the road. So the pain of birth is experienced again as you leave your warm house for the bright world, the unknown, walking that edge between awe and terror. And really, dying is much easier. For that, you just stop doing anything at all. You retreat as far away from the peopled world as you can and wait, and wait, and one day you are no more. But why do that when you can go for walks, which, despite all the difficulties, take you from place to place, and with each new place is a new possibility. Of all else, this is what hominids desire most, new possibility: a new day, a new chance, a new place. "Wayfaring," writes Merlin Coverly in his book *The Art of Wandering*, "is the fundamental mode by which living beings inhabit the earth. . . . The act of walking becomes a means of reading a landscape." So Scott and I walked and read out the signs that would lead us through the dirty tracks over the snowfields, the thick, squatty sentinels of the cairns in the mists, the swirl and spin of the clouds we walked inside, which led us out onto the other side, where we descended at an angle across a steep snowfield, down, down, until we dropped below the clouds at last, and a blue sky greeted us in a bright day. From here, as yesterday, we could see our way out ahead, down the long slow slope across the boulders to the waters at the head of Veiðileysufjörður. My heart warmed and felt at ease, as it appeared that we were almost home. "He who enters it is lost," writes Ibn Battuta, that twelfth-century prince of travelers, "and he who leaves it is born."

And yet the way seemed to resist our going, for when we hit the rock at the bottom of that sharp, snowy descent, we found no more cairns to lead us. The problem was not that we would not find our way, as the waters of the fjord were in sight before us, but that we would not find our way very soon. The cairns marked the easiest passage, the way most walkers would go. We struck out across the pathless lands, keeping watch for piles of stones. We skirted around great boulders, over streams and their companion patches of mud and swampy grass, and back to the boulders running out before us. In time, a pile of rocks that looked like a pile of rocks became a cairn, and, back on track now, we followed the faint path down. Behind us, the storm and cloud descended, spilling over the pass and filling the void below, pushing us down the fjord to the water. Out of the distance, a younger walker overtook us—a Frenchman with a big camera—and he beat us in to the safety of our camp.

We found a little depression in the land at the camp and pitched the tent, tying out the wind anchors, setting them firm in the ground. We cooked and ate as the sky grew darker, and just as we'd finished up the dishes, the rain came down the fjord on the wind. It blew, forcing the rain at the fly, bending the tent poles in.

One subject of every poem, one of my teachers taught me, is the poem itself, and so seated there in the tent in the wind, I made my notes on the day and the unfolding events of the moment. The journey is not over until you have told its story, I wrote. Then I sketched a little picture of our tent in the wind and regretted the angle at which we had pitched it. If the narrow end were facing the wind, we would ride out the storm a bit better. But no matter. Scott woke from a troubled sleep and said, "Here, I'll just press my big ass up against the tent so we don't blow away." I scribbled down my page and thought of the Welsh writer Arthur Machen, who made walking one of his primary arts. "For the essence of this art [walking]," Machen writes, "is that it must be an adventure into the unknown, and perhaps it may be found that this, at last, is the matter of all the arts." The storm raged on, and I slept fitfully, if at all.

Rising to the light of day, it was not raining anymore. I stepped out of the tent to find two new tents in the camp, late arrivals in the storm last night. A seal lifted its head from the waters of the fjord. I watched it bob away in the waves. After coffee and hot cereal, Scott and I retreated from the cold to our shelter—"It is best to leave up the tents," Jon, the ranger, had told us. "The boat can be delayed for many hours"—until we heard the voice of the man himself. Jon had arrived, a little pack on his back, still wearing those rubber boots.

"Did he walk in in those boots?" I said.

"Shit," Scott said. "I bet he did."

Jon told us he departed his Höfn cabin at 8 a.m., and it was now 10:30 a.m. What had taken Scott and me all day to walk, he had accomplished in two and a half hours.

"Now that's walking," Scott said.

I wondered what the Hornstrandir felt like to Jon, who negotiated its steeps and boulders and snowfields with such ease, its stream crossings and marshes and bogs, the beach sands, the grassy swales running up the fjord bottoms, the winds and rains and snows of summer. Did he feel perfectly at ease in the land, and if so, did that feeling come from outside, from the place itself, or from somewhere inside, a feeling he created? If the land out there was empty, if nature is indeed indifferent, perhaps it is still possible to love a place, to love a landscape, when that love is projected onto it. We cast the net of ourselves into the void, and instead of drawing it back, we leave it there so that next time, there is a there in that place to go to.

The boat appeared in the fjord, a white line in the waves drawn out behind it. Scott and I broke down the tent and packed it away. We still had a good string of days to explore the north and east of Iceland, and as the boat pulled in, I was ready to be moving on.

GETTING TO GREY OWL'S CABIN

Saskatchewan, 2012

On the Kingsmere Road west along the narrow arm of Waskesiu, I drive with the window down. Nine cow elk with calves graze the summer roadside grass, their mouths moving together in easy time. A little farther on, two bulls as big as dump trucks, racks spreading like the branches of oak, silent, soft in their eyes, watch me as I watch them. The sun is coming up off the tree line, and in the glowing track of the road, two wolf pups explode from the barrow pit. Was that dark presence at the corner of my eye their mother? But my gaze is forward, pushing hard on the brakes to slow the heavy truck. One of the pups breaks right and vanishes in the underbrush. The other runs right down the middle of the road. It's a little fur ball bouncing along on its big feet, loping like a teenager, its ears pinned back in terror (I would be terrified too). I'm coming up fast, still pressing hard on the brakes, harder, harder, hoping it will move out of the way before I push through, and then it does, cutting right to the cover of safety. I count myself lucky to see them—these elk, the wolves—and drive slower now, sunrise flooding the north woods, an eagle at the jaggedy edge of the spruces and larch and pine. Though I know this is a national park, where elk and wolves are safe from hunters, I've traveled in the boreal for-

est before and didn't see so many big animals. Maybe this is going
to be a good day.

When I mentioned to a Canadian friend that I wanted to make a
journey to Grey Owl's cabin, he said, "Really? Why? He was a fraud."
I suppose he was, at least in part, an Englishman who co-opted an
Indian identity. He was born Archibald Stansfield Belaney in the
seaside town of Hastings, southeast of London, 1888. He immigrated
to Canada and cobbled together a living as a trapper and seasonal
job-hopper. He took on the name Wa-Sha-Quon-Asin, Grey Owl,
He Who Walks by Night, given him by the Anishinabe, and buried
his past so deeply that it came to light only after his death in 1938
from pneumonia brought on by heavy drinking.

By his own count, Grey Owl was the son of an Apache mother
and a Scots father, and he spent his boyhood in Mexico. His father,
he said, was a close friend of Buffalo Bill Cody. After arriving in
Canada, Grey Owl settled in with the Anishinabe at Bear Island,
Ontario. There he learned a great deal about hunting and trapping,
perfected his skills at knife throwing, and became a crack shot with
a rifle. He was regarded as a heavy drinker, a sometimes brawler,
a man of "dark moods." He got into trouble with the law. But he
was also a welcome traveling companion and a man with a sense of
humor. He could play the piano and sing. He quoted Shakespeare.
During the First World War he enlisted in the Canadian army,
where his independent spirit and expert marksmanship made him a
top-rate sniper. He was married five times, however loosely he inter-
preted that word, and had two daughters and one son, each with a
different woman. Anahareo, his fourth wife and the mother of his
youngest daughter, Shirley Dawn, was the love of his life, but their
marriage dissolved a couple years before he died.

The problem with Grey Owl is not that he was an Englishman living among First Nations people in Canada, but rather that, over the
final eight years of his life, he became a notable writer and one of
the preeminent conservationists of the time. He sold his four books,
along with his Indian persona and his message that human beings
are not above nature, but part of it, to an impressionable public in

Europe, the United States, and Canada, nations on the brink of the Second World War. Lovat Dickson, Grey Owl's publisher and eventual biographer, writes in *Wilderness Man: The Strange Story of Grey Owl,*

> His appearance in London in October 1935 created a sensation. Not only did he look romantic, he spoke pure romance. His thrilling voice brought the wilderness and its inhabitants, animal and Indian, alive to his audiences. . . . In contrast with Hitler's screaming, ranting voice, and the remorseless clang of modern technology, Grey Owl's words evoked an unforgettable charm, lighting in our minds the vision of a cool, quiet place, where men and animals lived in love and trust together.

As his fame grew as a writer and conservationist, Grey Owl was commanded to appear before King George VI at Buckingham Palace. The strict protocol demanded that the audience take its place and then rise as the footmen threw open the door to make way for the king and his family. But Grey Owl demanded that the scenario be reversed, so that the king and his court would rise, and "he, Grey Owl, would enter." And so it was. King George, the queen, the queen's parents, the Earl and Countess of Strathmore, and Princesses Margaret Rose and Elizabeth, along with much of the palace staff, rose to their feet as Grey Owl entered in full buckskinned regalia. The lecture was a great success, and especially delighted Princess Elizabeth. When it came time to leave, Grey Owl put his right hand out to the king, touched him on the shoulder with the other, and famously said, "Goodbye, brother. I'll be seeing you."

Grey Owl really did live the life he wrote and spoke about, but despite the truth of his satisfying vision of the wild, his fans and readers had paid for an Indian. What they got, they only later discovered, was a white man playing dress-up. If Grey Owl had lived out his days quietly in the north woods, no one would have cared. But there is no faster way to make enemies than parting people from their money in a lie. On Grey Owl's death, a waiting horde of newsmen discredited him, slandered him, cursed him, and cussed

him, and his books and his message of environmental conservation
were lost in the fray.

To get to Grey Owl's cabin, I drove to Prince Albert National Park,
Saskatchewan, from my house in west Texas. It's about 1,725 miles
from Lubbock to Waskesiu, but I didn't drive in a straight line. I
made a number of detours over several weeks, camping along
the way: the Medicine Bow National Forest near Cheyenne, Wyoming, where great mushrooms of smoke from the High Park Fire
savaged the sky; Deadwood, North Dakota, because of that HBO
series; Devil's Tower, Wyoming, because N. Scott Momaday (Kiowa)
writes that "it has to be seen to be believed," and I believed him;
Lake Sakakawea on the wide Missouri River, North Dakota, where
Lewis and Clark once camped; then on up over the US/Canada
border to Crooked Lake, Saskatchewan, where I watched a terrible
wind come in over the quiet waters; then out to Riding Mountain
National Park, Manitoba, where Grey Owl also lived for a short
time; and finally, to Prince Albert National Park where he lived
out his days and now is buried. So, to get to Prince Albert National
Park, I drove 2,450 miles. Inside the park, I drove another 100 miles
over a period of four days. So now I was at 2,550 miles of driving to
get to Grey Owl's cabin. Of course, I would also have to eventually
drive home.

   I drive a 2002 Ford F250 4-by-4 supercab, with a 7.3-liter V8 Power
Stroke diesel engine (yeah, the last of the good ones). The paint
is peeling and the truck has 200,000 miles on it, but it's still going
strong. I'm running Firestone Destination A/T tires at LT285/75R16,
which is a little bigger than the factory tire, so that reduces my
fuel economy just a bit. Then I have an eight-foot cabover Alaskan
Camper on the back, which weighs 1,750 pounds, dry. The thing
about the custom-made Alaskan is that it's the only hard-shell pop-
up camper made in North America. The top raises for camping
and lowers for driving on a hydraulic system, which dramatically
reduces drag and thus helps maintain reasonable mileage. I've got
a canoe on top of that and a whole lot of gear stowed in the cab

because I'll be making a long canoe trip out of Stanley Mission, Saskatchewan, after I visit Grey Owl's cabin, plus books, clothes, pots and pans, food, assorted tools and other miscellaneous gear, 35 gallons of fresh water, 20 pounds of propane, and at least, *at least*, a case and a half of beer.

On a good day, my truck can pull down 18 miles to the gallon. I use a diesel fuel conditioner, because the EPA changed the diesel fuel standards to remove most of the sulfur, thereby reducing emissions of oxides of nitrogen and particulate matter. That's good news for all living things that respire, and those that don't too, and a good step toward curbing climate change, but the process reduces the potential energy of the fuel, decreasing the work it can do, which lowers fuel economy, which means burning more. This new ultralow-sulfur diesel fuel (ULSD) is rated at 15 parts per million (ppm) of sulfur and isn't so good for diesel engines built before 2007 because they are designed to burn low-sulfur diesel (LSD), rated at 500 ppm. One of the problems is lubrication, so the fuel conditioner lubricates older diesel engines, like mine, and can also increase fuel economy. Instead of buying this, you have to buy that. Now, this ULSD fuel is good news for European diesel engine manufacturers because they build engines designed to burn ULSD fuel, so now Europe can compete with North America in the marketplace. But I suppose this is not so good for North American diesel engine manufacturers, who until now had less competition at home, which is probably why the diesel fuel was made that way for so long to begin with. This is a more complex issue, though—it includes a world campaign to lower sulfur content in diesel fuels for the sake of the entire planet, and I have no business reducing it to market exclusion. The point here is that with all this weight on and in my truck, and with this fuel and my engine, I probably average 15 miles per gallon. That's not too bad for an outfit that weighs upward of 15,000 pounds, but I'd do much better with a Toyota Prius. At any rate, to get to Grey Owl's cabin, I burned 170 gallons of diesel. According to my source, 1 gallon of diesel produces 10 kilograms of carbon emissions. So to arrive at the parking lot where I will unload my canoe to paddle up to Grey Owl's cabin, my truck alone has produced 1,700 kilograms of carbon.

Grey Owl's cabin is at the southern edge of the Canadian Shield country—a vast region of exposed Precambrian rock and glaciated lakes that covers half of Canada and most of Greenland, and extends south into the midwestern and northeastern United States. It was the first part of North America to be uplifted, and most of the great mountain ranges of the ancient past have long since eroded away, the land pressed flat by advancing and retreating glacial ice. This process of glaciation (which occurred 1.6 million to 10,000 years ago) carried away most of the soils and carved out the many thousands of lakes. The land is an undulation, like the surface of a golf ball—lake to exposed rock to thin soils over bedrock and the boreal forest stretched across it. Few roads penetrate this country, and many are seasonal, relying on winter ice to connect passages over solid ground. It is a country so filled with itself that to travel here is to accept it on its own terms—water to land, land to water by canoe or motor boat in summer; and ice to snow, snow to ice by dogsled or snowmobile in winter.

This early in the morning, the parking lot at Kingsmere Lake is empty. I park my truck, unload my canoe, and carry it to the put-in on Kingsmere River, the lake's outlet. To get to Grey Owl's cabin from here, I will paddle upriver a short distance to a rail portage around Kingsmere Rapid. It's an easy two-thirds-of-a-mile walk, pushing my canoe down the tracks and through the woods on a rail cart. Back on the water, I will paddle a bit farther upriver and then out into Kingsmere Lake. From there, it's about eight miles of paddling along the eastern shoreline to a trailhead at the north end of the lake, and then another two miles on foot to Grey Owl's cabin on Ajawaan Lake. In Grey Owl's day, there was no road from the village of Waskesiu to the parking lot here on Kingsmere River. To get to Grey Owl's cabin, you had to paddle the length of Waskesiu Lake, another sixteen miles, or more, if the wind was up and you paddled the shoreline.

I reach Kingsmere Lake at about 7:30 a.m. and follow the east shore, easy in my canoe. The water is quiet, like a library, and I hear loons calling, but I can't see them, nor can I see any other boats. The sky is empty of clouds, and I am alone. Right now the wind is down, and I enjoy good paddling. I dig in and move my boat along at a good clip. It's a bit like mountaineering, in that I want to get out to Grey Owl's cabin and start back by 1 p.m. because the wind usually comes up in the afternoon, wind from the leading edge of the great billowing summer thunderclouds that crack open and let forth the deluge. If it comes at all, it always comes from the sky, a spectacular catastrophe for a little boat on a big lake. On Kingsmere it often blows from the northwest across the lake, which would push me back to the parking lot. That would be OK, if it doesn't push too hard. I've heard that this lake, like any large body of water in the Canadian North, can become dangerous quickly, waves so big you can't see the opposite shore. If I capsized out here alone, it wouldn't be any fun, but, barring major injury, I'm pretty confident I'd be able to swim my boat and gear to shore, empty the water, and paddle on. And if I can't get my boat to shore, I can get myself to shore, and then I'd walk the trail just there inside the cover of the woods five to ten miles back to my truck.

I'm paddling the boat my father gave me when I finished my undergraduate degree: a solid all-around canoe, a blue Old Town Discovery 169. I've modified the outfitting with cane seats and installed tie-down eyelets under the gunwales with pop rivets. I've added a few stickers to the outside: permits from paddling in Yellowstone, one from my canoe club when I lived in northern Japan. The hull is faded and scarred by twenty years of use. I'm using a paddle I carved myself from ash and alder wood from my native Northwest. The blade is wide and squat, a good all-around touring design, and the grip is an asymmetrical pear shape. This is my paddle's first voyage.

Another source of carbon from my outfit is the propane I burn to cook inside the camper, run the refrigerator, the hot-water heater, and sometimes the heater. My Alaskan Camper comes with a 20-pound propane tank, and to get to Grey Owl's cabin, I emptied it. A 20-pound propane tank holds 4.7 gallons of liquid propane. One gallon of propane will produce 91,690 British thermal units (Btus) of energy, and so 430,934 Btus for my tank. To put that into perspective, 1 Btu is the energy required to raise the temperature of 1 pound of water 1 degree Fahrenheit (usually from 39°F to 40°F). Another way to think about this is that 1 Btu equals about 253 calories, which is the potential energy in four medium-sized eggs. So my propane tank holds the energy equivalent of 1,723,736 eggs. Burning propane emits about 63 kilograms of carbon per 1 million Btus of energy. So this means I produced another 27 kilograms of carbon to get to Grey Owl's cabin. My carbon total is now at 1,727 kilograms.

I paddle on. It's cool on the lake, and quiet, and still. Sitting in the kneeling position, my knees on the bottom of the canoe, my butt leaning against the seat, I keep my back straight as I plant my paddle blade forward of my knees and unwind my torso, flare the blade to correct the boat, and glide a moment before taking another stroke. It's a good rhythm, and I like how it feels, almost better than anything else. I pass the Westwind campsite, conspicuously marked on the eastern shore, and think I'm making good time, but I can't yet see the far shore on the north end. I hear an outboard motor somewhere off to the west—fishermen, probably, who would have come in on the same route that I did, pushing their aluminum fishing boat up the rail trail on a cart.

Two loons fly by overhead, then a few more. I see ducks of several kinds that I can't identify. I hear more loons, and then the sound of the outboard fades around a far point. It's quiet again, and I dip my paddle, dip my paddle, dip my paddle. I listen to the water run from the blade between strokes, and I lean over the gunwale to look into the lake. I can see the bottom, the various algae and water plants, the flash of a few fish, likely northern pike—or jackfish, they call them around here—but not big ones. And the trees lining the shore are thick, so thick it would be difficult to walk between them.

After arriving in Canada, Grey Owl made most of his living as a trapper, but he soon began to see the end of that life. A season's work once easily netted him $1,500 to $2,000, but by the time he met his fourth wife, Gertrude Bernard, a nineteen-year-old Mohawk-Iroquois woman, who became known as Anahareo, or sometimes Pony to Grey Owl, he was bringing in less than $600 each season. Anahareo, whom Grey Owl describes as able to "swing an axe as well as she could a lipstick," encouraged him to stop trapping. If she could in fact swing an axe, she probably learned it from Grey Owl. She was a town girl, raised and educated in Mattawa, in the Ottawa Valley, Ontario, and unused to life in the bush. She found trapping cruel and thought her husband should find a better way to make a living. He resisted for a time, until one day he trapped a beaver with two kits. Grey Owl collected the dead female for its pelt, as he had been doing for years now, while the kits cried and cried. As Grey Owl reports in his book *Pilgrims of the Wild*, Anahareo could not stand their suffering. "Let us save them," she cried out. "It is up to us, after what we've done." It was in this moment that Anahareo changed Grey Owl's life. "And truly what had been done here looked now to be an act of brutal savagery," he writes. "And with some confused thought of giving back what I had taken, some dim idea of atonement, I answered, 'Yes, we have to. Let's take them home.'" In taking them home—these two beavers that became known as McGinty and McGinnis—Grey Owl started down the path to world fame as an environmental conservationist.

You may remember similar experiences doing as much for Aldo Leopold, and for an earlier American writer and conservationist, William Bartram. Leopold's historic land ethic hangs on that moment he watched the "fierce green fire dying in [the] eyes" of a wolf he had just shot in southwest New Mexico. Before this moment, he believed ardently that killing predators *was* environmental conservation. And Bartram, writing in the late eighteenth century, a time when good biology always included killing and collecting species for later study, was "affected . . . very sensibly" watching a black bear cub bawling over the body of its mother killed moments before by a rifleman as they traveled down a river in the South. He charged himself "accessory to what now appeared to be a cruel murder," and, "moved to compassion," he implored the rifleman to stay his hand. But too late, as "[the rifleman] fired, and laid [the cub] dead upon the body of the dam." Such moments are enough to unhinge a man, to change him, as it did these three, each taking a place in the story of the environmental movement in North America.

According to the Union of Concerned Scientists, the average American produces about 19.18 metric tons of carbon per year. By comparison, the average Canadian produces 17.27 metric tons of carbon; the average German, 10.06; the average Chinese, 4.91; and the average Brazilian, 2.18. The average Afghan produces almost no carbon at all. One metric ton is equal to 1,000 kilograms. To get to Grey Owl's cabin, I produced nearly 2 metric tons of carbon-burning diesel and propane fuels alone. But there is more, of course.

The truck I'm driving has a carbon footprint too. The footprint of building the truck is fixed (it is only built once), but each time I have the truck repaired, change the oil, or buy news tires and the like, the footprint grows. For now let's stick to the fixed carbon cost of manufacturing. Energy is required for every step in the process: the extraction of ore from the earth, the manufacture of the engine and components, the various plastics and such that make up the interior and exterior, the shipping of parts from all over the world, the energy required to run the plants where parts are made and the truck was assembled, and then the workers while at work. Even the workers' clothes and what they had for lunch have a carbon footprint. And after that is the footprint of the sales people and their facilities. It's staggering, really. It's hardly possible to calculate a precise carbon footprint for my truck, but it is possible to make an educated guess. Two journalists at the *Guardian* report that the carbon footprint of an average-sized car is about 17 metric tons. At the high end (the report cites the Land Rover Discovery as an example), the footprint is 35 metric tons. To build a truck like mine, surely the cost must be at the high end. The truck is ten years old, and I traveled in my truck for two months getting to Grey Owl's cabin and back again. A simple calculation puts my truck at 292 kilograms of carbon per month over its lifetime, which means adding another 584 kilograms. My total now is 2,311 kilograms.

And there is more still. My truck is carrying the camper and the canoe and all the gear and clothing and other supplies. All of this has a carbon footprint. The food I buy to stock the camper has a carbon footprint. Doing my laundry has a carbon footprint, as do the books I've brought with me, my laptop, even the beer. My source estimates 900 grams of carbon for a single bottle of good beer with a fairly extensive transport history. And this is what I have, good beer from Wyoming and Colorado. Let's estimate two beers a day for two months, and so add another 108 kilograms of carbon in beer alone.

So far my calculations have been fairly precise, and I've accounted for the big ones. The calculation of the carbon cost of getting to Grey Owl's cabin breaks down from here into a dizzying complexity "too flattering-sweet to be substantial," as Shakespeare said. I don't really want to try to come up with an accurate number for every little plastic gizmo in my kit, and as with the calculation for the manufacture and upkeep of my truck, I'd then have to calculate the carbon cost of that plastic gizmo only for the duration of time that I use it to get to Grey Owl's cabin. You would be bored to death, and I would never finish this essay. So to account for the rest that is nearly incalculable, I'll double the total I have now and call it good. Let's say that 2,311 kilograms doubled is at the very least the carbon footprint of getting to Grey Owl's cabin: 4,622 kilograms of carbon. And then, double it again to get home, and add the beer. To get to Grey Owl's cabin it cost me—no, it cost the world—9,352 kilograms of carbon, or 9.35 metric tons, plus or minus a kilogram or two. That sum is nearly half of the yearly carbon footprint of the average American, and nearly double the average Chinese. If I want to remain near the average for my country, there's no room for travel for the rest of the year, and no room even to drink good beer. I can stay home well enough, but giving up beer is hardly American. It's hardly even civilized.

By the time I reach the Sandy Beach camp on the eastern shore of Kingsmere Lake, I am starting to hope for the end. The sky, clear and Canadian blue, leads me on, and my gaze drifts to the water, from sky to water, water to sky, until I hardly know whether I am paddling or flying. I paddle into a raft of loons that part and make way for me. I wave to two figures squatting on the shore next to a canoe. The wind hardly shows itself at all, and I can hear them talking. One of the good things about traveling in Canada is that most people speak American.

"Is this Sandy Beach?" I call out.

"Yes," one of them calls back.

"So I'm not far from the trailhead to Grey Owl's cabin?"

"It's just on a bit farther. You see those reeds up there? That's the trailhead."

And so on I paddle, stroke after stroke, winding up along the shape of the lake until those reeds come within reach, and I beach my canoe on the shore. I brought food with me to have a lunch, but I worry about the afternoon wind and storm. I drink down a half liter of water and set out on the trail. A few dozen feet from my boat, a sign welcomes the traveler with a few words from Grey Owl:

> Far enough away to gain seclusion, yet within reach of those
> whose genuine interest prompts them to make the trip, Beaver
> Lodge extends a welcome to you if your heart is right.

Walking through the woods, I wonder if my heart *is* right, and how I would know. I climb a hill and come over it, head down into the basin of Ajawaan. At the top of a boardwalk, I find an old moose antler wired crosswise to a spruce tree. It is weathered, gnawed by mice, and green with algae at the edges. I wonder if Grey Owl himself put this up to mark my way. The trail takes me down to the lake edge and then comes away into a tunnel of trees. I stop to admire an immense bear shit in the trail, the bulk of which, could he produce it, any man might be proud of. It looks fresh, very fresh, a riotous cake of berry seeds and other dark matter. Alone and on foot, I feel a nervous energy rise up in my body, a light caution, a sudden alertness. I pick up a heavy limb to quiet my hand, and I begin to sing a little to Grey Owl's woods, a silly song about trekking:

> Oh, I love to go a-wandering
> along the mountain track,
> and as I go, I love to sing,
> my knapsack on my back . . .

It makes me feel better, and I think then that fear is a permeable membrane. One may walk in and out of it, but it is far easier to walk in. Walking out is a tremendous feat, and each time you make it out, you become a hero, however temporarily, however privately.

I walk and sing and no bear comes, and the trail begins to feel too long. Just as I am tiring of the day, a loon cries overhead and Grey Owl's cabin appears before me. I stop there at the portal from the woods. That, I tell myself, is Grey Owl's cabin. I feel a little shy of it, the cabin, not like I'm an intruder really, but rather that I shouldn't go right in. I stand a moment in its presence, the sunlight on the quiet lake, and though I do not think much or often of ghosts, I sense a spirit in the woods. Laugh at me if you want to, but some know what I mean. It's like walking with the bear that isn't there and singing to it as you go. And Grey Owl, after all, *is* here. He's buried just there on the hill.

Grey Owl died in the spring of 1938 after that impossible lecture schedule in Europe. At the height of his exhaustion on the tour he said to a friend, "A month more of this will kill me." His chief desire was to return to his cabin at Ajawaan. "If I am to remain loyal to my inner voice," he writes, "I must return to my cabin in Saskatchewan . . . and take time to think." He did so. A park ranger checked in on him on April 8, reporting that Grey Owl "seemed all

right, and very happy . . . to be back." On April 9, Grey Owl called
the park station at Waskesiu to report he was feeling ill. A party
arrived to take him to a hospital in Prince Albert. Within twenty-
four hours he developed a fever, and soon after he fell into a coma.
On April 13, he was dead. Lovat Dickson writes that Grey Owl died
of exhaustion, "exhaustion of hope and purpose which are born in
the imagination and signal the heart when to stop." His daughter,
Shirley Dawn, was buried next to him near the cabin in 1984, and
then Anahareo in 1986.

Though he probably can't hear me, I decide to say hello before
I enter Grey Owl's cabin. "Hello, Grey Owl," I say aloud and then
make my way to another signpost where he has left a few words more
just for me:

> I hope you understand me. I am not particularly anxious to
> be known at all: but my place is back in the woods, there is my
> home, and there I stay. But in this country of Canada, to which
> I am intensely loyal, and whose heritage I am trying to interpret
> so that it may be better understood and appreciated, here at
> least, I want to be known for what I am.

And what was he? To me these sound like the words not of a fraud
but of a quiet, thoughtful man who loves this country. Yet the public
outcry against Grey Owl in the years since his death runs the gamut
from "fake Indian" (which he was) to "wanton cultural appro-
priator" (which is arguable) to "pervert" (which I can't believe).
Scholar Albert Braz has pointed out that the "level of vitriol that
Grey Owl's 'masquerade' still attracts" is perplexing, and it "has
been so unrelenting [as to overshadow] every other aspect of his
life," especially the simple fact that in the 1930s, he emerged from
obscurity to become one of the preeminent voices for environmental conservation. He was one of the very few Canadians who publicly
recognized that the nation's natural resources have a limit. Some
even credit Grey Owl with saving Canada's national animal, the
beaver, from extinction. In support of him, Major J. A. Wood, then
superintendent of Prince Albert National Park, wrote that he cares

not whether Grey Owl "was an Englishman, Irishman, Scotsman or Negro. He was a great man with a great mind, and with great objectives which he ever kept before him." Canadian prime minister John Diefenbaker (1895–1979) echoes this sentiment, claiming that "Grey Owl was one of the most remarkable men Canada has ever produced. He was a genius; no doubt a charlatan, a poseur, and a faker, but no one in North American history ever left behind him such a treasure of concern for what he described as his furred brethren of the soil and his feathered brethren of the air."

Grey Owl, you might notice, did not look like *an* Indian so much as he looked like *the* Indian as imagined by white people, the Indian of Hollywood, the Indian of that Romantic vision of the New World unspoiled by European colonization and the filth of the Industrial Revolution. Grey Owl wore a costume of buckskins, dyed his hair black, colored his face with henna, and practiced his stoic scowl in a mirror to perfect this costume. Still, it is difficult to separate the costume from the man, as Grey Owl didn't just wear it but became it, utterly, seamlessly, ceaselessly. Braz points out that N. Scott Momaday, himself a person of mixed heritages, has written that "we are what we imagine" and "an Indian is an idea which a given man has of himself." Certainly Grey Owl possessed such an idea of himself, but does this make him an Indian? I don't know. But I wonder. If a man can travel to Trinidad, Colorado, and change his sex to become a woman, why can't a man change his heritage to become an Indian? Poet Gary Potts, a former chief of the Bear Island Anishinabe in Ontario, where Grey Owl first lived when he immigrated to Canada, points out that what troubles white people most is not the lie, but rather that one of their own went native. He argues that white people are not overly troubled by Indians who assimilate into their culture, but when it goes the other way, it "troubles them to no end." Braz reports that the Canadian poet Gwendolyn MacEwen asserts "there is nothing necessarily nefarious about Grey Owl . . . since his journeys through the Canadian wilderness are really 'in search of himself.'" And Anahareo, Grey Owl's wife, writes, "He was an Indian, as I was."

So what or who was Grey Owl? He was a boy trapped inside an identity that did not agree with him, an identity he eventually threw off when he moved to Canada, the one place he could live out his best idea of himself. And I think we are all complicit in his transformation. If you want to condemn Grey Owl, perhaps you might condemn yourself as well, a member of the culture that helped create him. Grey Owl was the Indian we all wanted him to be, a spokesman and symbol for the North American wilderness we simultaneously love and destroy. Perhaps, too, what is so difficult to accept is that Grey Owl ventured out to live the life he imagined, while most of us stare out the front window or at the computer screen and only dream.

I approach the cabin, the door already ajar. I push it open. Before me is a wood cookstove, rusted by decades of disuse, and across on the opposite wall, a crude desk or table next to an even cruder split-log sleeping platform. The cabin is not a replica, as in the case of Thoreau's cabin at Walden Pond. Grey Owl lived here. At the far end of the room is a space cut away from the floorboards with a collection of beaver sticks and mud, remnants of the famed beaver lodge built inside the cabin with access to the lake so his pet beavers could come and go as they pleased. On the desk is a drum propped against the wall, apparently a gift from the son Grey Owl had with Marie Girard, a Métis woman whom he abandoned when he was a young man. Girard died of consumption shortly after she gave birth in the winter of 1914–15. Written on the skin of the drum:

> To: Grey Owl
> & Anahareo
> Rest in peace Dad
> Your loving son #2
> Todd—SK

I walk up the hill to another cabin, the place Anahareo had built just for her. Apparently she didn't take to living with beaver; she wanted a space of her own. Next to that, the three graves: Grey Owl,

Shirley Dawn, and Anahareo. I linger there for a time, linger near the gravestones in front of the depressions where they went in. I leave a quiet space for them, not moving or making noise at all, and then I move on.

There isn't much else to see or do but for the sunlight streaming through the trees and the sparkling waters of Ajawaan. I wonder if the wind is getting up out on the lake, so I turn and make my way back down the trail.

I sing my way to my boat and find that the wind has indeed come up. The lake can look so small when it is calm, but when the waves are high it's like the sea. Great rollers are washing down the shore-line of Kingsmere Lake. Off to the north and west, thunderheads build against the sky. I stow my pack and push off into the waves, which push my boat along. I don't have to paddle very hard. My strokes keep the boat at a good angle, and I ride along with a happy heart.

Paddling, I begin to think of all the journeys I have made and how many of them likely had a much greater carbon footprint than this one. All you have to do is step onto an airplane. A round-trip flight from Houston to London, for example, comes in at about 1,700 kilograms of carbon for each person on the plane. The plane itself produces that sum multiplied by some four hundred seats: 680 cubic tons of carbon. But this is merely the plane's emissions; it does not include all the other carbon sources that I so tediously considered for my truck. Air travel produces more carbon than any other sort of travel. And, to boot, air travel is fast, which means you can produce more carbon in far less time. My truck racked up a good carbon sum, but it did so over a period of two months. Let's say you were to fly 1 million miles, as several of my friends have, as Hillary Clinton did in four years as secretary of state. If you never get off the plane, you can fly that million in 2,000 hours, the equivalent of just over 83 days. In my truck it would take 15,385 hours to make the same distance, an equivalent of 641 days. And of course, if you are doing the driving, you have to stop now and again to rest and drink beer, so it would take much, much longer. Not so with air travel; air travel allows you to drink beer and produce carbon at the same time.

So, what about the great travelers who roam the world? What about the immense journeys of the environmental writers and conservationists of our time, the women and men whose work has been my steady diet since I was a boy? What is the carbon footprint, for example, of a writer who travels to all the cold places in the world to bring back a story about melting glaciers or the decline of polar bears, writing that may help change public policy in order to curb the environmental pressures that are causing the melting and the decline to begin with? What is the carbon footprint of a writer who flies off to the site of some terrible disaster—Banda Aceh, Sendai, or the path of Hurricane Sandy? Or a writer who travels to a dozen landscapes in as many countries to consider the fate of humanity in relation to water? What is the carbon footprint of a UN conference on the environment? And how does the work of these writers and their carbon footprints compare to the work of writers who stay home, who inhabit one place, one landscape, for the whole of their life and so come to know it intimately and write from that intimacy? What are the impacts of those two bodies of work? The John Muirs of the world, who roam, and the John Burroughses of the world, who stay home?

The question I have to ask myself is this: is researching and writing a story on climate change worth its weight in carbon? Or are writers who travel extensively really just documenting the failure of our species, even as the process of documenting it hastens that failure? Perhaps you've asked these questions before. Eventually it becomes personal. I want to know how to justify my own journeys, those I've made and those I wish to make. How do I justify the carbon cost of my journey to Grey Owl's cabin? Surely my seeing Grey Owl's cabin will not help save the world. Of course it won't.

But I can't worry about this right now because the wind is gusting harder, pushing my boat into the shore. I turn the bow out to face the waves. I paddle up and over them. Up and over them. This will go on for hours, I think, because the thunder boomers are building against the sky, and the wind is intensifying, the waves growing and pushing against the shoreline. I miss a few strokes to switch from my new wood paddle to my fiberglass whitewater paddle, and the waves slap my boat up onto the beach. I give in and leap out, pull the boat up on the finely sorted pebbles. It's 1 p.m., and I've been moving and pushing the route pretty hard all day. I feel it now as I stand at the lake edge. I'm tired. I feel a little lost and deeply alone. I don't have that vibrant presence with me anymore, the presence of that bear, the presence of Grey Owl. This emptiness passes in a moment, though, because I begin to line my boat up the beach. It's not easy, and it doesn't make a lot of sense. The waves keep pushing the boat back onto the shore. I can't go very far anyway because ahead of me the trees come right to the water and cut off my path. I need to get back out into the surf and ride the waves again. There is no better antidote for loneliness than going on, so I paddle out and take that good tack on the wind and ride the storm down the lake. I see an eagle on the wing, and I sheepishly hope it is a gift from Grey Owl showing me the way.

Perhaps you have heard that the modern environmental movement is dead, that environmental organizations have themselves become corporations, and corporations, despite the good intentions of their members, are self-sustaining and self-preserving. A corporation is an entity working for the good of itself, not the good of the world. Kenneth Brower, in his article on Grey Owl, remarks that

> those old clarion voices in the wilderness and from the wilderness—Thoreau's, Muir's, Leopold's, Grey Owl's—have done their job in alerting mankind to the environmental threat. . . . The era of the "stars," those seminal, charismatic, flawed, larger-than-life characters whose eloquence and example brought the natural world back into the world; is finished—or so the bureaucrats themselves assure us.

Brower argues that what we have now are the bureaucrats, the lawyers and lobbyists, people who "know the art of compromise and can work effectively with Congress and Parliament." Certainly we need them, but we need Grey Owl too. Or at least *I* need Grey Owl.

My world and what I know about my world would be diminished if the writers whose work I admire stayed home. Truth is, I want them to get on airplanes and fly about the world. I want them to bring back stories of places I've never been and may never go. The truth is *I* want to get on airplanes and fly about the world. I want to go find stories in places I've never been. I don't know what to do about this, and I doubt they do either. Nobody knows what to do about it. And could we stop even if we were asked to, even if we wanted to?

A friend of mine has suggested (as others also have) that perhaps the adaptations that have allowed our species to take dominion over biological niches in virtually every climate on earth—our big brains, language, the opposable thumb—are maladaptations. Evolution is like that. A successful adaptation in one set of conditions may be or become a failed adaptation in another. I must confess that I no longer believe that we are going to get ahold of this thing called climate change. I no longer believe that we are going to exercise restraint and end or even curb our consumption of fossil fuels in order to make the world a better place for future generations, future generations of human beings and everything else. I don't feel hopeless. I just believe we're going to use it all up. What about you? There is no short-term incentive to stop mining the earth for resources. None. And for all our powers of imagination, we are still a species that functions better on brief time scales. We can hardly bother to imagine what's going to happen next week, let alone in a hundred years. Or a thousand. I think it's best for me, for my peace of mind, to plan for life in a hot future rather than try to stop that future from unfolding. I'll still recycle and walk to work and do all those things a thinking person should do, but I just can't allow myself to lay awake nights and worry anymore.

A few days before I wrote this essay, Al Gore made several hundred million dollars selling his "green" TV network, Current, to Al Jazeera, a fine news organization that is backed by big oil money from Qatar. After stating that he could see no hypocrisy here, he was asked if we still have time to save the earth from climate change. Yes, he answered, we still have time. I have nothing against Al Gore, but folks, he doesn't know. While he is a fine spokesperson, he's not a climate scientist. He's not even a man with a reasonable carbon footprint. Besides, climate scientists don't really know either. They work in probabilities, not in the absolute of *yes* or *no*. If the climate change spokesman of the world can't get out from under oil, how can you? How can I?

When I reach Westwind Campground again, the shape of the lake and the shore is a shelter for me. I can see the big waves out in the middle, and I'm happy to be where I am doing what I'm doing. I'm happy I paddled so hard and consistently to arrive back here so early in the day (it's 3:30 p.m.). I've not had any food since 5 a.m., and I feel worked. I relax for the first time on my trip, letting my boat drift into the weeds. I drag my hand in the water, and the sun is warm on my back. The thunder clouds are building still, wrapping the west and north shores of the lake. I've got beer and good food waiting for me back in my camper, and I'm eager now to paddle home.

I enter the outlet that is the Kingsmere River, and it takes me down into its quiet waters. I like how it feels in me that I've been to Grey Owl's cabin. I don't know what that feeling is really. An expansion? A depth? A clarity? I feel like I've pushed out the boundaries of my world a bit and now have new space to breathe. I've made other literary pilgrimages: Thoreau's Walden Pond; Hemingway's Idaho and Paris and Spain; Frost's cabin at Bread Loaf; Wordsworth's Lake District. This pilgrimage to Grey Owl's cabin won't save the world, but it has enriched my life, and I will add my story to those others. And perhaps this is enough to justify the expense in carbon. Though I still don't believe we're going to stop or even slow climate change, I feel a bit more hopeful about something. I have to believe that to keep such hope alive is the single most important endeavor in a time of crisis. A story can do this. And so can a journey on a lake in a canoe.

The river takes me out of the lake and back to the boat landing where I began. I paddle up to find a man and a young woman loading to paddle out. We exchange greetings, and he asks if I need help with my boat. We can load it on his car and take it up to my truck, which is parked about a quarter mile away. All right, I say. His name is Howard, from Saskatoon, and he introduces me to his daughter. They're headed up the west shore of the lake to camp for a few nights at Pease Point. He's a retired teacher, he says, and used to run canoe trips for his students. I tell him some of my story, and we find we have a great deal in common.

"So, were you out soloing overnight, or just for the day?" he asks. "I see you don't have much gear."

"Just the day," I say. "I made a trip up to Grey Owl's cabin. Started early this morning."

"Oh, Grey Owl's cabin. Good for you," he says. "Good for you."

A SHORT WALK IN
ANASAZI COUNTRY

Utah, 1996, 1999, 2001, 2006

In southeastern Utah, off the high plateau known as Cedar Mesa, an unassuming draw leads down from the highway's edge. It leads to the west, gradually at first, and, after passing a copse of aspen just below the rim, plunges steeply through the sandstone layers and across broken scree fields of soft rock. Where it turns sharply south, the canyon meanders, this side and then that, like the slick body of a bull snake, down to the banks of the San Juan River. All told, the canyon stretches 52 miles from top to bottom and drops 2,500 vertical feet. Not overly dramatic as canyons go, but in those upper reaches, willing travelers can find a rich complex of ruins, the remnants of an ancient Puebloan culture known to most people as the Anasazi.

It's a modest walk to make the circuit down Kane Gulch from the Bureau of Land Management (BLM) station there and up Bullet Canyon, requiring just a few days under a light pack. At about 6,500 feet elevation at the highway, the country is not beyond average fitness. I have made the walk a half dozen times and passed other parties with small children, who seem to manage just fine. The trail is well worn, and with the canyon walls rising up around you, it's difficult to become disoriented and get lost. You'd have to really fall asleep on the job. This Grand Gulch, as it is named, is a BLM primitive area. It gets steady use, with small parties leaving most days during the high season—the spring and early summer, and early to late fall—but it is still possible to make a private journey here, to tuck back against the rocks with a sleeping bag and cookstove, mostly unseen.

The Anasazi—who they were and what became of them—are not the great mystery too often purported in the literature of the American Southwest. In the late nineteenth century, when two cowboys, Richard Wetherill and Charlie Mason, walked into the pueblos at Mesa Verde and found pottery and pitch-lined water baskets sitting around, sandals and jewelry and children's toys, great panels of rock art, and great towers and dwellings constructed of mortar and stone, it did appear as though an entire people had stood up one day and walked off. Or that they were abducted before they had time to gather their things, by ships from the outer realms of space. But these people did not vanish without a trace. Archaeologists tell us that following thirteen hundred years of occupation, a combination of pressures over time—drought, depletion of resources, internal strife, and, likely, insurgent tribes like the Navajo and Apache—forced the people to move on. Some researchers argue that the threat of looting, warfare, and cannibalism pushed the Anasazi from the bottoms into rock shelters and crevices high in the canyon walls, and then eventually out of the canyons altogether. What happened next is more difficult to discern. Just as a modern traveler might slip from the world unseen by descending into the canyon, the Anasazi did so by ascending out of it. They reemerged as the Hopi, Zuni, and other Puebloan peoples. It's no wonder, then, that the creation stories of the indigenous peoples of the Southwest center on migration and emergence from the lower worlds into this one.

In Grand Gulch, as in other places in the Southwest, much of the material culture of the Anasazi walked out of the canyons too, with archaeologists and amateur pot hunters. You can find beautiful pieces in various museums all over the world and possibly on black markets. Still, even today the average traveler will discover worthy treasures in these village ruins: dried corncob and pieces of gourd, pottery sherds, arrow points, brittle lengths of woven cord, and petroglyphs and pictographs in dizzying arrays. Most of it is relatively recent, perhaps seven hundred to a thousand years old, but the Anasazi occupied Grand Gulch for at least twice that long. Their economy and culture is classified into two major periods: the early Basketmakers, characterized by pit houses, woven baskets, and hunting and gathering; and the later Pueblo period, marked by the development of pottery, the cultivation of corn, beans, and squash, and the construction of mortar and stone villages. Anasazi cultural complexity reached its pinnacle at Chaco Canyon in northwestern New Mexico. Eighteen major villages—indeed, they might be called cities—supported a population of some five thousand people and were bound to cultures across the Southwest and deep into Mexico by a system of roads and waypoints.

One spring afternoon camped at Junction Ruin, some four miles from Kane Gulch station, I sat in my camp chair with a view of the stonework high in a crevice below the canyon rim. A moderate breeze carried off the stiff-sweet scent of juniper. A canyon wren called from somewhere out in front of me. The ladder high on the wall, broken by the years and precariously pinned to something I could not see, allowed me to imagine people dwelling here, milling about in the final moments of the day, the metronomic rhythms of the corn grinders, the laughing and crying of children, voices in reverberation in the rock shelters where the continual repair and expansion of the adobe dwellings cycled on. Village life.

Nights in the canyon can be cold this time of year, even into the single digits, and as I sat there lost in this meditation, the temperature fell as the sun-line climbed up the canyon wall. The woman I was married to in those days once remarked that the sun sets backward in canyons, rising up from the bottom. I pulled on a fleece. The change I felt in that moment, the difference that urged me to pull on a warmer layer, awakened me to the passage of time in an otherwise timeless moment. I realized that in the moment previous to that awareness, nothing out there beyond the canyon walls concerned me, that I had been first cut off and then suspended as if by a great net that held me apart from the goings-on of the workaday world. The canyon was all I knew.

This was not the first time I had had this experience, not an anomaly, that coming into this country you feel a soft blend of comfort and agitation, a strange awareness when you crawl from your tent and the sun is sparking an eager light high on the canyon rim, illuminating the soft sandstone stained by eons of rainfall and stormwater as you blink at the beauty and simplicity of the way the people must have lived here, how they must have hungered and fought and made love and sang and despaired and lived, and also died, in the shadow of the canyon and in the glow of a springtime moon. On any average night, or any average morning, in Grand Gulch you feel the presence of this presence, as if you have passed through a wormhole, a breach in space and time.

In May 1996, I walked the canyon up to Kane Gulch station from Collins Springs, just fifteen miles up from the river. Those fifteen miles of canyon that I would not see, the boulders and the hot, dry emptiness of the canyon where even the Anasazi dared not go (there is little evidence of Anasazi occupation in the lower reaches), gleamed like a bright temptation in my mind. For one thing, Everett Ruess is said to have traveled in Grand Gulch, and at the river, he carved the word "Nemo" into the sandstone. This was his assumed identity, inspired by Captain Nemo from Jules Verne's *20,000 Leagues under the Sea.* "Nemo" is Latin for "no one," which was Ruess's plan all along: to give up his ego, his identity, and become little more than another desert creature dwelling there, to be absorbed by the canyon so completely as to pass through unnoticed. The hitch in his plan is obvious: if he wished to leave no trace of himself, why did he leave a trace of himself? Well, the inscription has vanished too, or has at least been lost, as the few who claim to have seen it are either dead or believe that the river may have claimed it. Now all we have is the story. On that trip, I was leading a group of a dozen high school freshmen, part of the spring outdoor program at the private school where I was teaching, and it was not a time to be wandering about in search of Nemo.

To say something more of his story, Everett Ruess traveled alone in the desert Southwest during the summers of 1930 to 1934. Sometimes he traveled with a donkey, sometimes a horse. And for a time, with a dog as his companion. He was a young man, only sixteen when he made his first journey. His mother had taught him to paint, and, afflicted by his art, he decided to make himself into a painter. To do so, he knew, he needed to fill the wellspring of his imagination with experience. He needed to make known in his body what was knocking about in his head. To be a painter, Ruess knew, he needed to make his life into his art. He needed to become a person. Curious that the more he traveled in the canyons, the more of his identity he gave up.

Most of what we know about Ruess's life comes from the many letters he sent home during his travels. In a letter to his father dated July 16, 1931, euphoria erupts from Ruess's immersion in the wild deep of the Grand Canyon. "For a week I was in the depths of the canyon," he writes.

> The heat was over 140 degrees at one time. I followed obscure trails and reveled in the rugged grandeur of the crags, and in the mad, plunging glory of the Colorado River. Then on sunset I threw the pack on the burro again and took the long, steep up trail. I traveled for several hours by starlight. A warm wind rushed down the side canyon, singing in the pinions. Above—the blue night sky, powdered with stars. Beside—the rocks, breathing back to the air their stored-up heat of the day. Below—the black void. . . . My life has continued as I have wished.

His life didn't continue much longer, however. Everett Ruess disappeared in 1934, last seen somewhere in Davis Gulch, in southeastern Utah. A search party found his burro but not his bones. The story of what happened to him is still a mystery. *National Geographic* broke a story in 2009 claiming that the remains of Everett Ruess had been found—but that claim has since been disputed. How did he die? Perhaps he starved to death: in 1933 he wrote, "I have been living on raw carrots and banana sandwiches." Or maybe he offed himself as he faced the horror of returning to school: "How could a lofty, unconquerable soul like mine remain imprisoned in that academic backwater, wherein all but the most docile wallow in a hopeless slough?" But, more than likely, he fell to his death, as during his last two summers, he came to taking greater and greater risks: "Hundreds of times I have trusted my life to crumbling sandstone and nearly vertical angles in the search for water or cliff dwellings. Twice I was nearly gored to death by a wild bull," he wrote; and then, "I have been flirting pretty heavily with Death, the old clown." And finally: "He who has looked long on naked beauty may never return to the world. . . . Alone and lost, he must die on the altar of beauty." The novelist John Nichols claims that Ruess did just that, "fashion[ing] a magnificent obsession that probably killed him. . . . It was his life," Nichols writes, "that was his greatest work of art."

On a trip in the spring of 2001, one of my companions, a self-made man who, at that time, ran a backhoe business and portable lumber mill, operated and maintained a small hydroelectric dam, patrolled for a lumber company, and outfitted wilderness trips with llamas, found a human femur at Turkey Pen Ruin. We were neighbors in California's southern Cascades, our wives were close friends, and this was his first trip in Anasazi country. As he is also a potter and maintains and operates a wood-fired kiln at his home, he was at first interested in the many pot sherds travelers had set up on slabs of sandstone, and those exposed in the sandy soil. He inspected the sherds, detailing the firing process and pigments. "Most of this stuff," he said, "was fired at very low temperature. And notice how much care went into making these lines. That's almost a right angle. You can see the brushstrokes here." He then pointed out veins of color in the sedimentary layers of the canyon walls, a bright band of yellow-stained rock: possible pigment sources. "If I was looking for a yellow, for example, I'd look up there. Some kind of mineral seep or something." Then, studying the long black streaks on the canyon walls known as desert varnish, the path water takes when it rains, he became convinced that the black, geometric patterning on Anasazi pottery was made with the canyon in mind. "They were re-creating their home landscape," he said. You could see this easily, how the canyon, a negative space, took shape in the positive space of the pot, which itself contained another negative space inside.

The femur lay exposed at the back of the rock shelter near the remains of a dwelling with two small doors. My companion came upon it easily, without much enthusiasm. It was one of many objects the people had left behind. Long, white, delicate, the bone was not cracked or broken. I have seen hundreds of bones in the desert. Cow, certainly, but also horse, sheep, deer, coyote, mouse, skunk, pronghorn, bobcat, even javelina. This was none of these. We knew right away what it was, and we did not doubt what he had found. My companion held the bone against his thigh, and you could see that it belonged there.

The sun comes in early at Turkey Pen and warms the sands, so standing there that morning, the light was good. We could see everything. On the wall curving up over our heads, a collection of pictographs: handprints, a few sheep, and two ghostly figures in white, hovering over the site. Wetherill is said to have discovered and then removed human remains from Turkey Pen, and holding the femur with those figures dancing along the walls, I sensed that I was trespassing.

Inspecting the bone, I noticed a series of striations near the greater trochanter, some horizontal, some vertical, like a game of tic-tac-toe. The markings looked old, but I didn't know enough to know. I noticed how the shaft hides a web of fractures, most of which look to be superficial, a result of the stresses of time. Near the lateral epicondyle—something remarkable to both of us in that moment—a thick flake of tissue, translucent red, and stiff-sharp beneath my thumb. I came to think of the bone as that of a man, but there was no way for me to know. Against my own leg, it was several inches shorter. Perhaps this man stood five foot eight, or five nine; he would have been smaller than me, anyway. And perhaps he even stood where I stood, a long time ago, with the light coming in just like this.

Turkey Pen was quiet that morning until we heard below us another party coming up the trail. Their presence jogged us from our reveries, and we had to acknowledge the miles we planned to walk that day. We needed to get moving. My companion then took up the femur, pulled back some of the cool dry sand that had fallen into the trough where he found it, laid it in, and buried it.

I led my group of high school freshmen up-canyon from Collins Springs, leaving those bottom fifteen miles for another day. This was a hardy group of kids, and we moved at a steady pace, pushing along the trail through the stands of desert willow and across the sandy bottoms where our boots slipped back and turned the walk into a slog. We paused at Bannister Ruin, Deer Canyon, and Big Pour Off Spring. At Polly's Island on our second day, the group followed a faint trail through the cacti and dense sage. I heard a scream up ahead, and the line stopped.

"What is it?" I called out.

"Nothing," one of the boys said. "A snake."

"A rattlesnake?" I asked.

"I don't know," he called back. "A snake. But it's gone."

"I think the trail is gone too," someone else said.

And the trail was gone, vanishing into the thick brush and sage where we stood waist deep, bearing the weight of our packs, a pale midday sun hammering our heads. I heard the first boy say, "I think we're lost."

"Are we lost?" someone called back to me.

"Certainly not," I said.

"OK," he said. "But do you know where we are?"

I didn't. I had not looked at the map all morning. The trail and the canyon led you easily in the direction you wanted to go, and when a ruin or panel of rock art or anything interesting came along, you always noticed. To me, in that moment, it really didn't matter if we knew or didn't know, and had I been looking at the map, I would have confirmed this to be true. Had we bushwhacked on up the west side of Polly's Island, a massive butte that splits the canyon around it, the sage and dense brush might have been challenging, and might even have ruined our fine attitudes. Once around the point, the passage opens up, and a good trail leads back to the main canyon. At that point, we would have known precisely where we were, that understanding coming in after the fact, not before.

"Good point," I said. "I'm not sure where we are. So. Yeah. Where are we?"

"Ohmygod," another student said. "We're totally lost."

"What are we going to do?" the first asked.

These were the days before everyone had a cell phone, and before backcountry travelers routinely carried GPS locators or sat phones. We had no way of contacting the outside world. The world of the canyon was all we had. I carried my running shoes in my pack for this very reason. If we needed help, my plan was to find a place to climb up to the rim and run east through the desert until I hit the highway.

"Don't worry," I said. "We're not in danger in any way."

"But we're lost," the first student said.

"We're not lost," I said.

"But you don't know where we are," the second said.

"Right. I don't know where we are, but we're not lost."

"I'm out of water," someone said.

"Ohmygod," someone else said.

"Let's go back," the first student said.

"Look. We're all fine. Is there no trail ahead?" I asked.

"Nope," the first student said.

"So, let's go the easiest route. We can turn around, no problem."

And so, a little agitated, a little panicked, the group turned back, and we made our way to the main canyon and around Polly's Island.

"That wasn't so bad," the first student said. "Being lost, I mean."
"Nope," I said.

That morning in the spring of 2006, I was leading another group
of students, college juniors and seniors, on a twenty-four-hour solo
fast in Bullet Canyon near Jailhouse Ruin, just down from Perfect
Kiva. Base-camped beneath a massive juniper, my coleader and I
waited. The stoves kept breakfast warm and the coffee hot as the
students walked in, one by one, from their private solo sites. We
formed a welcome circle, but no one spoke just yet. To break the
silence, we would give a rousing cheer, then open the pots to serve
out the food.

What happened to them out there during the long bright day
and the long dark night? Fear. And personal struggles. And pres-
ences visiting in dreams. But then one of them asked if back here
at base camp my coleader and I had heard a flute on the wind just
as the light of the sun was going out. No, we told them. We heard
nothing. They looked at each other. We did, they confirmed. A
flute song. It went on for about ten minutes, maybe fifteen, they
said, and hearing it helped them feel better, helped them not to
be afraid.

Up Shiek Canyon, a mile from the Bullet Canyon junction, a spring
forms a pool near a few small cottonwoods. The shelf above and
opposite is a fine camp, with views across the spring of a massive
panel of pictographs. These shapes and figures and handprints,
one of the major draws for most travelers, were likely made over
many hundreds of years of occupation: A series of headless figures
in red pigment, their wide, squared bodies stippled to reveal other
shapes in the negative space. A row of bulbs on top of long lines,
and, hovering over them, a circle with wavy lines radiating from
each side that look like wings. Another figure with a death's head,
the shoulders and torso in yellow. A complete figure with a rectangular body, an impressive phallus dropping straight down, and two
immense horns on its head, likely the ceremonial headdress of a

shaman who walks between worlds. And not far off, another picto-
graph, the green mask, for which this place, Green Mask Spring, is
named. The long hair along each side of the face is red and looks to
be bound with white cord in the middle and at the ends. The face
has no visible eyes; instead it consists of alternating bands of green
and yellow, edged in white. It really is a tiny thing, about fifteen cen-
timeters wide and twenty high, and is positioned high on the wall,
so it is not easy to find with all the business and chaos of the panel.
It may take some time before you see the green mask, but once you
do, it glows like a beacon.

At the mouth of Step Canyon, farther down, I find a terrifying
face on the wall with gawking white eyes and lion-sharp teeth. The
eyes are a little too close together, so that they penetrate in gazing back at you. It is a demon, or a man possessed. Handprints are
everywhere, also human figures, some with pendulous phalluses; a
few coyotes; a three-foot-tall quail with one red eye. All these eyes,
watching. This place feels loaded, like something happened here,
the memory of which could not get out. Great plates of sandstone
peel from the wall, as if shaken loose, and have fallen and settled
upright on the ground.

And farther down still at Big Man Panel, that day after not getting lost at Polly's Island, concentric circles beneath the left hand
of the "big man" on the right. These two huge figures—their high,
squared shoulders, their hair like bulbs below the chin-line—look
like shaman who may move between worlds. Three concentric
circles, according to some sources, are the sun's light on the outside, the sun itself, and then the portal, the umbilicus, the gateway
through which flows a life energy between this world and the other.
The shaman may use this gateway to get in and to get out.

Concentric circles are not to be confused with the spiral, which
some authorities say is the *sipapu*, the emergence place where the
Anasazi were born into this world. This was a birth through water
and through the womb of the earth. Do not forget the great flood of
Genesis and *Gilgamesh*, and the flood that moves the people along
on their migration route in the Navajo creation story. And do not

forget that all human babies are born into this world through water from the mother's womb.

Think of the canyon from above: A wound in the skin of the earth where birds and lizards and coyotes live, and, long ago, people. Where cottonwood and willow and juniper hold the fragile soils, and the soil itself is alive with cryptobiota. Orange globe mallow, sage, Mormon tea. Like a cut in your arm, or like the opening of a woman, water made this gash in the earth, and life rushed in to fill it. One archaeologist has put it this way: "It seems everything goes into the canyon and nothing goes out."

On one walk in the canyon, a BLM ranger came upon me filtering water below a great sandstone knob that towers above a ledge where the water runs clean and pure. Lots of people stop here for water. I stopped here for water.

"Have you been up to the panel above?" she asked.

"No," I said. "I didn't know there was a panel above. I didn't know there was an *above* above."

She was dressed in her BLM uniform, a small government-issue day pack on her back, hair about shoulder length, curly, sandy blonde, lovely muscular legs, and a lovely shapeliness to her from walking the canyon. She was young, maybe midtwenties. I was young too, maybe late twenties.

"Let me show you something not many people have seen," she said.

"That's very generous of you."

"Go right up that slick rock there," she said. "It doesn't look like you can make it, but you can. Take your pack up if you like. Nice campsite up there too. Go right up the side of it all the way to the top."

"What will I find?"

"How about I show you?"

"That's very generous of you."

I dropped my pack and up we went, up the side of the slick rock at an impossible gradient. It really was an impossible gradient, and I said so.

"This is an impossible gradient," I told her.

"It looks that way," she said. "But see how easy it is."

At the top, she led me along a faint trail to the canyon wall, the nose of another great tower that rose to the rim and made an outline against the sky. You could see where a great slab of the canyon had come away; pieces of it were scattered about.

"Here," she said. "Come closer. Have a look at this."

I thought I was playing a role in a movie. Now we would stand in awe at the panel, see the figures and animals pecked into the stone, notice two figures making the beast with two backs, and feel a sudden rush of adrenaline and lust, at which point we'd exchange glances, ask the other what books, what coffees, what movies we liked, and inquire "Do you like to travel?" She would turn to me and say something like, "Oh, God, how beautiful," and I would say nothing, the strong silent type, then take her by the wrist, wrest her pack from her, drop it on the ground, and strip her of her desire there on the bare rock under the warm sun as clouds wheeled overhead like my darkened loneliness.

We stood there staring at the panel together. Kokopelli skipped lightly over the face of it with his long flute. Kokopelli the trickster, the spirit of agriculture, the music man, the fertility god. Between his legs, his cock like a long snake, unfolded far below his feet and extended off the face of the rock.

"Well," she said. "Have fun."

And then she walked out of my life forever.

Up Bullet Canyon, I descended the ladder into Perfect Kiva with my friends from California and the woman I married. The kiva is a round room the Anasazi used for community events and for ceremony. Most villages had at least one. Inside, we crouched in a circle, our eyes adjusting to the darkness. How evenly the sun angled in through the door in the roof, even on an overcast day like this one, a straight shaft of light. I wanted to locate the sipapu, the little hole in the floor symbolic of the gateway where the Anasazi, at the direction of Grandmother Spider Woman, the creator, ascended from the underworld into this world. Every kiva has one. And the door of the kiva itself, as the people climbed in and out of it, is a re-enactment of this original moment of emergence.

In *Roads to Center Place*, Kathryn Gabriel suggests that Spider Woman also urged the people to find the center place, and then she gave it to them. She lay down on the earth, her long legs extending outward to the four directions, thereby making her heart the center place. For Gabriel, this is Chaco Canyon, a great Anasazi complex in northwestern New Mexico, from which a series of roads radiate outward to the villages, like these at Grand Gulch. The roads tend not to skirt around mesas and mountains but to cut through them, or over them. Seasonally, the people made a pilgrimage to Chaco Canyon to worship, following these roads back to the center place, back to the original sipapu, grandmother's heart. "The ultimate duty is to walk the straight road," Gabriel writes, "and the ultimate blessing is to finish one's own road, or to attain an equilibrium in old age, and to return to the underworld through the sipapu."

But nothing is this simple, this straightforward. The straight road is not always straight. Gabriel explains:

> Just as the emergence became a metaphor for migration and leaving one's ancestral home, taking the straight road became a metaphor for a centering process. One follows the straight road without deviation throughout a life of service to one's pueblo. Migration is symbolized by a coiled snake, the sign for water. . . . Ultimately, the straight road takes one back to the place of emergence. Thus the straight road becomes a circle, a snake swallowing its tail for all eternity.

Walking out of Bullet Canyon in 1999, the sky fell in on top of us. It rained, soft and light, then a cold wind blew in and the rain turned to snow. We took shelter for the night under the juniper and pinyon, sat under the branches with cups of hot tea. It rained much of the night. In the gray morning, we loaded our packs. Patches of snow melted over the sandstone in the finicky air. The desert varnish showed jet black against the white. As we ascended the narrow canyon, the woman I had married spotted a lovely little pool in the rock, the water black and cold. She was just the sort who would do that kind of thing. We told her, yes, we would wait for her. She made her way through the towers of stone down to the pool's edge, stripped off her clothes, and dove in.

At first we could see the white form of her body beneath the black water, and then (maybe it was the shifting light on that gray day) we could not. She seemed to be down for a long time, longer than a person might hold their breath. Had she found the way through? Bubbles rose to the surface just as one of us might have said something, and her head appeared and then her astonished face. A breeze kicked up, rustling the juniper and pine as the woman emerged from the water, cold, wet, and alive.

CROSSING OVER THE MOUNTAIN

Idaho, 2006

> But all the waters of the world find one another again,
> and the Arctic seas and the Nile gather together in the
> moist flight of clouds. The old beautiful image makes my
> hour holy. Every road leads us wanderers too back home.
>
> — Herman Hesse, *Wandering*

Dawn. A few rain drops on Lookout Peak. I woke to the sound of the *plink, plink* of the rain against the rain fly, and the bloodstain on the mesh wall of my tent from the border collie pup that now slept in my vestibule. The night before, I had only just crawled into my tent in the dark when I heard Rambo, a border collie/heeler mix as fierce and violent as his name, savage this little pup that had dared approach the food bowl. Rambo had little interest in the sheep, and little interest in people, as he had warned me away several times when I approached him to remove the ticks that ringed him like a necklace of grapes. But he was hell on coyotes. His only mission, it seemed, was to chase coyotes, or kill them if he could. And the pup, savaged in the night, his ear a torn and bloody rag, came sadly to my tent. I knew that Hector and the other sheep herders, Edwin and Freddy, would laugh at me if they knew, as a dog that can't make it on its own out here isn't a dog at all.

We packed and loaded and left without coffee or breakfast as storm clouds came careening in and the rain came down with thunder and lightning. Today we had to cross over the mountain, Lookout Peak, and descend onto the west side of Cascade Lake, near Cascade, Idaho. I'd become used to this routine: an early, fast wake-up, heavy labor for an hour, and a hasty departure on a hard stomach. It was cold, colder than any morning I'd been out with the sheep, and the air was wild and high. As thunderheads settled in over the top of us, Hector mounted his horse—the horse with no name—and rode ahead pushing the band of sheep up over the mountain. He sang an old Peruvian song as he went:

> Hoy estoy aqui
> Mañana ya no
> Pasado mañana por donde estaré

> [I am here today
> I won't be tomorrow
> Who knows where I'll be the day after tomorrow.]

Hector Artica is one of about twenty Peruvian sheep herders working for the Soulen Livestock Company, a third-generation Idaho sheep and cattle outfit. I was traveling with him this summer, as I had last summer, for three reasons: to see wolves, which had recently been reintroduced to the mountain West after about one hundred years following eradication; to get a story; and to live out my romantic vision of the shepherd's life.

The Soulen ranch consists of about fifty thousand deeded acres, with another sixty thousand acres of grazing allotments with the BLM, and other allotments with the Forest Service and the state of Idaho. These allotments have dwindled in recent years due to a number of pressures, especially concern for bighorn sheep, which contract a deadly pneumonia-like disease carried by domestic sheep. Phil Soulen; his daughter, Margaret; and his son, Harry, share management of the ranch. Margaret focuses her efforts on the sheep operation (between 10,000 and 14,000 sheep divided into five to seven bands, depending on the time of year), while Harry mostly works the cows (about 1,000 head). Each sheep band is assigned a herder, charged with the safety and health of the sheep; and a camp tender, charged with the safety and health of the herder. The camp tender takes on the tasks of cooking, camp setup and takedown, and moving camp on a mule and horse pack string. The sheep graze a vast expanse of country, making a long loop from their winter range on the Snake River south of Nampa, Idaho, to their summer range in the mountains near McCall, Idaho. As spring turns to summer, the sheep follow the grass into the high country. Every mile between these distant points, the sheep must walk. The lambs are born on that range, the ewes live and die out there with the guard dogs and the herding dogs, and the shepherds, too, live on the range year-round with the eagles and trout, the coyotes and bears.

Hector's Idaho driver's license claims he is five feet tall, but I wager he is sub four-eleven. He comes from Lima, the capital city of Peru, but has spent much of his adult life with his wife and young son in a village on the Altiplano, the high plains of the Andes, which average about 12,000 feet elevation. His family is there still, and he has not seen them in a couple years. Working through the Western Range Association, the herders contract with the ranch for three-year work visas, with an option to renew after returning home for a few months. Hector is near the end of his second contract cycle.

The herders are compensated with a salary of $750 per month, with all other expenses paid—food, shelter, supplies, transportation, health care. This may not sound like much to Americans who love, above all things, to consume, but living a modest life without expenses, the herders are able to send most of their money home, where the per capita gross domestic product (GDP) is $5,600 per year. Compare that to the per capita GDP in United States: $40,100.

The pattern here, the relationship between herder and sheep and dogs, is as old as the hills, even those hills rooted in the mythic past and first grazed by Abel's sheep, born out of Eden with his brother Cain, who slew him. The story goes that Abel was beloved of God, and in his jealousy, Cain rose up against him. Imagine, though, the tension between these two men, one a bondsman to the land, devoted to it, imprisoned by it, unable to live a single day that the land did not need him. The other, a man as free as the bully winds that blew in over the fallen world, who roamed from place to place with his sheep and dogs, from good grass to good grass, from good water to good water. First there is the tension between bondage and freedom, and then, would not Cain defend his fields from the insatiable hunger of his brother's sheep? When Cain says to God, "Am I my brother's keeper?" he means that he is not, and he means that in fact his brother is a keeper of sheep, and he is the keeper of his fields, which must be kept even at the expense of his brother.

The tension between Cain and Abel, and the deed that was inevitably to come, is seeded in the men's names, too. "Cain" is rooted in the Hebrew word *kanah*, meaning "to possess or acquire," and *koneh*, which means "to create, shape, or form." Cain is the created man, having taken shape in his mother's womb. He commands space and identity. He acquires and possesses the material world. This is precisely what he does in his occupation as farmer: he owns and controls the land, takes dominion over it. "Abel" is from the Hebrew word *hebel*, which means "vapor, breath, or breath that vanishes." As a shepherd, he is a creature who roams, drifts, floats, and may be nowhere and anywhere at any time. He is a wanderer, a transient, a vagabond, which mirrors the fleetness of his very life, taken from him by Cain, the possessor.

After Cain murders Abel, God issues his punishment. He is to be "cursed from the earth," which opens "her mouth to receive [his] brother's blood from [his] hand." Now when Cain tills the earth, it will not yield "her strength; a fugitive and a vagabond shalt [he] be in the earth." The earth is explicitly female here, so that among Cain's crimes (murder, betrayal, lying) is the violation of the feminine, of the creative power of procreation, even the violation of Eve, Cain's mother. God commands that the source of Cain's identity and power (his ability to bring forth fruit from the feminine ground) will be denied him. The strength of the earth, and so the strength of the feminine, will not be known to Cain again. It will be known to Abel, however, who is accepted by the feminine earth as she opens her mouth to receive him. The fertile soil accepts Abel and rejects Cain. In effect, the two brothers exchange roles: Abel as farmer (or, more literally, he becomes the farmed land), and Cain as wanderer. Yet Cain will be a different wanderer than his brother, for Abel was at home with his flocks in the wild lands, and Cain will remain a drifter, always out of place wherever and whenever he is. To compound this eternal state of exile, Cain will be forever pursued by the guilt of his crimes, and only a state of continual wandering will allow him to atone for his brother's murder.

Cain departs the only home he has known, traveling "out from the presence of the Lord" and dwelling "in the land of Nod, on the east of Eden." The name "Nod" corresponds with the Hebrew word for "wanderer," so Cain dwells in the land of wandering, which is to say that he lives everywhere and nowhere, where Abel once roamed free before him. Cain is truly alone, lost, without support or anchorage of any kind, and what he does next is remarkable.

Cain fathers a son, Enoch, which begins the ages of humankind. The story continues as a genealogy of who begat whom, alongside the construction of civilization, a civilization based on an economy in agriculture, which will prove intolerant to a nomadic way of life, to Abel's way of life. Later, along Cain's line is born "Tubal-cain, the master of all coppersmiths and blacksmiths." As metallurgist, Tubal-cain possesses the power to fashion the tools that drive the agricultural machine and shape the weapons of war against nomadic raiders. Metallurgy is a dark art, a sacred art, one which, during the Iron Age, was both honored and feared. The metallurgist does not perform his art alone, however; he requires the miner and the blacksmith.

In his three-volume series *A History of Religious Ideas*, Mircea Eliade writes, "Mines [were] assimilated to the womb of Mother Earth," where metals were thought to grow and change. Mining metals from the womb of the earth is a process of interrupting the gestation period. The immense spans of time required to transform metals and make them perfect, it was believed, could be hastened in the forge. This is why miners practice "rites involving a state of purity, fasting, meditation, prayers, and cult acts," writes Eliade. Together, the miner, blacksmith, and the metallurgist—three parts of one process—assume "responsibility for changing nature," by taking "the place of time." What would have taken Mother Nature "eons to ripen in the subterranean depths," writes Eliade, "the artisan believes he can obtain in a few weeks; for the furnace replaces the telluric womb." Such powers were considered both "sacred and demonic." Metallurgists and smiths "[were] highly esteemed but [were] also feared, segregated, or even scorned." Like Adam and Eve before him, Cain's desire to master nature and so master time will play out in a cycle of violence and subjugation of those peoples who live by the will of nature and time, the nomads and pastoral nomads, whom Abel himself embodies. It is the farmer, and the civilization built on that economy, who seeks mastery of the weathers and seasons, who amasses wealth to fill a spiritual emptiness that comes with the subjugation of nature, who is obsessed with youth and immortality and so disgusted by the limitations, humors, and pleasures of the body. Ironically, it is Cain, not Abel, who is a slave to time, who falls prey to the very thing he wishes to control.

I hurried along on foot behind Hector's horse, as lightning gave us the tree-lined horizon in flashes. Hector, I knew, hated lightning. He feared it. I'd heard it told that during a storm, Hector would not go near his rifle, and sometimes he would leave it a long way out of camp, thinking it would attract lightning. He has good reason to fear. A few years ago, a bolt struck the stovepipe of a herder's tent and blew him out of his shoes. Hector once visited a Forest Service fire lookout and noticed the glass insulators on the legs of the chairs and the bed. Later, he happened across such an insulator lying derelict on the forest floor. He wore the insulator around his neck as a talisman against a blue bolt from the heavens. Under the flash and boom of this storm, he looked possessed, driving those sheep on, hard and fast, to get over the top of the mountain before God struck him down.

"Lightning no no good for me," Hector said.

We came upon a bag of dog food in the trail that must have fallen off one of the mules in the pack string ahead of us. Freddy, the camp tender, had gone on ahead with the camp hoping to set up near Cascade Lake on the other side before we arrived with the sheep. Edwin pushed his band out ahead of us, and Hector and I followed up the rear with his band. Our camp, a tidy kit packed on five horses and mules, consisted of one canvas wall tent, a wood-burning cookstove, four wooden boxes for storing the kitchen and food, four five-gallon water jugs, and various bundles of other gear: bedding for the men, their clothes and personal items, a rifle and a shepherd's crook for each herder, the dog food, a couple small folding stools on which to sit. Food was resupplied by the fore-man, Cesar Ayllon, when the camp's location allowed road access. Everything we needed to live comfortably was here, and not much else. The herder's kit has changed very little since Abel's time.

The dog food was safe inside its sack from the rain, but even if it had gotten wet, we couldn't afford to leave it. The dogs needed this food, as hard as they worked. They were so footsore, so beaten down by the mountains, that when we hit camp at dusk, they ate hurriedly, then crawled up into some quiet shelter alone to sleep off their fatigue like the dead. I hefted the bag onto the back of Hector's horse, tied it down, and we went on.

We trailed the rear of the band now, Hector mounted and me on foot, and we followed behind a little lamb, limping, its left front leg spattered with brown ooze. It dragged that little leg helplessly with each step. I recognized it then, the same lamb that Hector responded to so tenderly the day before. The rain came down harder, and my Gore-Tex raincoat was shiny and slick with the rain. Lightning flashed all around us, and Hector's eyes were wild and afraid.

"Stupid bitch!" Hector yelled at the lamb and the storm and his fear.

The little lamb just could not do it today, could not, after all these days, push on so smartly as before with its useless leg. It stopped. Hector rode up on it with the horse, and frightened it. It bolted forward, moving along a little farther over the mountaintop. Soon it slowed and sputtered and stopped again. Hector rode up on it with his horse, which pushed it on a bit farther. This went on for half a mile or so, until Hector dismounted, shoved the reins of his horse into my hands, took off his coat and used it to whip the little lamb to make it go. It woke from its stupor once again and ran, a burst of surprising speed, before it realized the leg didn't work, and it stumbled and fell, as tired as it was. It rose again with all its might, got up, wanted to move on with the great band flowing out in front of it, the ewes and lambs baaing and bawling, a tremendous force of sheep in a fluid grace pouring over the mountain. But the lamb could go no more. Its front legs buckled and down it went onto its knees, its nose just touching a bit of soft moss to hold it up. Hector took up his coat again like a mace and beat the little lamb. It started and ran. He whipped it, yelling "Stupid bitch!" as the lightning flashed and the rain wetted us.

But that whipping, that rage, that ferocious abuse was not enough, was not more frightening than the fatigue and pain and destitution the lamb must have felt, for it stopped again. It was done, this lamb, finished with dragging its broken body over this great hump of Idaho. If we did nothing more, surely it would die. It would lie down and wait to die, wait for the coyote that would surely come, or the wolf, for we were now in wolf country. But what more could we do? I doubted we could bring the lamb in to safety. How could we carry it all the distance we had yet to go? And why not let it go? What's one lamb in a band of two thousand? Let it go, I thought. I can't stand watching this poor thing struggle against death anymore. The rest of the sheep are hitting the crest of the mountain and are maybe even headed down the other side. We're getting soaked to the skin. It's cold. The lightning is close, and these great tall pines surrounding us are sure to attract that fatal flash from heaven you fear so much. Let it go. Let it die. Let's go on.

"No good," Hector said, calmer now. "No good, this little lambs." The lightning didn't seem to bother him now. The lamb needed him, and I think, somehow, he needed the lamb.

Hector moved the dog food bag forward onto the saddle, picked the lamb up, and laid it gently over the horse just behind the cantle. He took hold of the front feet, set them side by side, and tied them down with the leather saddle strings. He came around the rear of the horse, set the lamb's back legs side by side, and tied them off tight with the saddle strings. He moved the dog food bag, all fifty pounds of it, up behind the lamb now, pressed it in over the lamb to keep it in place, and tied it off with the horse's lead rope.

"You go the horse," Hector said. "I push the sheep." Then he left me, vanishing down the trail.

I stood awhile in the downpour, the reins in my hand, the horse standing with one hind leg bent, the little lamb laid over its body. I looked down the watery surface of the path through the rain, which ran out before me and then angled sharply down. I coveted a dry shelter and the simple indoor life that came in reading and studying books. I no longer desired to be a lone shepherd on a distant promontory, staring into this wet and boundless forest. Yet I had only one choice, and that was to lead the horse and lamb on and to embrace the lonely roads, which in his optimism Wordsworth claims are an "open [school] in which [he] daily read / with most delight the passions of mankind."

Our species, mankind, evolved out of a nomadic economy. Agriculture does not appear in a meaningful way until about ten thousand years ago. Before that, all the way back to *Homo habilis* and *Homo erectus* (2.5 million years ago), we were nomads, foraging for plant foods and hunting the great beasts of the veldt. Most of our species's past (more than 99 percent of it) has been spent living as nomads, in "small-scale, highly egalitarian groups who shared almost everything," writes Christopher Ryan and Cacilda Jethá in *Sex at Dawn*. And that economy, that way of life, encouraged a very different kind of social structure than the American way, which is based on the individual (the hero, even), based on consumption, based on the "every man for himself" principle. "Foragers divide and distribute meat equitably," write Ryan and Jethá, "breastfeed one another's babies, have little or no privacy from one another, and depend upon each other for survival. As much as our social world revolves around notions of private property and individual responsibility, theirs spins in the opposite direction, toward group welfare, group identity, profound interrelation, and mutual dependence." Because sharing everything was at the heart of our ancestors' lives for so long, the authors' maintain, this practice "extended to sex as well."

This is not New Age idealism, a hippie utopia, or even socialism, Ryan and Jethá assert, but rather the only system that made sense. In a nomadic economy, a reliance on the group, as opposed to the individual, made life possible. An early human would not have survived alone for very long. He faced far too many dangers: predators, injury, starvation. You are better off sharing what you have gathered or killed with others, who will in turn share what they have gathered or killed with you. In this system, everyone eats a little all the time, instead of eating a lot some of the time. Think of sharing in this system not as altruism, but rather as a means of distributing risk. In this light, such community-mindedness was not idealistic, but highly pragmatic.

The agricultural revolution that came later is generally regarded as a great leap forward, but according to the American scientist and writer Jared Diamond, it was the worst mistake in human history. While it does make civilization and all its wonders possible—especially beer—it is also the genesis of slavery, class divisions, large-scale warfare and genocide, the rapid spread of epidemic diseases, habitat destruction, species extinction, and the divorce of human beings from nature. In an article in the May 1987 issue of *Discover*, Diamond reports that the quality of life in early agricultural communities decreased dramatically from that of nomadic cultures. Early farmers faced increased malnutrition and anemia, infectious disease, and degeneration of the spine, probably due to heavy labor. By about 4,000 BCE, the average height of peoples adopting agriculture fell dramatically, along with average life expectancy: twenty-six years before agriculture, and nineteen years afterward. Most nomadic peoples were reluctant to adopt farming. In his book *The Third Chimpanzee*, Diamond writes, "Agriculture advanced across Europe at a snail's pace: barely one thousand yards per year!"

But advance it did: slowly, slowly, farmers outbred and overpowered nomadic groups, because, as Diamond writes, "ten malnourished farmers can still outfight one healthy hunter." Even so, as Diamond asserts, agriculture brings with it a world of ills, and it has delivered us to our present state, here at the dawn of the twenty-first century. Growth of the world's human population is out of control, and we are fast consuming the very planet on which we depend for life. Like a plague of locusts in a crop field, most of us will perish when the crop is gone.

I started down the watery path over the rocky mountaintop, leading the horse with no name and the lamb. Down, down, down, picking my way among the boulders and rocks, I was "voyaging through strange seas of thought, alone," to use Wordsworth's words. There wasn't much more to do, and there wasn't much of a path either, just an open track of land where the sheep had traveled year after year, for the past one hundred years. The clouds were almost within reach, they were so low and we so high. The lamb lay there with its eyes open, blinking, helpless either way—walking or being walked, it had no will, no way to choose what would become of it. I put my hand on its little head. There, there, little lamb.

With the advent of agriculture come property rights and the ability to amass wealth. When you have wealth, you need an army to protect it from those who don't have wealth, and you need an heir to pass it on so the poor landless people (in some cases, nomads) remain poor and landless. Class systems, patriarchy, and monogamy are all products of agriculture, as men appropriated reproduction rights through marriage and essentially took ownership of women's wombs.

Since sex was readily shared among early humans, so was parenting, according to Ryan and Jethá. Children were raised by the village, not solely by the biological parents, and one of the reasons is that men did not really know who had fathered which child. In a world without monogamy, it didn't much matter. Everyone was a member of the community, and so each child was everyone's child. There are in fact zero "monogamous primate species that live in large social groups," and "adultery has been documented in *every* ostensibly monogamous human society ever studied," write Ryan and Jethá. It's nice to think we're monogamous, but our behavior proves otherwise. Monogamy is not even present in human societies in which anything but monogamy is a crime, especially a crime for women. Jews, Christians, Muslims, and Hindus have all punished adulterous women with death, and even that threat is not enough to change our behavior. "Think about that," Ryan and Jethá write:

> *No* group-living nonhuman primate is monogamous, and adultery has been documented in every human culture studied—including those in which fornicators are routinely stoned to death. . . . It's hard to see how monogamy comes "naturally" to our species. Why would so many risk their reputations, families, careers—even presidential legacies—for something that runs *against* human nature? . . . No creature needs to be threatened with death to act in accord with its own nature.

Hector had melted into the band of sheep, somewhere below. I could hear them bawling a hundred yards ahead, and now and again, I caught sight of sheep emerging from beneath the pines. We fell farther and farther behind, me, the little lamb, the horse with no name. Where was camp tonight? Where were Freddy and the pack string? Where were Edwin and the other band? Where was Hector? I did not know. The rain fell steadily now as I led the horse on. There was only one way to go: down, down to the lake, which spread out before me as I caught glimpses of it between the trees. From there, I might hear the four thousand sheep in a meadow nearby, and find the welcome shelter of the tent.

The horse stepped down into the slick muddy steep, slid forward, and rode up on me. I leaped out of the way as the horse caught himself and stopped. It angered me to be frightened this way by that huge animal almost toppling over me. We walked on, and the horse fought to keep his feet in the rain-slickened mud as I struggled to keep out of his way. We made a quarter mile, maybe a bit more, when I looked back at the lamb. It had slid over the horse to one side, and hung from its four feet like a sacrifice, helpless, its head lolling dangerously up and down as if it might come off with the horse's rhythm.

I stopped the horse, made him stand, and rescued the little lamb, lifted it up and back over the horse, repositioned the dog food sack to hold it there, and we went on. The trail steepened and the horse slid and arrested itself, slid and arrested itself, me walking alongside it now as it drew out the reins in front of me until I was walking near the rear of the saddle near the lamb that had slid down again into a little sling, slinging that way, its head lolling like it was barely attached. It looked unaffected, poor thing, blinking at me, helpless, hardly aware of its body, detached from any knowledge of having a will of its own, waiting for whatever cruelties would befall it. I set the lamb back up onto the horse, and it just lay there, that position as good as the hanging position, I suppose. It didn't seem grateful at all. I felt awful, though, terrible in letting it suffer this way. I stood there in the rain a bit, listening for the band down the mountain.

I looked back at all my troubles, the little, innocent, helpless lamb. High up on the horse now, the lamb craned its neck back to browse the green leaves of a mountain alder where a branch came down over it. Christ, I thought, what was it doing browsing the leaves as if this were an ordinary day? Didn't it know it couldn't walk, that its leg and its body were broken? Didn't it know that it was a lamb on its way to the slaughter? That its life wasn't worth more than the going rate of a few pounds of meat on the supermarket shelf? Didn't it know that it was a prisoner, not only on this horse's back, but in this world, its being locked away in this lamb's body, hardly a body of its own, a body owned by a world apart, like a carrot in the ground, an apple on a tree, a loaf of bread on a kitchen counter? Does it not desire to break free of its prison and run and bound through the boundless world, to face its life and death on its own terms, to face the coyote even, its jaws and teeth, so long as it were free? Still, it went on nibbling the leaves, impervious to my questions, my pains, the way I ached for it, the fucking lamb.

Not far from where humankind was born, the Tuareg, one of the great nomadic Berber tribes of North Africa, regard agriculture as "an occupation for slaves and the lower classes," writes Michael Brett and Elizabeth Fentress in *The Berbers*. "Even today, no noble will willingly take up a hoe." The basic property of a Tuareg family consists of a few mats and maybe one precious rug, as well as the tools of their work and a tent to live in. As in so many traditional cultures, women in such nomadic communities possessed a great many freedoms. The tent belongs to the woman, and a new husband would move into her tent for "as long as the marriage lasts." Despite their "extremely simple material culture," writes Brett and Fentress, "the Tuareg possess a social culture of great complexity." And it includes, among other highly articulated and rigid rules of behavior, an enduring love for poetry.

Things went on this way with the lamb for some time, for a life-age. I went on, leading the horse as before, trying to stay out of its way as it struggled to keep its feet in the slick mud where the sheep had trammeled the ground between the rocks. The rain came down. The sky flashed and I waited for the thunder to shake the mountain. Wham! It was beautiful and terrible too. Wham! I hated it. I'd never leave home again. Wham! I loved it. I'd never go home again. Then the horse lurched forward and slid on all its feet, its back legs splayed out and then back under it. I leaped to the side to save myself. Soon we gentled out onto the next little flat into the taller grass. I had not yet looked back to see what I knew I would see: the lamb hung loosely again over the side of the horse.

I stopped and made the horse stand. I hefted the little lamb back up, pulled its front feet over, positioned it just so, and dropped the dog food into place against it. What an impossible situation. I walked alongside the horse now, the lead rope in my left hand, and my right hand on the lamb's backside to keep it there from falling. We ambled on through the grassy swale and the rain. It worked, at least for now, to lead the horse and hold the lamb, and we made up a little ground because I could hear the sheep again out in front.

Farther on I saw a ewe, its broad back exposed where its head was inside the branches of a pine. Hector must be somewhere nearby, I thought. Then I felt something warm and comforting, but I couldn't place it. I didn't know where or why I was having this sensation. I looked up at the sky and into the wet clouds hung low above me, and across the horse into the green treetops. And then at the lamb, which was pissing over the top of my hand and down the side of the horse.

Who knows what words issued forth in that moment, but I also felt for that little creature that had not even the dignity of its body's functions. Of course it would need to piss. Of course it couldn't help but piss. And where was it to piss? Right where it was, strapped down like a sack of dog food half under a sack of dog food, probably dog food made from lamb meal. I stopped then and stood beneath a great pine out of the rain. I shook my hand off and held it out to let the sky clean it. Where was Hector, anyway, and why, why, why had he left me with this lamb and his horse? Why didn't he take the horse and let me push the sheep? There wasn't anything to it. They knew where to go. He's out there walking free, or sitting under a dry tree while the sheep mosey down the mountain to camp. I scanned the mountainside and the sheep scattered here and there, and back up behind me, all around, everywhere. No Hector.

I pushed back the dog food bag, untied the lamb's feet on both sides, lifted it up and off the horse, and set it down. It crumpled into a little pile. Now not one of its legs worked. It couldn't move at all. What a pitiful sight. I picked up the lamb and walked with it up to the base of that great pine. There I set it, positioning its legs so as to make it comfortable. What was I doing? I couldn't abandon the lamb this way. I couldn't leave it here to the coyotes and the turkey vultures. Would this terrible sin hang on my soul? Would guilt consume me and nightmares trouble my sleep in the coming days, in the long cold nights? Would beasts appear from the darkness to mete out reparations? If I walked away now, the lamb's fate would no longer be tied to mine. I would be free. I wondered again what I was doing. I could not abandon the lamb this way.

But I did. I turned and walked back to the horse. The band of sheep had moved on, and, now unencumbered, I took the lead rope and, with the horse, chased after them.

As I made my way to the band, I consoled myself. You've done the right thing. You've done the right thing. Hector would have abandoned the lamb, too. He had already abandoned that ewe a couple days back, her wool mostly gone, her face gaunt and tired, her last moments upon her. What was that night like for her, I wondered, the dark coming on, the temperature dropping, alone among the silent trees as the band moved farther and farther away, she calling out with no one listening, no one coming for her except the coyotes now, barking and calling to each other with excitement, one appearing out in front of her, another behind, a few more coming down off the hill, coming in on her from all sides. What was that moment like as the first coyote determined the ewe was alone and it was safe to come in. So in it came, circling a little and then circling back, just to be sure, because to be cautious is to be alive, and then when it was so close it had to, the coyote rushed in taking the ewe's throat in its teeth, holding her in its bite, turning her neck back, twisting her until she went down onto her side. And once down, she waited to die, the teeth deeper in her neck where now she bled into the coyote's mouth while other coyotes arrived, some pulling on her legs, the young ones leaping up around her in excitement and confusion. She made no sound at all, her throat clenched tight until the bleeding weakened her and weakened her, waiting for it to end, her breath slowing and slowing until it stopped and her eyes went stone cold black.

Where was Hector? He wasn't anywhere. I walked down, descending with the horse into the sheep. Closer and closer now, the ewes and lambs calling out in the wet rain, until one appeared in front of me, and a few more, and I came to the edge of them. The great pine in front of me, dry beneath, looked like a good place to tie the horse. I wasn't certain why I needed to find Hector now, except that I wanted him to acknowledge my choice and tell me it was the right thing to do, that no shepherd would have kept on with the lamb, that it was done for, and this is the way of things on the sheep trail. Some lambs don't make it. Some ewes don't make it. The dogs die out here, from time to time, the mules, the horses, the herders. But where was Hector? He wasn't anywhere, and I became worried that now I too, like the lamb, had been abandoned in the rain, here under a great pine, the camp surely down the mountain by now and the tent erected there in a green meadow at the lake edge where Freddy and Edwin and Hector now relaxed near the stove with coffee and cheese and crackers. I turned off to the north, scanning the trees and the sheep band, then to the west, the south, and the east. I looked down for a moment, watching the rain run from my hat brim. I looked up, and there Hector was.

"The little lambs?" he said. "You bring the lambs?"

I pointed up the mountain.

I have been a wanderer too, a nomad, journeying out of Eden with the first man and the first woman, dying into the ground with Abel, and walking the pathless wastes into the cities with Cain. It is easier and stranger to love and yearn for home when I am wandering in the wet woods in a lightning storm with Hector, Edwin, and Freddy, two bands of sheep, a dozen dogs, and all the wild predators of the West. But this life, the life of the nomad, is mostly gone now, replaced by getting and spending, replaced by the city, which is built on an agrarian economy; and yet the world is full of wanderers, or people with wandering hearts. So what is a wanderer?

In his book *Wandering*, the German writer Herman Hesse writes, "I belong to those windy voices . . . who love only love." Then, in the next paragraph, he offers the baseline of his being:

> All of us wanderers are made like this. A good part of our wandering and homelessness is love, eroticism. The romanticism of wandering, at least half of it, is nothing else but a kind of eagerness for adventure. But the other half is another eagerness—an unconscious drive to transfigure and dissolve the erotic. We wanderers are very cunning—we develop those feelings which are impossible to fulfill; and the love which actually should belong

to a woman, we lightly scatter among small towns and mountains, lakes and valleys, children by the side of the road, beggars
on the bridge, cows in the pasture, birds and butterflies. We
separate love from its object, love alone is enough for us, in the
same way that, in wandering, we don't look for a goal, we only
look for the happiness of wandering, only the wandering.

So the wanderer's condition is a love for the world. The bliss of
being "lightly scattered" completes wanderers because it allows
many places and experiences into their lives. An object of beauty in
the wanderer's path is not the object of love, but rather a reminder
of the passion of love empirical that may be expressed in so many
ways, among so many features in the land, among so many small
pleasures, so many small freedoms. Whereas the farmer concen-
trates his love in one field, one place, one life, the wanderer leaves a
little love in many fields, in many places, and lives many lives.

On looking at a small rectory, Hesse imagines becoming a priest.
He imagines what kind of priest he would be, what kind of life he
would have as a priest, and how he might live that way, content. He
imagines it but then confesses a deeper truth: he will always be a
wanderer. His fantasy of becoming a priest is the fantasy of a wanderer who steps into and out of possibilities, into and out of lives. It
is not the priesthood that allows him to tremble, but the excitement
he feels in its possibility. "I feel life trembling within me," he writes:

> in my tongue, on the soles of my feet, in my desire or my suffer-
> ing, I want my soul to be a wandering thing, able to move back
> into a hundred forms, I want to dream myself into priests and
> wanderers, female cooks and murderers, children and animals,
> and, more than anything else, birds and trees; that is necessary, I
> want it, I need it so I can go on living, and if sometime I were to
> lose these possibilities and be caught in so-called reality, then I
> would rather die.

In these possibilities, in the many forms of love and of the self,
Hesse feels most alive. Indeed, he knows that he cannot live unless
he is free to feel so.

I expected some kind of judgment—I did. I still do. I expected that in every situation in the sheep herder's life there was a right way and a wrong way. There was a protocol, or a procedure, or a system in place to determine what to do. Instead I think there was only what was possible and what was not possible, and what was possible for Hector was not necessarily possible for me.

"Show me," Hector said.

We trudged up the muddy path in the rain, up the steep mountain to the tree. The lamb lay there still, curled into a shivering ball. Hector knelt there in the mud and whispered something to it. An apology, perhaps? He took it into his arms, cradling it like a child, then lifted it over his head, draped it around his shoulders like a shawl, and carried it down the mountain.

Through the rain and mist of that big blow, I saw smoke in the trees: Freddy and our camp. He had the tent set and a fire glowing in the woodstove. The rain continued to fall, and I saw a warm light from the flap door as Hector and I approached.

"You go in," Hector said.

I went in, and inside it was warm and dry with the glow of the fire in the stove, and Freddy handed me a cup of hot coffee. Water streamed from my raincoat and fell onto the wet grass that was our floor. I lifted the cup to my mouth and drank, then stood at the open flap of the tent with the coffee in my hands and watched Hector work in the rain. He set the lamb down in the grass not far from the tent. Its legs would not work, and it lay there, unable to get up. Hector knelt beside it, put his hand on its head and then on its hindquarters, as if transferring some vital energy or offering it a blessing. Lifting his hand now, he rose and came away to the tent.

"It can't get up," I said to Hector.

"No. No walk," he said, taking a cup of coffee.

"So it will die?"

"Maybe die," Hector said. "But maybe live. Slowly, slowly, it can get up."

We needed to be vigilant, Hector warned, please keep an eye out, because the lamb, if it gets on its feet again, might wander back up the trail to return to our camp of the night before, and then back up the trail farther still, back to where it came from, wander into the dark wood where the wolves were surely waiting. All the ground we gained today, all that distance we traveled these past days crossing over the mountain, Hector cautioned, the little lamb might undo.

"This lambs maybe want to go home," Hector said.

"What do you mean?" I asked. "Go home where?"

"Go back to where born."

Standing out of the rain with the hot cup in my hands, I imagined the homing instinct in that lamb, as broken and feeble as it was, the power of its desire to return pushing it beyond its body's function, beyond its knowing of the way, a desire to retrace the route to its origin place. I thought then that this might be the expression of all living things, a journey back to one's origin place, to the center, or to the edge, or to the end. I felt a surge of love for the day, for this day more than other days, for the day of hardships and trials and curses, for the rain and the storm and the little lamb, and the difference in being out of the rain and the storm with the little lamb: a shepherd's life. I thought of the meal we would soon cook in the shelter of the tent, a dish of rice topped with a hash of carrots, potatoes, celery, garbanzo beans from a can, garlic, and Spam, salt and pepper to taste, as much as we wanted to satisfy who we were and who we would become. I loved the day, and I thought of those effusive lines of love from Wordsworth, those lines from a lost world from a poet who is the master of effusive lines from lost worlds, but what better lines with which to end a day?

> I loved,
> Loved deeply all that had been loved before,
> More deeply even than ever.

"Now," Hector said to me. "Freddy cook the lunch. I go in the sheep. You drink the coffee."

"You don't need help?"

"No," he said. "You drink the coffee."

Freddy filled my cup, and I stood in the flap door of the tent watching Hector on his way to the sheep in the rain and watching the little lamb just there, tottering on its weak legs in the wavering grass of spring.

ACKNOWLEDGMENTS

Though my name alone appears on the cover, a book is a community effort, and this book rests on the guidance, advice, criticism, friendship, and love of the following entities and individuals: my family (hi Leah!); everyone at Trinity University Press, especially Barbara Ras and Steffanie Mortis, who have made me a better writer and maybe a better person; the staff and faculty of the Honors College at Texas Tech University, and my students there, who are an inspiration to me; the staff, faculty, and students of the Vermont College of Fine Arts, where I taught for a time and hope to one day teach again; the good people of Arborwear, makers of the best pants in the world, who generously supported and outfitted my journey through Iceland; the Office of Research Services at Texas Tech University, whose financial support made my journey through Iceland possible; James M. Hargett, who helped me understand Fan Chengda; Steven Churchill at Duke University for help with Neanderthal; Margaret Soulen and Joe Hinson for their generosity and support in my travels with their sheep herds; Bruce Walsh; Duncan Campbell; Barry Lopez, who has fathered my work, first unknowingly, and then knowingly, since I was fourteen; Curtis Bauer and Idoia Elola, who reviewed my Spanish and encouraged my journey in Iceland; Scott Dewing, who has been my friend now for thirty years, and who helped make many of these journeys possible; and Karen Clark, for her guidance, editorial interrogation, Canadian-ness, and love, especially during that dangerous summer in Saskatchewan in the never-ending rain, and the storm and sun on the road in, and on the road out. Thank you.

KURT CASWELL is a writer and associate professor of creative writing and literature in the Honors College at Texas Tech University, where he teaches intensive field courses on writing and leadership. He has also been on the faculty at the Vermont College of Fine Arts. His other books include *In the Sun's House: My Year Teaching on the Navajo Reservation*; *An Inside Passage*, which won the 2008 River Teeth Literary Nonfiction Book Prize; and an anthology of nature writing, *To Everything on Earth: New Writing on Fate, Community, and Nature*, which he coedited. His essays have appeared in *ISLE, Earthlines, Matter, Ninth Letter, Orion, River Teeth*, and the *American Literary Review*. He lives in Lubbock, Texas.